WHITE LAND, BLACK LABOR

Charles L. Flynn, Jr.

WHITE LAND, BLACK LABOR

Caste and Class in Late Nineteenth-Century Georgia

Louisiana State University Press

Baton Rouge and London

790515

Designer: Barbara Werden
Typeface: Linotron Aster
Typesetter: G & S Typesetters, Inc.
Printer and Binder: Thomson-Shore, Inc.

Library of Congress Cataloging in Publication Data

Flynn, Charles L.
  White land, black labor.

  Bibliography: p.
  Includes index.
  1. Reconstruction—Georgia. 2. Afro-Americans—
Georgia—History—19th century. 3. Afro-Americans—
Georgia—Economic conditions. 4. Georgia—History—
1865–   . 5. Georgia—Economic conditions. I. Title
F291.F58   1983   975.8′00496073   83-721
ISBN 0-8071-1097-3

To

Robert F. Durden
Stephen G. Kurtz
and
Edwin B. Lee, Jr.

Contents

Maps

Acknowledgments

The Historic Chattahoochee Commission has given me permission to quote from its microfilm publication, *John Hory Dent Farm Journals and Account Books, 1840–1892*, eds. Ray Mathis, Mary Mathis, and Douglas Clare Purcell (University, Ala., 1977). So has the Auburn University Archives, where some of the original journals and account books are housed. The University of Georgia Libraries, Rare Books and Manuscript Department, Athens, and the Georgia State Archives, Atlanta, have given me their permission to quote from materials in their collections.

The Denison University Research Foundation helped me to pay my cartographer. The Department of Geography, University of North Carolina at Chapel Hill, prepared the maps for this volume from data in the *Tenth Census*, the *Eleventh Census*, Rand McNally, *Indexed Atlas of the World, Historical and Statistical: United States* (Chicago, 1898), and Carlton J. Corliss, *Development of Railroad Transportation in the United States* (Washington, D.C., 1945).

I would like to reiterate publicly the thanks I hope I have already shown to my colleagues at Millsaps College, the University of North Carolina at Charlotte, and Denison University for all sorts of personal and professional support; to William J. Cooper, Jr., for encouraging Louisiana State University Press to consider my manuscript; to Steven Hahn for suggesting valuable lines of research; to Judith Bailey, Donald C. Butts, John W. Cell, Paul D. Escott, Lisa J. McDonnell, John R. Martin, and Richard L. Watson, Jr., for recommending ways to improve this work; and to Robert F. Durden for all these and innumerable other things.

I would also like to thank my parents, Charles L. and Winifred Carocari Flynn. Besides understanding and support, they gave me a more unusual gift. They never placed any question off limits, not even challenges to their most deeply held convictions. They asked only that my own views be carefully considered and that I not compromise on a commitment to excellence. They were courageous enough to want their children to be adults.

WHITE LAND, BLACK LABOR

INTRODUCTION

S TUDIES OF SOUTHERN HISTORY since the late 1930s may be divided somewhat arbitrarily into two broad groups. The liberal tradition has focused on racism and racial oppression as the foundation of southern society and has been primarily concerned with racial injustice. The works of Charles S. Sydnor and Kenneth M. Stampp exemplify this group.[1] The second interpretive tradition, not limited to but increasingly dominated by Marxists, sees racial oppression as a function or subset of a more general class oppression. The writings of C. Vann Woodward, the most commanding figure among southern historians and no Marxist, fall in this group. In *Tom Watson: Agrarian Rebel* and in *Origins of the New South, 1877–1913*, Woodward portrays the Redeemers as bourgeois exploiters of agrarian elements, white as well as black.[2] More recent works have undermined Woodward's attempt to distinguish between postbellum southern leaders and their antebellum counterparts, between capitalists and planters, but these studies retain Woodward's characterization of racism as one more tool of class oppression, as a means of increasing upper-class exploitation of poor groups.

Both the liberal and the class-conscious traditions draw upon substantial evidence. Racism was, of course, a powerful social doctrine that afflicted the minds of most if not all white southerners. According to the prevailing white social ideology, race was the primary division of southern society. Whites disagreed about the severity with which the racial division should be drawn, but they agreed that all blacks should be beneath all whites. Whites described a racial caste system: an inherited, in-

1. Charles S. Sydnor, *The Development of Southern Sectionalism, 1819–1848* (Baton Rouge, 1948); Kenneth M. Stampp, *The Era of Reconstruction, 1865–1877* (New York, 1965).
2. C. Vann Woodward, *Tom Watson: Agrarian Rebel* (New York, 1970); C. Vann Woodward, *Origins of the New South, 1877–1913* (Baton Rouge, 1951).

flexible system with a literally moral authority. All whites were supposedly equal above the black laboring caste. Yet despite the *Herrenvolk* faith that described whites as equals, there is plentiful evidence of class oppression of poor-to-middling whites at the hands of large landowners.[3] And there is plentiful evidence that poor-to-middling whites resisted that abuse. To focus on racism alone, as have liberals, is to see the South as many white southerners claimed it was supposed to be, a simple pattern of white over black, and to discount as unimportant or nonexistent the substantial evidence of divisions among whites. On the other hand, to explain the coexistence of—the relationship between— class abuse among whites and the caste system requires something more than the class-conscious historians have offered. It requires something more than pointing to the racist diatribes and political corruption with which poor-to-middling whites were supposedly kept either deluded or impotent. It requires something more than submerging racial oppression within a supposedly larger pattern of class interests and denying the very real and important differences between the treatment and fate of poor whites and of blacks. At its worst, the second interpretive tradition is as facile as the first; it affixes pejorative labels to the wealthy, exalted labels to the poor, and rather than explaining the southern tragedy, blames the prominent and powerful for just about everything.

This book assumes that the central theme of southern history has not been racism, nor has it been class oppression, of which racism was one part. Although both interpretive traditions draw upon substantial evidence, each is incomplete. Instead, this book assumes that the central theme of southern history can be found in the interplay between the South's culturally defined caste and economically defined class systems. It is a call to appreciate the complexity of the tragedy of southern history. It searches for an understanding of the cultural mechanics with which the caste and class systems worked simultaneously both in harmony and against each other to create the South's social system, to limit

3. On the concept of *Herrenvolk* democracy, see Pierre van den Berghe, *Race and Racism: A Comparative Perspective* (New York, 1967), 17–18, and George M. Fredrickson, *The Black Image in the White Mind: The Debate on Afro-American Character and Destiny, 1817–1914* (New York, 1972).

the ways in which southerners understood their problems, and thus to define the terms in which those who resisted oppression did so.

The class structure among whites was a child of the caste system and of the wealth, power, and prestige of the planters it sustained. But children and their parents are often at odds, and tension between the system of class divisions among whites and the system of caste superiority dividing whites from blacks was evident long before the Revolution. Tension grew during the decades before the Civil War as up-country, yeoman whites pressed for improved education, improved transportation, equitable systems of taxation, and democracy among white males. In fights over public policy, planters interpreted any challenge to their interests or power as a challenge to the system of subordinate labor upon which they depended. Yet poor-to-middling whites repeatedly showed themselves deeply committed to the caste line. In their resistance to abuse from planters, they insisted that *Herrenvolk* democracy become a reality. If some powerful southerners used racist rhetoric to quell dissent, if they used racism manipulatively, it is equally true that others less powerful justified their demands for change as demands to fulfill their rights as members of the supposedly superior race.

This book examines comparable tensions between class and caste in the postbellum South. The Civil War and Reconstruction by abolishing the clear racial line between slave and freeman created a social system that was more fluid than whites believed it ought to be. Although planters attempted in the black codes to create a new system of coerced labor, northern free-labor Republicans changed the federal Constitution and left whites permanently unable to define the caste line as absolutely as they wished. Because of these congressional actions, blacks were able to use their freedom and the demands of the marketplace to force planters to compromise somewhat on the terms of employment. The result was a new decentralized plantation system, distinguished from its antebellum counterpart in the degree of latitude it allowed labor but governed by landowners according to unchanged caste values. Rather than seek prosperity through improved productivity, landowners sought to increase their income through new systems of exploitation. Blacks might be exploited harshly or gently. If they were lucky, they might escape whites to live in impoverished independence. But prosperity was not an option, for the policies of landowners created an unnecessarily dense poverty for the great mass of black labor.

In a second, unrelated transformation of the South's labor system, the postwar years also brought rapid growth to the landless white laboring class—a development that further clouded caste and class lines. Like large landowners, white laborers assumed that the caste line should be rigorously drawn, but because of the same federal laws that freed blacks from the harshest of planter demands, landless whites found themselves working on decentralized plantations and subject to a system of labor originally designed for freedmen and predicated upon the urge to exploit a racially defined laboring caste. Caste values were, however, a two-edged sword. Although trapped in an exploitative system of plantation labor, landless whites were free to press for the privileges of their race. Like employers, they reaped economic and social benefits from the racial discrimination that gave them a real if also shortsighted and emotional stake in the caste system.

Small-to-middling white proprietors had a crucial position in the socioeconomic system of the late nineteenth-century South. They were outside the plantation system, and they were collectively willing and powerful enough to resist planters in order to serve their own interests. They were the major constituency of every substantial reform movement. Yet like other white groups, they were dedicated to a social ideology that was at odds not only with the long-standing oppression of themselves and poorer whites at the hands of the relatively well-to-do but also with the mobility of blacks. Small-to-middling white proprietors justified their resistance to planters as the privilege of membership in the supposedly superior race; yet like planters, they defined their interests narrowly and ignored the needs of even poorer white groups. In seeking solely to improve their own economic position, middling whites did not challenge but rather ratified the values of caste and class superiority that defined the plantation system. Thus they also ratified and, in their reforms, intensified the unnecessarily dense poverty that the plantation system created and the severe limits that it placed on southern economic development. The values of caste and class superiority kept the South poor not only because of actions on the plantation but also off it as well.

The mechanism through which the South's socioeconomic system was created was an interplay of caste and class selfishness. Each white group fought for its own interests against those above it while ignoring those below and all the time justifying its cause with the same inherently unjust ideology. The white social ideology defined the economics of the plantation system—a system that planters manipulated in order to exploit black labor instead of seeking economic growth. The white social ideology provided the avenue by which white labor was ambiguously incorporated within the plantation system—simultaneously extending to landless white workers both exploitative practices and dividends from racial discrimination. And the white social ideology defined the efforts of small-to-middling white landowners to resist oppression by planters and to try to change their society in ways that served their needs. Yet in a poetic retribution of epic proportions deserved by all but its most thorough victims, in a blindly self destructive insistence that is part of every tragedy, the caste and class selfishness of whites brought a plague of impoverished misery on most of themselves and much of their region.

This work is not, however, a study of the entire South. It is a case study of late nineteenth-century Georgia. I chose Georgia because it was an important and in many ways representative southern state. Its black belt, upper piedmont, mountain, wiregrass, and coastal counties typify all important subdivisions of the South except the sugar districts of Louisiana. Georgia, like the rest of the South, was overwhelmingly rural. The rise of New South cities was dramatic, and a study of caste and class relations within them would have added an important dimension to this work, but I believe that the social history of the countryside is the background against which the cities must be understood and that historians have assumed they understood rural life better than they do. I have every reason to believe that my conclusions about Georgia hold true for the South in general. For that and stylistic reasons, I have frequently referred to southerners in general rather than Georgians in particular.

Chapter I

THE VALUE OF BLACK LABOR

Aside from the assumption that the negro will not work without physical compulsion, there appears to be another popular notion prevalent in the south. . . . It is that the negro exists for the special object of raising cotton, rice, and sugar *for the whites*, and that it is illegitimate for him to indulge, like other people, in the pursuit of his own happiness in his own way. Although it is admitted that he has ceased to be the property of a master, it is not admitted that he has a right to become his own master.

—Carl Schurz

FRANCES BUTLER was not a harsh mistress. She tried to rule under the paternalistic code of the Old South. Like her Georgia plantations, her paternalism was part of a legacy. She did not earn her land or the affection of her black workers so much as she inherited both from her father, Pierce Butler, who died in the summer of 1867. Rather than abuse the freedmen's loyalty, she consciously used it, as perhaps her father had taught her, to control her work force better. Her control was never absolute; it could only precariously bridge the space between the freedmen's attitude toward work and her own wish that they spend long, productive hours in the field—a closer approximation to the discipline of slavery than they wanted to bear. Her black workers kept the manager of her Sea Island plantations "in despair," she wrote. They just could not seem to understand that emancipation had not canceled their obligation to toil in her fields. "They don't do more than half a day's work" (about eight hours), and to get that, the overseer "has often to go from house to house to drive them out . . . and then has to sit under a tree in the field to see they don't run away." Butler's frustration was endless, her solution clear: "From the first, the fixed notion in their minds has been that liberty meant idleness; they must be forced to work until they become intelligent enough to know the value of labour," a generously offered lesson they seemed a bit hesitant to learn.[1]

Such comments, common during Reconstruction, became the planters' litany for the remainder of the nineteenth century. The Civil War had barely ended and free labor was yet untried when, in the summer of 1865, Carl Schurz traveled across the South to prepare a report for President Andrew Johnson. Southerners, he declared, had already concluded that free labor would be a failure: " 'You cannot make the negro work without physical compulsion.' I heard this hundreds of times, heard it wherever I went, heard it in nearly the same words from so many different persons, that I [concluded it is the] prevailing sentiment." Nearly fifty years later, white Georgians pronounced their views unchanged. In response to a survey conducted by Professor Robert Preston Brooks, planters still stressed the need to discipline black laborers to keep them at work. Other travelers in 1865 and other scholars fifty years later reported or shared similar views.[2]

Incontestable evidence that blacks worked hard and the comments of southern whites who praised black labor have tempted historians to dismiss as racist drivel the grumbling of employers during and after Reconstruction.[3] But as postbellum white land-

1. Frances Butler Leigh, *Ten Years on a Georgia Plantation Since the War* (London, 1883), 76, 53, 124.

2. Carl Schurz, "Report of Carl Schurz on the States of South Carolina, Georgia, Alabama, Mississippi and Louisiana," in "Message of the President of the United States . . . in Relation to the States of the Union Lately in Rebellion, December 19, 1865," *Senate Executive Documents*, 39th Cong., 1st Sess., No. 2, p. 116; "Inquiries I," 1912, in Robert Preston Brooks Papers, University of Georgia Libraries, Rare Books and Manuscript Department, Athens. For additional examples from Reconstruction, see James L. Roark, *Masters Without Slaves: Southern Planters in the Civil War and Reconstruction* (New York, 1977), 101, 116–17, 123, 138, 168; Whitelaw Reid, *After the War: A Tour of the Southern States, 1865–1866*, ed. C. Vann Woodward (New York, 1965), 146–51, 361, 363; Sidney Andrews, *The South Since the War, as shown by Fourteen Weeks of Travel and Observation in Georgia and the Carolinas* (Boston, 1865), 321. On scholars, see Matthew Brown Hammond, *The Cotton Industry: An Essay in American Economic History* (Ithaca, 1897), 186; Albert Bushnell Hart, *The Southern South* (New York, 1910), 93, 122–23.

3. Based upon what he had seen in the South, Albert Bushnell Hart anticipated later scholars in dismissing charges that blacks would not work as "race

owners and their antebellum counterparts complained about black workers, they meant something substantial (no matter how poorly conceived) that makes it possible to examine the canons of their faith in the labor of others. In fact, by listening closely to both the critics and the champions of the black work force, one can find a cluster of shared values among their apparently contradictory clichés. Experience with slavery, its attendant racism, and the touch of cupidity had nurtured among whites a group of coherent assumptions governing their perception of black work habits and their definition of the role of free black labor in southern society.

The collective experience of whites in a society with black slaves had taught them to think of blacks as a racially defined laboring caste. After the war, blacks remained a caste to be systematically excluded from southern society. They stood apart. What southerner was ever described as black? What black was ever described as a southerner? Blacks were a resource, something between man and beast, to be worked like a mule, to be worked like a forest or a mine. But whites went further than this. After the war as before, they defined blacks as a resource more important than any other, for they believed that society (which in their minds consisted solely of whites) depended upon the labor of blacks for its wealth.

Before the war, despite poor agricultural techniques, the exploitation of slave labor seemed to compensate masters reasonably well. To whites this was only right; blacks were meant, perhaps even destined, to produce wealth for whites. Slaveholders frequently complained about the shiftlessness of black labor not because slaves failed to work hard but because they tried to avoid work or fell short of harsh demands.[4] After the war a nostalgic haze enveloped the Taras of the Old South and allowed

---

slander." Hart, *The Southern South*, 122–23. See also Peter Kolchin, *First Freedom: The Responses of Alabama Blacks to Emancipation and Reconstruction* (Westport, 1972), 30–48, *et passim*; Joel Williamson, *After Slavery: The Negro in South Carolina During Reconstruction, 1861–1877* (New York, 1975), 45–47, 164–65; Roger Ransom and Richard Sutch, *One Kind of Freedom: The Economic Consequences of Emancipation* (Cambridge, 1977), 21–22.

4. Edmund S. Morgan, *American Slavery—American Freedom: The Ordeal of Colonial Virginia* (New York, 1975), 317–19.

whites to forget the complaints of slaveholders.[5] Their memories of ideal black slaves became indistinguishable from the ideal against which they judged free black workers. Since the freedmen failed more completely than the slaves to live within that narrow role to which white expectations consigned them, landowning employers labeled them idle and unreliable and attributed their own economic troubles to a collective failure to subordinate black labor adequately.

With these assumptions about the role of black labor, whites greeted emancipation. With these same assumptions, unaltered by years of conflict with and begrudging concessions to black workers, whites greeted the twentieth century some thirty-five years later. In a sense, the social history of slavery was not yet over in 1900. It was still being written in static patterns of assumption and behavior.

Whites left many records that, while expressing their own point of view, also obliquely noted the attitudes of blacks toward work. After the war, the chronic repetition of white complaints about black workers testified to the irreconcilable differences between the normative assumptions of white landowners and the performance of their newly freed and dismayingly willful workers. The complaints of 1867 were the complaints of 1900. Whites complained when the freedmen did not go the fields but dried fruit or tended gardens, when they would not work on Saturdays or put in the sixteen-hour days of slavery, when their wives and children refused to work in cotton under a white supervisor, and when they bargained over the terms of new contracts.[6]

5. Paul M. Gaston, *The New South Creed: A Study in Southern Mythmaking* (Baton Rouge, 1970), 181–83; Williamson, *After Slavery*, 37–38.

6. Illustrations appear in both primary and secondary sources. See, for example, J. D. Collins to John A. Cobb, July 31, 1865, Howell Cobb to My Dear Wife, December, 1865, both in C. Mildred Thompson, *Reconstruction in Georgia: Economic, Social, Political, 1865–1872* (New York, 1915), 71–73; "Suggestions Submitted by a Committee of Planters," n.p., November 24, 1864, in Schurz, "Report of Carl Schurz," Accompanying Documents, No. 3, p. 84; *Southern Cultivator*, February, 1875; Hammond, *The Cotton Industry*, 187; James Atkins, testimony, October 24, 1871, in *Testimony Taken by the Joint Committee to Inquire into the Condition of Affairs in the Late Insurrectionary States: The Ku Klux Klan Conspiracy, House Reports*, 42nd Cong., 2nd Sess., No. 22, Vol. VII, p. 524, herein-

But when freedmen did these and other things that whites saw as evidence of idleness and unreliability, they were making choices that helped to determine the economic structure of the postwar South. It was these choices on which whites often blamed their own economic troubles. Thus, to understand the political economy of the New South, it is important to understand how the freedmen defined their own interests: what they did and why they did it.

Although the records left by whites are wrapped in self-interest and racism, they nevertheless record the occasional incident or phrase that helps to describe and explain the behavior of freedmen. Like whites, blacks seem to have understood their new freedom in terms of slavery. But while whites believed with remarkable unanimity that the regimen of free black labor should approximate as closely as possible to that of the ideal slave, blacks defined freedom as an end to the specific abuses that slavery had encouraged. From the very beginning of Reconstruction, they sought to escape the long-borne hardships of slavery that were reflected in the concrete questions they asked before agreeing to contracts: How long would they have to work in the fields? What would their duties be? Would there be an overseer? Would whipping be prohibited? Could they have gardens and keep pigs? And most of all, how much would they be paid, in cash or shares, with rations or without?

The expectations whites and blacks had gathered from their common experience were so different and the authoritarian norms of whites were held so dogmatically that conflict was inevitable. It was one of the clearest and most predictable legacies of slavery, for even as slaves, blacks were not fully resigned to the role whites defined for them. The conflict that followed emancipation was the much-repressed conflict of slavery suddenly burst free.

---

after cited as *Joint Committee Report on the Ku Klux Klan*; W. O. Atwater and Charles D. Woods, "Dietary Studies with Reference to the Food of the Negro in Alabama in 1895 and 1896," U.S. Department of Agriculture, Office of Experiment Stations, *Bulletin* no. 38 (Washington, D.C., 1897), 18; Williamson, *After Slavery*, 36, 45–46, 89, 91, 100, 102, 104, 107, 114; Leon F. Litwack, *Been in the Storm So Long: The Aftermath of Slavery* (New York, 1979), 227, 292–304, 329, 337, 340–46, 416–25, 432–37; Paul D. Escott, *Slavery Remembered: A Record of Twentieth-Century Slave Narratives* (Chapel Hill, 1979), 148–58; Vernon L. Wharton, *The Negro in Mississippi, 1865–1890* (New York, 1965), 81.

The conflicts of slavery often occurred as masters tried to control the diligence, amount, and pace of labor.[7] They usually worked their slaves from dawn to dusk, watched carefully, punished severely, and extracted five and a half, six, or sometimes seven long days of work a week.[8] The simplicity of monotonous, grueling labor in the sun, of plowing, chopping, or picking cotton, encouraged the planters to make oppressive demands, but perhaps their power to make unchallengeable demands grated more than any particular oppression. There was a constant pulling between masters and their shirking slaves, and when a master or mistress stepped beyond the large limits of a slave's endurance, the result could be one of the quick outbursts of defiant resentment which were common during the history of American slavery. These outbursts were sometimes verbal, sometimes physical, but in any case their price was high. A bullwhip often arbitrated differences between a master and his slaves. While not used on every plantation, whips and threats of whipping were widely employed to maintain plantation discipline. In fact, whippings, more often than anything else, prompted the dramatic episodes of resistance that freedmen still living in the 1930s remembered.[9] Whippings were a grievance, but they also symbolized with pain and humiliation the white proprietors' demanding supervision of their black workers.

This symbolism was apparent not only in retrospect. It was an integral part of the masters' definition of properly controlled black labor and of the slaves' understanding of their bondage. After emancipation, as one freedman put it, blacks were free to "take no more foolishness off of white folks."[10] But even though emancipation had arrived with Union soldiers, freedmen still had to win slowly for themselves an end to physical abuse. After the war, as Carl Schurz and many others reported, white southerners continued to assume that they should repress the independent will of black workers. For that reason, in 1865 and 1866

7. Escott, *Slavery Remembered*, 40–61, esp. 86–87; *Unwritten History of Slavery: Autobiographical Accounts of Negro Ex-Slaves*, Social Science Source Documents, No. 1 (Nashville, 1945), 171–72, 182, 229. Despite numerous recent studies of slavery, Kenneth M. Stampp's *The Peculiar Institution: Slavery in the Antebellum South* (New York, 1956) remains the best single volume.

8. *Unwritten History of Slavery*, 18.

9. *Ibid.*, 21; Escott, *Slavery Remembered*, 79, 89, 92–93, Tables 3.7, 3.8, 3.10.

10. Escott, *Slavery Remembered*, 144, and see 127–28.

vigilante patrols, replaying the role of their legal antebellum counterparts, tried to force freedmen to stay on the plantations of their former masters, and southern legislators attempted to accomplish the same thing in black codes. The freedmen braved patrollers to exercise their new liberty, and they resisted other attempts to continue the demands and coercion of slavery. As a result, the conflicts that characterized slavery became endemic during Reconstruction as part of the turmoil through which a new system of labor relations gradually supplanted the old.

Several incidents in 1868 illustrate the painful transition to freedom. In Dougherty County in southwest Georgia, Mrs. L. Mott became furious when Robert Peck refused to obey her orders and answered her with "insolent language." She shot him. In nearby Lee County, Henry Calloway became so enraged at Edmund Johnson's "disobedience" that he punched him in the face, kicked him, and when Johnson tried to flee, "pursued him with an open knife" and shot at him twice. To employers like these, a worker was also insolent if he complained to the Freedmen's Bureau. In Dougherty, Henry Clay Caswell "was shot in the head" by Robert Bray "for having complained to [an agent of the Bureau] that his wages had not been paid" before he was dismissed from Bray's plantation. Although Bray was arrested, an empathetic grand jury refused to indict him. Caswell, on the other hand, recovered from his wound only to be tried and "sentenced to the penitentiary for four years." His offense was grave. He had made his mark on an affidavit swearing that W. C. Bray, not Robert, had shot him. Three months later in the same county, James Hall severely beat Anne Hampton "with a heavy stick" for "having made statements to an agent of the bureau contrary to his own." Between January and mid-November, 1868, in the congressional district that included Dougherty and Lee counties, at least 113 freedmen were murdered or "attacked with intent to kill." Fifty-seven of these cases had no reported cause or provocation. Twenty-six of these attacks occurred on one Saturday in September, as the energetic sheriff of Mitchell County and his posse made sure that "no Republican meeting should be held at Camilla." Of the remainder, fully one-half were directly attributable to some argument over work. One can hopefully assume that most disagreements between employers and freedmen stopped short of homicidal, but these cases are not even a full summary of incidents of conflict over labor. Many of the conflicts in the fifty-seven incomplete reports were, no doubt, over work, and local agents of the Freedmen's Bureau estimated that at least one-third of "the crimes of this nature" (murders and murderous attacks) went completely unreported. The officer for Clay County reported that he and every other agent could present "a long list of lawless and high handed proceedings which this bureau is powerless to correct, and which the civil authorities will not take cognizance of." [11]

These incidents tell of repulsive brutality. But retrospective repulsion is, in a sense, irrelevant except as it enhances the appreciation of other things that the pattern of violence suggests. White southerners were not some extraterrestrial breed with a peculiar penchant for violence. During Reconstruction decent people became so outraged at "insolent" and "disobedient" black workers that they struck out cruelly. Their violence reflected the sincere, elemental conviction that race defined appropriate social and economic roles. When widespread violence died out, it was because southern whites learned that violence could disrupt free labor as much as control it. Peace was, therefore, no sign of change. Whites had not converted to free-labor ideology. They continued to believe that the proper role of black labor was abject subordination.

Surprisingly, even those whites who praised black labor shared this belief in racially defined economic roles. Their assumptions are obvious in the words they used to defend black workers. "Employed in squads under skillful direction the negro is the best of laborers," wrote one supposed authority. "As a patient laborer the negro has no equal," claimed another. Besides being excellent, black labor was indispensable, as was admitted by Bill Arp, one of the most widely reprinted southern columnists of the day. Arp wrote in a down-home, commonsense style

11. "Report on Murder and Assaults with Intent to Kill Committed upon Freed People in the State of Georgia from January 1, 1868, to November 15, 1868," in "Conditions in Georgia," *House Miscellaneous Documents*, 40th Cong., 3rd Sess., No. 52, pp. 124, 126–27, 128, case nos. 11, 58, 32, 39, 61–86; George Ballou, report, in Brevet Major O. H. Howard to Brevet Major Frank Gallagher, November 14, 1868, *ibid.*, pp. 119, 130.

that reflected and affirmed the prejudices of his admiring white audience. "I like the nigger," he wrote indulgently. "For hard work, contented work, humble work, who could take his place? . . . He is grafted to the Southern tree."[12]

The similarity between the superficially contradictory views of critics and champions of black labor was reflected in a curious dichotomy. The opposite of idleness and unreliability was not industry; it was planter control and disciplined labor. "We have the best labor when it is properly utilized," admonished a planter from Stewart County, "and we have the means to control it."[13] To control labor properly was to keep it subordinate to and hard at work for whites; otherwise, the black presence was unwelcome. In a speech before the state agricultural society, Dr. W. S. Leland, one of Bill Arp's neighbors in Cartersville, Georgia, noted this attitude and the dichotomy in which it was expressed: "We needed them as slaves, we need them as freedmen. . . . It's nonsense to talk of their idleness. Call you the making of seven million bales of cotton last year not working! Uncontrolled the negro is a nuisance; properly managed he is a blessing to the South."[14] Objecting only to imprecise diction, Dr. Leland pointed to the link between critics and champions of black labor and agreed with both.

The fundamental agreement among whites was also reflected in their views on race. They could see their definition of the proper role of black labor written in the ever-self-justifying statutes of natural law. Negroes could supposedly "lie harder, get up sooner, [and] stand the sun better than any people on the face of the earth." The black man, "by nature, by the very organization of his mind and body," was "made for a laborer, and that," conveniently enough, "in countries where good rice, sugar cane,

12. John L. Black, "Cheap Labor in the South," C. J. Haden, "The Spectre of the Negro," both in *Southern States: An Illustrated Monthly Magazine Devoted to the South*, I, 307, 458; Atlanta *Constitution*, July 27, 1884. Bill Arp was the pen name used by Charles H. Smith. See also Robert Preston Brooks, *The Agrarian Revolution in Georgia, 1865–1912*, University of Wisconsin, *Bulletin*, No. 639, History Series, Vol. III, No. 3 (Madison, 1914), 21; Leigh, *Ten Years on a Georgia Plantation*, 24–26, 25 n.

13. Anonymous letter from Lumpkin, Stewart County, in *Southern Cultivator*, November, 1875.

14. Atlanta *Constitution*, August 16, 1883.

cotton and all other crops that need attention year round are raised." He was physically able and "content to work cheerfully ten to eleven hours daily." Whites asked, "who but he can make a cotton and corn crop on three pounds of bacon and a peck of meal a week?"[15] Who indeed?

But while made to labor endlessly on an unwholesome diet, the black man was supposedly also "by nature indolent and superstitious." Therefore, said whites, "when left to himself, he succeeds poorly as an independent farmer." He always did "best with a head over him to direct his labors." Blacks needed "intelligent white men to manage, direct and control them." Because they were constitutionally "unable to take care of themselves," the white men who forced them to work were doing them a great service. As Dr. Leland explained, "we need their brawn and muscles, and they need our brains."[16]

The justification offered by whites for the subordination of free black labor sounded unchanged from their defense of slavery.[17] Both implied a reciprocity that became even less obvious after the war than it had been before. As freedmen tried to lessen both the burden of work and their dependence upon white landowners, whites resisted point by point, and blacks learned quickly, if they did not already know, that the elaborate racial etiquette that had attended slavery still constrained them. To violate that etiquette invited a harsh, sometimes violent rejoinder. To push hard was dangerous.

During congressional hearings white Georgians frankly acknowledged their intolerance of assertive black workers. "Suppose that a white man and a colored man have some controversy

15. S. H. Bassett, address to the Georgia State Agricultural Society, in *Southern Cultivator*, November, 1884; R. M. Orme, letter, in Milledgeville *Union and Recorder*, September 1, 1885; Black, "Cheap Labor in the South," 307; Dixie [pseud.], "Nut Grass—the Labor Question," *Southern Cultivator*, September, 1869, quoted in Stephen DeCanio, *Agriculture in the Postbellum South: The Economics of Production and Supply* (Cambridge, Mass., 1974), 88.

16. Bassett, address; Haden, "The Spectre of the Negro," 458; Orme, letter in Milledgeville *Union and Recorder*, September 1, 1885; W. S. Leland, address to the Georgia State Agricultural Society, in Atlanta *Constitution*, August 16, 1883.

17. On antebellum justification for the subordination of black labor, see Winthrop D. Jordan, *White over Black: American Attitudes Toward the Negro, 1550–1812* (New York, 1977); Fredrickson, *The Black Image in the White Mind*.

about a matter of dealing between them," a congressman asked a planter from Floyd County. Would "the white man allow the black man to stand up and assert his side of a controversy, and his views, and his" claims? The planter replied, "No sir, not as a general thing. . . . that is impudence." The congressman asked another planter from Georgia, "Suppose that a negro man has been working for a white man and they have some difference or dispute in relation to wages, will your people generally allow a negro to stand up and assert his right in the same way . . . they would allow a white man without objection?" The witness was surprised that the question was even necessary. "O, no, sir," he said, "that is not expected at all." The congressman pressed on, "If a colored man does stand up and assert his rights, . . . that is considered 'impudence'?" The witness agreed, "Yes, sir, gross impudence." Finally, the congressman concluded his line of questioning, "Is that species of 'impudence' . . . considered a sufficient excuse by many people for chastening a negro or 'dealing with him'?" The witness hesitated uncomfortably; perhaps he had already admitted more than was wise. "Well, some think so," he equivocated.[18]

Even at the turn of the century, whites could remember the "insolence" of former slaves with a bitterness that reflected passionate convictions about the racial "foundation of civilization in all the Southern States." As one still indignant white educator remembered, "The family cook . . . demanded to be known as Mrs. Jackson and the chambermaid as Miss Marguerite." Thus, he said, "the negro was intoxicated with the licence of freedom; the North was blinded by the passions of war; the South was fighting for civilization and existence."[19]

Yet in the late nineteenth century there were incidents of paternalism—even reciprocal paternalism—that seem difficult to reconcile with the severity of white social cosmography. In 1887, for example, the Americus *Weekly Recorder* told of two freedmen supporting their former master. As a rich planter, he had

18. P. M. Sheibley, testimony, July 10, 1871, George P. Burnett, testimony, July 11, 1871, both in *Joint Committee Report on the Ku Klux Klan*, VI, 47, 67.
19. George T. Winston, *The Relation of the Whites to the Negroes*, Publications of the American Academy of Political and Social Science, No. 310 (Philadelphia, n.d.), 113–14.

been kind to them in slavery, and now that he was old, blind, and hopelessly poor, they were being kind in turn. The *Recorder* concluded this remarkable story with a confession that "such affection between master and slave rarely exists."[20] That it existed at all would be worthy of note in any society.

Other incidents of paternalism and loyalty were more obviously self-serving than they had seemed in slavery. "Dear Miss Mary," wrote Rena Hughes to her former mistress, "I shall ever think of you as a near friend and one who has had quite an interest in me and truly hope you will ever prove the same." With that pointedly affectionate introduction out of the way, Miss Hughes moved on to business. "I know I owe your husband, the Dr but dont feel I shall ever be able to pay him and hope he will consider the debt paid."[21]

More typical was a different sort of exchange. After a bad crop, or when the price of cotton fell especially low, an employer might have felt obliged, however reluctantly, to feed his penniless hands until the next planting season. Laborers were scarce, he would explain. If he did not supply them, they might go off to work for some other landowner who would.[22] Nor were these provisions of side meat and meal charity. They were charged, with considerable interest, against the following year's account. Similarly, if a freedman needed a doctor or lawyer—if he had some emergency—he would turn to his employer for help. Who else was there with money enough to pay the fee? If a loan were granted, it might carry 33 percent interest; yet both planter and worker would still consider it an act of generosity.[23] Kitchen scraps and worn clothing could no doubt be given with as much

20. Americus *Weekly Recorder*, January 11, 1887.

21. Rena Hughes to Mary Camak, July 14, 1884, in Mary Camak Papers, University of Georgia Libraries, Rare Books and Manuscripts Department, Athens. A case in which a son of a planter may not have lived up to his father's wishes by failing to care for a former personal servant may be glimpsed in G. E. Memford to Mr. Colson, August 7, 1890, in John Marshall Slaton Papers, Samuel Carter Atkinson Division, Box 53, Georgia Department of Archives and History, Atlanta.

22. Ray Mathis, Mary Mathis, and Douglas Clare Purcell (eds.), *John Hory Dent Farm Journals and Account Books, 1840–1892*, Microfilm (University, Ala., 1977), XV, December 6, 1883.

23. Clarence Herman Nixon, *Forty Acres and Steel Mules* (Chapel Hill, 1938), 34. See also Mathis, Mathis, and Purcell (eds.), *Dent Journals*, XVIII, December 1, 1886.

contempt as charity and received with as much stoicism as thanks; but as self-serving as white employers and black workers often were, some of the confusion of resentment, contempt, affection, and resignation that made opaque and inexplicable the antebellum relations between master and slave lingered on in the postbellum South. In part this testifies to the thoroughness with which blacks were kept in poverty and made dependent upon their white employers. In part, the friendships that developed despite the barriers of racial doctrine and oppression merely tell of the humanity of ordinary people living in an inhumane society.

All in all, however, it is clear that with emancipation or very soon thereafter, whites and blacks moved into ever more separated societies. As one southern scholar observed in 1889, "The diminished intimacy of the relation of master and servant is . . . moving the negro and white man further and further from one another." The statement was more redundant than explanatory, but the observation was accurate enough: "The two distinct societies do not join, when they come together at all."[24] For that reason, John H. Dent, the owner of a large plantation in Alabama who sold out, moved to Georgia, and employed several croppers after the war, noted little about the personal lives of his black hands, although he frequently mentioned his white neighbors. He could go on at great length in his voluminous, meticulously kept journal about the death of Bully, his Scotch terrier, eulogizing him for more than a page and calling him a "true friend, a constant companion to his master." But following a series of brief, daily entries marking the slow, painful death from rabies of the son of a black sharecropper on his place, Dent could record the boy's death with the note: "Jake's child died last night which put a stop to all fodder pulling and work on this place today. Niggers ought to die when there is not much work on hand, for when one of them dies, it stops the work of the whole neighborhood." This reaction was no anomaly. A month later Dent repeated it when another boy died and two days of work were lost. There is a temptation to dismiss Dent as a harsh, immoral, in-

24. Philip A. Bruce, *The Plantation Negro as a Freeman: Observations on His Character, Condition, and Prospects in Virginia* (New York, 1889), 44–48. See also Winston, "The Relation of Whites to Negroes," 105–106.

human man. Yet his journal shows him to have been like most other people—suffering from his share of unextraordinary faults but trying reasonably hard to live an honest, decent life. Indeed, he tried to treat his workers fairly and complained bitterly about landowners who did not.[25]

Despite such callous indifference, after the war as before, paternalism was not unimportant. The freedmen who worked for Frances Butler and John Dent fared better than did those who worked for employers of untempered severity. But it is possible to exaggerate the differences between whites who wanted to treat blacks kindly and those who did not. Like critics and champions of black labor, kind employers and cruel ones shared large areas of agreement about the rightful subordination of black labor. As a result, postwar paternalism became even less encompassing than its antebellum counterpart. Evidence of antebellum paternalism comes largely from the friendships between masters and personal servants that many whites upheld as the ideal against which to judge the treatment of slaves as a group. Postbellum paternalism could appear similar, but emancipation had destroyed the contradiction of man as property and the substantial investment in labor that led masters to treat slaves well—even if only in theory. Now, whites needed only to treat blacks fairly, which was a quite different standard, readily buried in legalistic severity. As John Dent observed, self-interest no longer commanded that whites provide even bare comforts for blacks. The freedmen were expected to care for themselves. If they fared poorly, it was their own fault.[26]

To say that paternalism faded in the postwar South in no way implies that slavery was not a brutal institution. Evidence from both periods suggests a none-too-pleasant "father." After the war, however, paternalism persisted as the exception to the rule while the old paternalistic ideal assumed a new function. Reminiscences of the wondrous, if atypical, friendships between masters and slaves cost whites little and satisfied them much. And

25. Mathis, Mathis, and Purcell (eds.), *Dent Journals*, XIX, August 28, 1890, XVI, September 5, 1884, October 15, 1884, November 13, 1877. Most of Dent's few comments on the personal lives of blacks had to do with the occasions they missed work. See, for example, XV, May 20, 1882.

26. *Ibid.*, XII, January 5, 1877, also January 10, 1877, XV, February [?], 1884.

even though whites had little trouble in conscience, these mythic memories, coupled with occasional postwar incidents of paternalistic friendship, could readily serve to excuse their past and justify their present.[27] Since individual whites were no longer directly responsible for the well-being of individual blacks, the paternalistic ideal turned from a practical guarantee that most blacks would eat reasonably well into abstract, impersonal, and often conveniently meaningless measures for the "best interests of the colored people." If many blacks were not as well-off materially after the war as they had been in slavery, if some starved or lacked clothing or a home, southern whites no longer felt responsible. Blacks, they said, should learn self-reliance.

In this way emancipation chipped away the veneer of paternalism while it left untouched the urge to perpetuate the exploitation of blacks that slavery had allowed. There were incidents of unselfish charity, as when whites helped a freedman on "the Barrow place" whose cabin had burned, but the sarcasm with which whites often discussed their occasional charity suggests substantive change as well. As historian George Fredrickson has demonstrated, little was left of paternalism in the New South not only because of the decreasing intimacy of employer and servant but also because it had lost its utility as a moral, normative standard against which to judge individual behavior and the obligation of whites as a group to blacks as a group.[28] Vestigial paternalism had become a convenient and increasingly chimerical justification for the continued subordination of a racially defined laboring caste.

There was a neat, tautological inevitability to the white man's understanding of the social order, for white southerners, like many other Americans, did not need the label of social Darwinism to assume many of its premises. After the war, white southerners became, if anything, more severe in their racially defined

27. See, for example, Winston, "The Relation of Whites to Negroes," 116–17, *et passim*; Gaston, *The New South Creed*, 181–84.

28. Americus *Weekly Recorder*, January 25, 1884; Bill Arp, in Atlanta *Constitution*, January 5, May 6, 1883, July 27, 1884; Fredrickson, *The Black Image in the White Mind*, 198–227. Fredrickson deals largely with the ideology of collective relations between whites and blacks rather than the relations between individual employers and laborers.

economic dogma. Blacks were born inferior, were less successful, and were destined to occupy their subordinate position for-
ever. In 1884 John Dent, as usual, repeated the typical white
point of view. "A generation of negroes has been born free and
raised as citizens of the United States," he wrote, "and today
they are the same race of Niggers yet, morally, socially, and materially. They were Nigger born, Nigger bred and will Nigger
die. As God made them, so they will ever be. . . . As slaves they
were better off, and more cared for than they are as freed men."[29]

Yet despite the leaden poverty of blacks, and despite the sincere conviction with which whites defined absolute control of
subordinate black workers as ideal, natural, and inevitable, the
complaints of white employers show that the postwar world refused to match their expectations. Those who complained most
were those small-to-middling farmers who were, unlike indifferent landlords and planter-merchants, dependent primarily upon
income derived directly from agriculture rather than from rents
or commerce. Their favorite target was the decentralized plantation system that evolved after the war. Under this system,
black share hands and renters acquired substantial day-to-day
autonomy even when landowners supervised closely. Where a
landowner was absent or indifferent, black autonomy increased
that much more.

Many complaints concerned destructive agricultural techniques. "A planter who cultivates on the share system," said one
observer, "must see his fences falling out of order, his manure
heaps a diminishing quantity, his hogs and cattle strayed, stolen
or starved." Claimed another, "when a farm is entirely in the
hands of negro tenants the deterioration . . . is something fright-
ful, the land is materially worn out." Not surprisingly, articles
on well-run farms, which appeared regularly in both the rural
and the urban press, directly linked the success of the farmer
with his control of labor. "I employ wage hands and have tenants," reported a "modern farmer" who cultivated eight hundred
acres near Eatonton, Georgia. "Both farm hands and tenants are
kept under fine control." And James Oliphant of Stellaville

29. Mathis, Mathis, and Purcell (eds.), *Dent Journals*, XV, n.d. (following last
entry, February, 1884).

advised: "Tenants must be able to support themselves." They "must be directed in pitching their crops and working them; they must be compelled to make manure and keep up fences. The land they work must not be allowed to become any poorer." [30]

Landowners who condemned inadequate supervision and control were undoubtedly correct in that inattentive landlords made less profit from farming than they might otherwise have made and that the productivity of southern agriculture as a whole suffered because of them. The agricultural techniques employed by blacks did not obtain maximum yields or preserve the fertility of the land. Even Albert Bushnell Hart, the northern historian who sympathized with blacks and condemned as "race-slander" the accusation they would not work, reported that the effects of their imposed ignorance could be seen in the slovenliness of their farms.[31] Yet many of those who condemned inadequate discipline were also saying something more than this. In their eyes, the failure of one planter to discipline labor had a directly adverse effect on the profits of his more diligent white neighbors and was responsible for southern poverty. Listen, for example, to an address by William J. Northen, president of the state agricultural society and future governor of Georgia, before a convention at Brunswick in 1889. Graphically, he described the consequences of allowing farms to be "run by indolent tenants in the absence of landlords." These farms, Northen claimed, demoralized "for miles about them, the labor that would [otherwise] be productive and prosperous." They ruined Georgia's agriculture; they destroyed "the confidence of business"; and they put "all farmers at a disadvantage in trade while they encourage[d] an idleness that festers with corruption." They spread "the contagion of their social, moral and political poison" throughout their neighborhoods. Like so many others, Northen thought white Georgians could solve all their problems if they would just place black labor "under a rigid system, to enforce industrious habits and efficient good service." He concluded, "When

30. Robert Somers, *The Southern States Since the War, 1870–1* (London, 1871), 60; Albany *News*, n.d., quoted in Sparta *Ishmaelite*, October 14, 1887; Americus *Weekly Recorder*, January 6, 1887; James Oliphant, letter, September, 1875, in *Southern Cultivator*, November, 1875.
31. Hart, *The Southern South*, 121.

this is done, we will give back to the rural districts the school house and the church, the centers of civilization and progressive development."[32]

Northen's view was not unique. In fact, his speech, widely published in county newspapers, received the kind of praise usually offered particularly adept statements of conventional wisdom. In 1894 Charles Otken published a study, *The Ills of the South*, that repeated Northen's claims as accepted truths. "The resident farmer[s]," he explained, "had less than half the number of negroes that they could provide with land. The worst feature was [that] those they had were demoralized by the labor on [absentee and] merchant places. To control them was a difficult thing. To get work out of them was a task. The danger of losing even these inferior negroes was great. Patience was worn threadbare. Other resident farms, with land and livestock sufficient for twenty or more hands, could not secure a single negro laborer." Resident farmers less prominent than Northen agreed: "These landowners are the culpable parties and the cause of the low state of farming throughout the country" because they allow "labor that could otherwise be productive and profitable [to be] taken away from productive farming." Even U. B. Phillips, the first great master of southern history, added only "poor soil" to the "slackness" of uncontrolled black labor as the cause of southern poverty.[33]

These critics of undisciplined, "demoralized" labor were not concerned with the profits of merchants or inattentive landlords, let alone black farmers. They were concerned with the liberty that unsupervised farms afforded black labor. They knew these farms allowed blacks to escape from white control, and they thought that this escape, or the possibility of escape, and the economic leverage it allowed made the employees of atten-

32. "Semi-Annual Address Delivered by Col. W. J. Northen, President, Georgia State Agricultural Society, at Brunswick, February 12, 1889," and accompanying clippings, Scrapbook, 1887–1889, pp. 1–4, in William J. Northen Personal Papers, Georgia Department of Archives and History, Atlanta.

33. Charles H. Otken, *The Ills of the South* (New York, 1894), 43; Mathis, Mathis, and Purcell (eds.), *Dent Journals*, X, August 8, 1872; Americus *Weekly Recorder*, August 26, 1884; Ulrich Bonnell Phillips, "Plantations with Slave Labor and Free," in Phillips, *The Slave Economy of the Old South: Selected Essays in Economic and Social History*, ed. Eugene Genovese (Baton Rouge, 1968), 268.

tive farmers, whether working for wages or for shares, difficult to control adequately.

A hundred years later, the belief that blacks were not as dependent upon whites as they should have been seems almost incredible. A late twentieth-century observer is tempted to see nineteenth-century blacks only as captured in poverty and subject to exploitation with varying degrees of efficiency. But from the very beginning of Reconstruction, the slightest autonomy of emancipated slaves was at odds with the planters' idea of appropriate relations between labor and capital. Historian James L. Roark has shown how the norms of the plantation governed the minds of landowners with undiminished power immediately after the war. Planters testified eloquently to their inability to adjust to the market relations of even partly free labor.[34] In 1874 James Oliphant of Stellaville thought undisciplined blacks had left planters "humbled, humiliated and worried. . . . Many are fast losing their self-respect, veracity, integrity and the noble independence of manhood." To prove his point, he described wage hands slowly bargaining their way through stages of cropping on "halves" and "thirds" until they became renters. "The negroes have been flattered and allowed latitude until they are well-nigh ruined," he concluded. A commentator from Lumpkin explained, "The farmer should be independent, and control his land, his mules, his crops, and his labor."[35] Ironically, as blacks were working their way up the agricultural ladder toward autonomy, they were proving their "demoralization" in the eyes of the planters. The latitude or maneuvering room of blacks within their subordinate position—their ability to demand share privileges, advance to "independent" tenancy, and occasionally even become landowners—was fundamentally offensive to the white sense of social order.

Significantly, however, planters and other critics did not describe the effects of "undisciplined labor" merely in terms of social status. Planters attributed their collective financial troubles to the quasi autonomy of blacks. They could count their money as well as anyone, and during the late nineteenth century

34. Roark, *Masters Without Slaves*, 111–205, *et passim*.
35. Oliphant, letter, in *Southern Cultivator*, April, 1874; Anonymous letter from Lumpkin, Stewart County, *ibid.*, November, 1875.

they found precious little to count. They thought that they had "given up their only claim to superiority and that the curse" was upon them "in a decrease in substance . . . and self-respect."[36] The plight of capital was the fault of labor; the plight of whites, the fault of blacks. "The unreliability of our present system of labor has become so palpable," reported one newspaper, "that it is getting to be a serious question in this country whether or not farming will pay at all." Labor can say to capital, "I'll chop your cotton or pick your cotton for so much by the day or hundred, while the farmer is fully convinced . . . that if he pays these rates he must lose by it." Whites thought this was "a most singular anomaly," and they asked, "When labor controls capital . . . are we not bound to admit that our present system is unreliable and untenable?"[37] Whites believed the South was poorer than it had been before the war because black labor was not being kept in its "God-given place."

As whites complained about black labor, they made it obvious they were not comparing it to free labor elsewhere. They had no reason to do so. They understood it in terms of their former experience as superior white masters dealing with inferior black slaves.[38] Therein lay the reason planters attributed their economic troubles to labor. Free black labor seemed "idle and unreliable" to Frances Butler and most other white southerners because they could not compel freedmen to work as many hours as slaves had worked, because freedmen had liberty enough to make economic choices and to act on interests at odds with or merely different from those of landowners, because black women and children would not necessarily work in the field, because free labor was too expensive, because it was, to use the planters' emblematic phrase, "too independent."

Economic historians Roger Ransom and Richard Sutch argue that the South was not poorer for emancipation. But, they say, the freedmen received their share of southern income, for-

36. Milledgeville *Union and Recorder*, July 28, 1885.
37. Dawson *Journal*, August 22, 1881.
38. The view of the plantation as a social institution has been most notably characteristic of the works of U. B. Phillips and Eugene Genovese. On the persistence of the cultural values of the plantation, see Phillips' lily-white, romantic, yet still important essay "The Plantation Product of Men," in Phillips, *The Slave Economy of the Old South*, 269–72.

merly expropriated by their white masters.[39] Their argument would have been small comfort to the planters. It would also have seemed incomprehensible or maybe just silly. When white landowners claimed that the South was poorer than it had been before the war, they meant that they were poorer. They were not making an unthinking conceptual slip. To whites, blacks were not a part of society.

Obviously this was a self-serving habit of mind, but it was consistent and powerful, and it was evident in their language. When a Georgia newspaperman during Reconstruction wrote of "the people of the North and South" groaning under the "burdens of national strife," he meant the white people. After all, he was protesting the passage of a civil rights bill for the protection of blacks. Another Georgia newspaperman advocated the forced overseas colonization, not of slaves, but of black American citizens in 1893 in order to solve the "race problem." The editor wrote that colonization was "altogether the best thing Congress could do with the subject in justice to the people of the South and to the negro himself." "What must be done with the negro?" asked a college professor. "Everything touching the subject must be of incalculable interest to every man of the South and every woman, too." What the professor felt no need to say, and what his white audience did not need to be told, was that he meant every *white* man and every *white* woman, too. When the editor of the Atlanta *Constitution* echoed the professor, he was no different from any other white southerner: "The truth is the negro is the situation and the situation is the problem, and the sooner the southern people take hold of this problem in earnest, the better it will be for the whole country. In the South and by the southern people alone is this problem to be solved." We can be sure it will be solved fairly, claimed the editor. After all, "there is no reason why any Southern man, woman or child should have any prejudice against the negro race." Even in the most casual ways, whites made their assumptions clear: "Egg nog was kept at the house or mansion for everyone," reminisced an anonymous author about the Christmas before the Cause was Lost. But *everyone* did not mean quite everyone. "For everyone and all

---

39. Ransom and Sutch, *One Kind of Freedom*, 4–5, Chap. 3.

the hands" was the complete phrase.[40] *Hands* was, of course, one of the several terms for slaves.

When white southerners discussed social and economic issues, there were southerners, and then there were blacks. There was society, and then there were blacks. There were people, and then there were blacks.[41] The equation of whiteness with membership in society was inseparable from the implicit equation of black labor with agricultural labor as a whole and of whiteness with capital. Whites assumed a bifurcated society. *White* equalled property equaled capital, equaled society. *Black* equaled poverty, equaled labor, equaled something somehow alien.

As historian Paul Gaston has shown, white southerners moved back and forth with ease between justifying their domination "on the basis of the wealth-intelligence-character formula" and what he describes as "a purely racial justification."[42] But while in Gaston's view this vacillation weakened their position, landowning white southerners felt no need to reconcile the two formulas. They assumed them to be synonymous. This assumption was part of the faith that defined and justified the caste system. Before the war, prominent landowners had with jesuitical obfuscation considered slavery the basis of democracy among whites rather than the prop of baronial pretensions.[43] Emancipation made no difference to the similar pretensions of postbellum white landowners.

Perhaps this delusion endured through the end of the nineteenth century not only because of intense racism but also because this cosmography was in a most vague and general sense true, especially in the black belt. But the class structure of southern society was a great deal more complex than the discussions of white landowners allowed. There was, for example, no

40. Covington *Georgia Enterprise*, May 29, 1874; *Banks County Gazette*, n.d., quoted in *Cherokee Advance*, May 5, 1893; Dawson *Journal*, February 1, 1893; Atlanta *Constitution*, May 10, 1883, and see May 11, 1883; *Carroll County Times*, March 24, 1876.

41. See Hart, *The Southern South*, 91. See also Gerald W. Johnson, *The Wasted Land* (Chapel Hill, 1937), 61.

42. Gaston, *The New South Creed*, 117–50 *passim*, esp. 134–35.

43. Wilfred Carsel, "The Slaveholders' Indictment of Northern Wage Slavery," *Journal of Southern History*, VI, 504–20. See also Richard Hofstadter, *The American Political Tradition and the Men Who Made It* (New York, 1948), 68–92.

place in their system for white agricultural labor, which was a large and growing group in the late nineteenth century. To understand the social structure and political economy of the late nineteenth-century South, one must understand the relationship between ideology and practice. Why were whites unable to create a system of labor that matched their social ideology? How did blacks escape absolute white control? How did middling groups—yeomen and white labor—perceive their role and interest in the bifurcated system? What happened to the values of a plantation economy based upon subordinate labor and justified by racial doctrines when landowners dealt with members of their own race who were laborers? What happened to the values of class and race, which were defined as synonymous but in fact were not, when they were brought into conflict? And what were the socioeconomic consequences of the disparity between the white social ideology and actual practice?

Chapter II

THE MORAL VIOLENCE OF THE CASTE SYSTEM

The negro was intoxicated with license of freedom; the North
was blinded by the passions of war; the South was fighting
for civilization and existence.
—George T. Winston

WHITES DISSATISFIED with the postwar labor system could hardly blame themselves. As Reconstruction began in 1865, planters in Georgia and across the South confidently set out to compel the kind of labor they wanted. Dominant in the politics of the state and region, they controlled the force of law and exercised coercive authority. They had no expectation that they might fail. All blacks were to remain beneath all whites. The bifurcated society would be true in practice as well as theory.

Planters assumed these things; they did not debate them. And their assumptions would have been reasonable if northern Republicans had not controlled the victorious federal government. But in the wake of the Civil War, prominent white southerners seem to have been remarkably naïve. Republicans were determined not to see a new system of coerced labor replace the old, to see a resurrection of the planter aristocracy and the social patterns they blamed for the "Great Rebellion." With Republicans dominant in Washington and white southerners intransigent, conflict over the status of black labor would pervade the politics of national reconstruction. This conflict would also entail widespread violence within the South directed against white and black Republicans. Clearly, the sectional conflict was a continuation of the Civil War. The violence among southerners, although somehow bound up with the status of black labor and in a sense an extension of the war, nevertheless assumed different configurations from the familiar sectional rivalry. Ku Klux violence has, therefore, attracted historians as a key to insights about southern society.

To explain why political rivalries within the South entailed great violence, historians have returned to the explanation offered by W. E. B. Du Bois in the 1930s: the propertied class sought to repossess the power of legal coercion essential to its exploitation of black labor. There is a good deal of merit in this argument. In Georgia between 1868 and 1871, as in all other southern states on a varying timetable, the socially prominent led bands of the poor and middling sort in violence to restore "white rule." Recent historians draw the lines of causality even tighter. One, for example, claims that, in South Carolina, Klan violence was most severe where planter control was most immediately threatened, that is, where the plantation system of gang labor was giving way most quickly to the share and rental systems. At stake, he says, was control of land and labor.[1] Unfortunately, this historian offers little evidence of a connection between the rise of share and rental arrangements and the incidence of Klan violence. He offers several examples of a correlation between Klan violence during Reconstruction and land tenure some ten years later, but he does not establish an overall pattern. And even if regions of intense Klan activity and of the new sharecropping and renting systems were the same, the dates of these developments did not coincide. Sharecropping began to become common in 1866.[2] Why would there have been a two-year hiatus before large-scale violence began?

There is still another, more serious problem with the explanation that attributes Klan violence to the elite and its need to subordinate black labor. Whether constructed loosely as by Du Bois or tightly as by some of his heirs, this theory understates or at least cannot explain the incredibly broad support that the repression of black labor commanded among whites in general or yeomen in particular. After all, the Klan and similar organiza-

1. J. C. A. Stagg, "The Problem of Klan Violence: The South Carolina Upcountry, 1868–1871," *Journal of American Studies*, VIII, 303–18. See also Vernon Burton, "Race and Reconstruction: Edgefield County, South Carolina," *Journal of Social History*, XII (Fall, 1978), 31–56; Jonathan M. Wiener, *Social Origins of the New South: Alabama, 1860–1885* (Baton Rouge, 1978), 61–66.
2. Brooks, *Agrarian Revolution in Georgia*, 46–47.

tions constituted a movement that every white male in some counties reputedly joined. Even people who agreed with its goals but doubted its methods would not criticize it for fear of being labeled "traitors to their race and section."[3] It does seem more than a little unlikely that a movement could receive such support or demand such dogmatic purity if it were based narrowly upon the interests of employers seeking to control land and labor. The prevalence of Klan violence across the South in hill and mountain counties where plantations were rare merely affirms these doubts.

It is conventional and important to acknowledge the private reservations and the less-frequent open opposition of some white southerners to the vigilantism of the Ku Klux Klan and similar organizations. It is more important for historians to explain the pattern of violence and the unusually broad support that Klan brutality received from otherwise good and decent people. To explain the pattern of vigilantism and the reasons it received broad support is to explain why it arose.

The vigilantism of Reconstruction, although of unprecedented scale, was in many ways a traditional folk movement aimed at upholding the white community's moral standards. Both the vigilantism itself and the widespread if sometimes tacit support it commanded among southern whites testified to the literally religious conviction with which whites subscribed to their racially defined caste system. But it is also true that within their near unanimity whites betrayed class divisions among themselves. Landowning employers were less consistently willing than white yeomen to use violence to maintain the purity of the racial order. Both groups were committed to a racially bifurcated society, but when vigilantism threatened the productivity of labor, the economic interests of employers tended to temper their norms of race somewhat. Employers, anxious to remain dominant but unwilling to sacrifice their economic interests, abandoned yeomen vigilantes, who fought on alone to make lines of caste and class superiority rigorously synonymous.

In 1865 Klan violence was a long way off. Conflict over the

3. Vernon Burton, "Race and Reconstruction," 37–38; Allen W. Trelease, *White Terror: The Ku Klux Klan Conspiracy and Southern Reconstruction* (New York, 1971), ix–xii.

status of black labor took different forms. There was plentiful uncertainty. In fact, the temporary absence of civil government following the defeat of the Confederacy was felt perhaps most severely in the relations between landowners and emancipated slaves. Much business might proceed on the assumption that things would be, in general, as they had been before, but emancipation meant uncertainty for both workers and employers. The Freedmen's Bureau worked to fill this vacuum by arranging and trying to enforce contracts between the freedmen and their former masters.[4] But in 1865 and 1866, as the head of the Freedmen's Bureau in Georgia reported, planters in the black belt "adamantly refused to pay the freedmen reasonable wages." He noted further, "In some cases they compel them by threats to contract for from one to three dollars per month, the laborer to furnish his own clothing and medicine." When officers of the bureau told planters "that such contracts would not be permitted, . . . the employers refused to annul" them or for that matter even to "allow the freedmen to go to other parts of the country where they are offered better wages. Citizens going to certain counties to hire labor, and offering reasonable prices, were arrested and imprisoned. . . . Every possible expedient was resorted to for frightening [blacks] and keeping them at home, in order to enable employers to hire them at shamefully inadequate wages."[5] Contracts that assured workers low wages gave planters nearly limitless authority. Frances Butler, for example, demanded that her hands "agree to do all the work required of them in a satisfactory manner, and in the event of any violation of this contract, they are to be dismissed [from] the place and to

4. Trelease, *White Terror*, xiii–xiv; C. W. Tebeau, "Some Aspects of Planter-Freedmen Relations, 1865–1880," *Journal of Negro History*, XXI, 133; William S. McFeely, *Yankee Stepfather: General O. O. Howard and the Freedman* (New York, 1968).

5. Davis Tillson to O. O. Howard, November 1, 1866, in Edwin M. Stanton, "Letter of the Secretary of War Communicating . . . Reports of the Assistant Commissioners of Freedmen and a Synopsis of Laws Respecting Persons of Color in the Late Slave States, January 3, 1867," *Senate Executive Documents*, 39th Cong., 2nd Sess., No. 6, p. 50. Some planters conceded that Tillson's complaints were just. See Milledgeville *Federal Union*, January 9, 1866, cited in C. Mildred Thompson, *Reconstruction in Georgia*, 75–76.

forfeit all wages due to them."[6] Since Miss Butler, like many planters, paid wages only at the end of the year, the last, not unusual provision invited fraud.

Carl Schurz noted that planters "adhered as much as possible to the traditions of the old system even where the relations between employers and laborers had been fixed by contract." Even whipping "continued to a great extent, although not in so regular a manner" as before.[7] Schooled in the Republican doctrine of "Free Soil, Free Labor, Free Men," Schurz was surprised that contracts did not matter. He thought employers were using the legal forms of freedom illegitimately to coerce labor. But white Georgians did not share the northern Republican's view of a free-labor system. To them the exploitative contracts seemed perfectly legal and acceptable. Planters may have resigned themselves to emancipation, but as a federal general stationed at Macon reported, they wanted to subject blacks to "a modified condition of Slavery similar to peonage." Other northern observers repeatedly came to the same conclusion. Like Carl Schurz, they believed planters had "absolutely no conception what free labor is."[8]

Northerners had good reason for this claim. Whites confirmed it by being unembarrassed about their intentions and sincere in expecting no interference from the North. They did not fully comprehend that their course might be unacceptable to the northern victors. It did not occur to them that blacks could have an unfamiliar role. "The institution of slavery, in my judgment, provided the best system of labor that could be devised for the negro race," wrote Howell Cobb. "I take it for granted," he continued,

6. Leigh, *Ten Years on a Georgia Plantation*, 115.

7. Carl Schurz, "Report of Carl Schurz," 19. C. Mildred Thompson (*Reconstruction in Georgia*, 68) and Brooks (*Agrarian Revolution in Georgia*, 27) came to the same conclusion.

8. J. H. Wilson to W. P. Whipple, June 15, 1865, quoted in C. Mildred Thompson, *Reconstruction in Georgia*, 53; "Views Expressed by Major General [James] Steedman in Conversation with Carl Schurz," August 7, 1865, in Schurz, "Report of Carl Schurz," Accompanying Documents, No. 6, p. 53. See also "Memorandum of Conversation Between William King, Esq., of Savannah, and Carl Schurz, Savannah, July 31, 1865," *ibid.*, No. 29, p. 83; Andrews, *The South Since the War*, 337–38; Reid, *After the War*, 151.

"that the future relations between negroes and their former masters, like all questions of domestic policy, will be under the control and direction of the State governments."[9]

Former governor Hershel V. Johnson agreed. His brief speech at the end of Georgia's first Reconstruction convention reportedly "brought tears to the eyes of many delegates." The convention ordered it printed in its journal, and it was widely reprinted in newspapers around the state. White Georgians frequently suggested that Sidney Andrews should read it because, they said, it epitomized their feelings. But to Andrews, a northerner traveling through the South at the time, the speech was remarkable for the lack of understanding it reflected, understanding of both the political situation and the consequences of defeat. Johnson said in part: "We are now to enter upon the experiment whether the class of people to which we are in future to look as our laboring class can be organized into efficient and trustworthy laborers. That may be done—or I hope it may be done—if we are left to ourselves. If we cannot succeed, others need not attempt it, and I trust that in the future we will be left alone in reference to this class of people." A veteran of General Longstreet's valiant Georgia troops showed a similarly obtuse sense of political possibilities as he suggested a program for national reconciliation. "You of the North must do one of three things," he told Whitelaw Reid. You must "reestablish slavery; give the old masters in some way the power to compel the negro to work; or colonize them out of the country, and help us to bring in white labor."[10]

To maintain a system of abjectly subordinate labor, however, southern employers did not turn to widespread vigilantism immediately after the war. There were reports of sporadic violence, but as northern travelers and the head of the Freedmen's Bureau in Georgia reported, for the most part planters from 1865 through 1867 tried to exploit black labor by combining the tools of contractual law with threats, whippings, and other forms of

9. Howell Cobb to Wilson, June 14, 1865, quoted in C. Mildred Thompson, *Reconstruction in Georgia*, 52–53.

10. Andrews, *The South Since the War*, 337–38, and see Andrews' report on an address by General John T. Morgan, C.S.A., in southwest Georgia, 324; Reid, *After the War*, 361.

intimidation that were more reminiscent of slavery than vigilantism. An "insolent" worker might be punished, a school established for freedmen might occasionally be burned, and some laborers might be driven off without pay, but such improvisation could not secure the system of labor that planters wanted.[11] White landowning employers expected to solve their new "labor problem" through the legal institutions they had always dominated. Just as law had defined slavery and helped make plantations possible, so whites now intended to define legally the subordinate position of black labor and thereby to enable themselves to live as they had before the war.

As southern legislatures convened in late 1865 and early 1866, they began quickly to enact so-called black codes, statutory charters of their plans for black labor. Among the early enactments, Mississippi's offers a good example. Through a series of laws defining vagrancy, apprenticeship, and various crimes especially for blacks, it effectively relegated them to a severe, compelled labor. Blacks were to work for wages, for they would not be allowed to own, rent, or lease rural land. Only in unusual cases would exceptions be made to allow them to live in towns or villages. They were to contract for a year's labor by the second Monday in January and were subject to harsh penalties for the slightest violation of the law or of their contracts. Penalties were debts to be worked off in apparently endless peonage.[12]

Georgia was different from Mississippi. Its legislature was among those that convened late and did not enact a harsh black code. White Georgians appeared more liberal than their fellow white southerners. In fact, they were not. In 1865 the state's first Reconstruction convention established a special commission to draft proposals for a black code. This was the same convention, it will be remembered, that Herschel V. Johnson addressed, the same convention that could not escape vassalage to the tradition

11. Oliver O. Howard, "Report of the Commissioner of Refugees, Freedmen, and Abandoned Lands, November 1, 1867," *House Executive Documents*, 40th Cong., 2nd Sess., No. 1, p. 675. Howard comments that such incidents became less common in 1867.

12. James Wilford Garner, *Reconstruction in Mississippi* (1901; rpr. Baton Rouge, 1968), 113–16; C. Mildred Thompson, *Reconstruction in Georgia*, 49. The codes of all southern states appear in Stanton, "Letter of the Secretary of War," 170–230.

of states' rights or the nobility of the Lost Cause and therefore repealed rather than nullified the Secession Ordinance of 1861. When the Code Commission reported to Governor Charles J. Jenkins in early 1866, it recommended eleven severe laws to control the freedmen. Governor Jenkins in turn recommended and the legislature intended to enact a code much like Mississippi's. But because the codes of other southern states had aroused unexpected anger in the North, political leaders decided to pull back. Following the advice of former governor Joseph E. Brown, the general assembly granted black workers ostensible equality. It validated marriages between blacks, made equal the rights and liberties of owning property, and made the crimes of whites and blacks subject to the same penalties. After some sparring with the Freedmen's Bureau, it even abolished required racial discrimination in the courts so that the state could repossess jurisdiction over blacks. As the legislature enacted new laws defining apprenticeship and new crimes, such as vagrancy and "enticing away workers" (which were the crux of Mississippi's black code), it made no distinctions of color. Whites simply assumed that the laws applied to blacks and knew they could amend them later if necessary.[13]

In one sense, Georgia's ploy worked well. Its black code occasioned no hostile comment in the North.[14] But this was not enough to satisfy northern Republicans. The course of Reconstruction may seem confusing when the details of one state's history are compared to those of another, but southern whites were relatively consistent overall. Reports of reluctant unionism among them, their refusal to repudiate their old leaders (the election of Alexander Hamilton Stephens, former vice president of the Confederacy, to the United States Senate from Georgia serves as perhaps the most impolitic example), and the black codes of southern states whose legislatures convened early—all these developments directly influenced the course of Congres-

13. The distinction between legislatures that convened early and those that convened late appears in David Montgomery, *Beyond Equality: Labor and the Radical Republicans, 1862–1872* (New York, 1967), 55–56; C. Mildred Thompson, *Reconstruction in Georgia*, 151, 157–58, 158 n; Stanton, "Letter of the Secretary of War," 55, 179–80.

14. C. Mildred Thompson, *Reconstruction in Georgia*, 159–60.

sional Reconstruction. As Elizabeth Studley Nathans wrote, the "understanding that they themselves had contributed to the process [by which Presidential Reconstruction gave way to congressional action] came only slowly to Georgians during the summer of 1866."[15]

What was true of white Georgians was true of other white southerners, and it was this consistency that impelled even moderate congressional leaders to action. They judged the behavior of southern whites against the same antislavery doctrines that had inflamed antebellum proslavery southerners. When congressional Republicans proposed the Fourteenth Amendment in 1866, they included a statement of purpose and justification. It would have sounded familiar to a person who had heard nothing since the political campaigns of the late 1850s: "Slavery, by building up a ruling and dominant class, had produced a spirit of oligarchy adverse to republican institutions, which finally inaugurated the civil war. The tendency of continuing the domination of such a class, by leaving it in the same exclusive possession of political power, would be to encourage the same spirit and lead to the same result."[16]

And so, one step led to the next: the Civil Rights Act of 1866, which, despite its questionable constitutionality, invalidated discriminatory black codes; the proposal of the Fourteenth Amendment, which would bar Confederate leaders from holding any office and make the Civil Rights Act constitutional and immutable; the Reconstruction Acts of 1867, which disfranchised former Confederate leaders and enfranchised the freedmen in a further effort to get what Republicans defined as "true unionist sentiment" dominant in the politics of the South and to get the Fourteenth Amendment ratified; the Fifteenth Amendment to try to protect the new political system; and the Ku Klux Klan Act to try to counter anti-Republican and antiblack violence. These congressional actions went much further than all but the most radical Republicans had anticipated at the end of the war. Each step was meant to protect the step before, but the cumulative

15. Elizabeth Studley Nathans, *Losing the Peace: Georgia Republicans and Reconstruction, 1865–1871* (Baton Rouge, 1968), 14; Montgomery, *Beyond Equality*, 67–68.

16. *House Reports*, 39th Cong., 1st Sess., No. 30, p. xiii.

effect was as great as a second civil war. This time the preservation of the Union was no longer at issue, but the status of black labor was still very much so.

The perceptions of northern Republicans were reasonably accurate. Although white Georgians did not enact a harsh black code, they would not abandon and were loath even to modify their definition of the proper role of black labor. In late 1866 after congressional Republicans had made perfectly clear their demands and their power to insist upon them, planters affirmed their own traditional stance with defiant stubbornness. General Davis Tillson, the head of the Freedmen's Bureau in Georgia, was finding it impossible to stretch his meager budget to hire enough local officials. He therefore "appointed agents from among the resident whites" who were "to serve without salary" but were to receive fees from "employers and freedmen for the witnessing of contracts." It was soon clear that the Georgia experiment would not work. "Resident white appointees . . . shamefully abused" their power and "occasionally inflicted cruel and unusual punishments," reported General Oliver O. Howard, commissioner of the national bureau. "The education they received under the slave system seems to have unfitted them for the responsible relation they were called upon to sustain to the interest of free labor. Some were less tyrannical than others, yet comparatively few escaped censure." After the Georgia bureau returned to a system of salaried, mostly northern agents in January, 1867, a group of freedmen in southwest Georgia was even blunter about the failed experiment. Planter agents, they said, had operated on the assumption that the "negro has no rights the white man is bound to respect. . . . The same couching servility required of us as slaves was now exacted of us as freed people, and deviation from the requirement subjected them to the overseer's cudgel or [prison]."[17]

But it was after all this had happened—after the Civil Rights Act, after white Georgians refused to ratify the Fourteenth

17. Howard, "Report of the Commissioner," 674; Robert Crumly and Philip Joiner on Behalf of the Civil Rights and Political Rights Association, "Memorial of the Colored Men of the Second Congressional District of Georgia, Setting Forth Their Grievances and Asking Protection," December 4, 1868, in "Conditions in Georgia," 92.

Amendment, after the Reconstruction Acts of 1867, after Georgia's Republican-dominated constitutional convention had met, even after the Republicans had won control of the state government—that white Georgians began resorting to widespread Ku Klux violence in the summer of 1868. If the dates vary among southern states, the sequence was the same everywhere. Tennessee had led the way. The only former Confederate state to ratify the Fourteenth Amendment in 1866, it alone was quickly restored to the Union and exempted from the Reconstruction Acts of 1867. However, in an effort to stay in power, Tennessee's Unionist-Republican regime adopted its own broad disfranchisement of former Confederates and enfranchised its freedmen. Vigilantism had increased gradually after the Unionist-Republicans came to power; it became endemic after they adopted these political measures.[18]

Since most of the violence in Tennessee, Georgia, and across the South was directed against politically active freedmen and white Republicans and since Klan violence intensified just before elections, the political connection cannot be ignored. Nonetheless, the resort to political violence does not explain itself. It was extraordinary primarily because it occurred at all and secondarily because it appeared over so much of the South; because, even though it was perpetrated by numerous organizations with different names, it assumed a consistent pattern; and because it was—despite this widespread, consistent pattern—basically a local rather than a regionally coordinated movement.[19]

In Georgia, the incidence of Klan violence was greatest in a cluster of about seventeen counties running from Atlanta east and southeast to the South Carolina border. This area included counties in both the upper piedmont and black belt. In 1880 (the first year for which statistics are available) these counties had patterns of share and rental arrangements that were typical of their respective regions as a whole. A second major center of Klan activity included eight counties to the northwest and west of Atlanta along the northern and western boundaries of the state. In 1880 these counties also had patterns of land tenure

18. Trelease, *White Terror*, 73–74, 3–27. On scattered incidents before the election of a Republican governor and legislature in 1868, see pp. 76–79.

19. *Ibid.*, xlv–xlvi, 51, 226.

that were typical of their regions—whether the mountainous counties of northernmost Georgia or the upper piedmont. Several had a rate of tenancy higher than that of their immediate neighbors because they were located in a river valley in which the terrain was more conducive to farming than was the more broken country immediately surrounding it. Even these counties, however, did not differ substantially from other counties in the upper piedmont.[20] What is most peculiar about the centers of concentrated Klan activity is that, with only two exceptions, the mountain and upper piedmont counties involved were never controlled by local Republicans. Even some of the lower piedmont counties in the black belt were consistently dominated by Democrats.[21] In other counties in these areas, though not in all others, Republicans were in a majority. It seems, therefore, that neither an explanation associating Klan violence with the rise of share and rental arrangements nor a simple political explanation based on the desire to redeem government from Republican control nor even an explanation directly relating these two can adequately explain the situation in Georgia.

When southern whites explained Klan violence, they did so in amorphous terms that offer a vaguely moralistic justification for their behavior. Their reasoning deserves attention because they were not at all apologetic. "There is a kind of vague notion with a great many people," testified C. D. Forsyth of Floyd County, "and it is an honest conviction with them, that they are in danger from the colored population. As a general thing," he continued, "when a person . . . attempts to justify the operations of the Klan, they do it upon that theory, that it is necessary to keep the colored people down, to keep them in subordination. And [in] my opinion . . . that is the ground of the whole of it. The idea of the liberation of the slaves and the conferring upon them universal suffrage, is so obnoxious to the people of that country that I think it is the cause of the whole of it." At the turn of the century a former Klansman, who had not changed his views since 1868, corroborated Forsyth's testimony: "While it [the Klan] was not originally intended to interfere with the white men, still where they would stir up the negroes and take their

20. *Ibid.*, 318, C. Mildred Thompson, *Reconstruction in Georgia*, 376, 361–63; *Tenth Census, 1880: Agriculture*, 40–45.
21. C. Mildred Thompson, *Reconstruction in Georgia*, 362, 375.

part against the whites, they would naturally become *persona non grata*, and at a meeting of the Ku-Klux Klan . . . a decision [would be made] as to what to do." In our country, he explained, there was a white fellow who started "impressing upon them that they were just as good as the whites and ought to assert themselves. It began to make them very restless and retractable [*sic*] and it became necessary to take action." When the first whipping did not work, "it began to look as if he would have to be killed," but finally he relented. Had they not taken this course, the Klansman continued, "every little insolence . . . would be bragged about by its perpetrator and fellow observers among the negroes. The news would spread with great rapidity, and there would be no telling where it would end." Anne Cooper Burton could write with similar authority about the righteousness of the Klan. She was, after all, both the daughter of a Grand Cyclops and in 1916 the president of the Wade Hampton Chapter No. 763 of the United Daughters of the Confederacy in Los Angeles, California. She knew that "no other power in the world would have saved the suffering South from the disorder which prevailed during the awful period following the War Between the States." And she declared, "Their purpose was to scare into submission the unruly free negroes and the troublemaking carpetbaggers." [22]

In 1868 in Emanuel County, Thomas Allen's brother-in-law was killed, but the target had been Allen, a politically active black preacher. The following morning a friendly white neighbor was distraught; it is unclear, however, what exactly he was distraught about: "By God, Allen," he said, "I told you six months ago that we would not submit to negroism in this State; did I not tell you that they would kill you?" Allen said, "Yes, but I did not believe it. I preached for you all during the war, when you could not get a white preacher, for all had gone into the army." [23] Like those historians who have deeply submerged racial hostility be-

22. C. D. Forsyth, testimony, July 10, 1871, and see E. H. Chambers, testimony, October 26, 1871, both in *Joint Committee Report on the Ku Klux Klan*, VI, 23, VII, 604; Richard C. Beckett, "Some Effects of Military Reconstruction in Monroe County, Mississippi," *Publications of the Mississippi Historical Society*, VIII (1904), 177–86; Anne Cooper Burton, *The Ku Klux Klan* (Los Angeles, 1916), 5, 9–10. See also Warren P. Ward, *Ward's History of Coffee County* (Atlanta, 1930), 142–43.

23. Thomas M. Allen, testimony, October 26, 1871, in *Joint Committee Report on the Ku Klux Klan*, VII, 608.

neath divisions of class interest in their interpretations of Klan violence, Allen underestimated the independent, sovereign authority of racism in the minds of many whites.

General Nathan Bedford Forrest, titular head of the entire Klan, reflected its inexact purpose and local orientation by justifying its violence solely in terms of conditions in Tennessee. He said that Governor William E. Brownlow "was drilling the negro militia all over up there, and bad white men, and they [the Klan] had organized for the protection of society in Tennessee."[24] Even the Klan's own statement of purpose reflected this moralistic, if amorphous, understanding of the group's behavior:

> This is an institution of Chivalry, Humanity, Mercy, and Patriotism, embodying in its genius and its principles all that is chivalric in conduct, noble in sentiment, generous in manhood, and patriotic in purpose; its particular object being, First: To protect the weak, the innocent, and the defenseless, from the indignities, wrongs and outrages, of the lawless, the violent, and the brutal; to relieve the injured and oppressed; to succor the suffering and unfortunate, and especially the widows and orphans of Confederate soldiers. Second: To protect and defend the Constitution of the United States, and all laws passed in conformity thereto, and to protect the States and the people thereof from an invasion from any source whatever. Third: To aid and assist the execution of all constitutional laws, and to protect the people from unlawful seizure, and from trials except by their peers in conformity to the laws of the land.[25]

As historian Allen Trelease has noted, few statements could seem a greater mockery of Klan violence, but the incongruity is all the greater because so many white southerners were so sincerely unable to see it. The statement of purpose and the violence it was meant to justify reflected two assumptions on their part: first, that Congressional Reconstruction was an unconstitutional usurpation of power destructive to their society and, second, that blacks were not a part of that society.[26]

24. Trelease, *White Terror*, 21–22.
25. Anne Cooper Burton, *The Ku Klux Klan*, 18–19.
26. Trelease, *White Terror*, 16–17.

The explanations that southern whites offered for Klan violence went far beyond racial justifications for economic relations. Whites defined values of caste—values with a literally moral authority reflected not only in the conviction with which whites expressed themselves but in the kind of violence with which they enforced their views. If in the twentieth century that sounds like a contradiction in terms or yet another literary excess, to them it was neither. The racially, economically, and politically motivated violence grouped under the heading of the Ku Klux Klan had an ancient pedigree both in the United States and Europe. It was part of a system of coercion used to maintain standards that its perpetrators understood in moral terms. Although the political violence that most attracted the attention of congressional Republicans largely disappeared after Redemption (at least for a couple of decades), the more general though less intense pattern of vigilante justice at the hands of disguised bands remained common. Known before the war as Regulators, after Reconstruction these groups continued to be called Ku Klux or were sometimes called White Caps, after their usual headgear. Even when a group of blacks gathered to whip a white man who habitually beat his wife and then left her to take up "with a negro woman, living with her as his wife," the case was reported under the headline "Colored Ku-Klux."[27] The interchangeable names show that these groups were understood as synonymous in a fundamental way. Their violence reflected racial, economic, political, and moral values that they sought to protect as an unsympathetic, even self-contradictory whole (like the values of almost any group) rather than as separable by genre and motive.

Gangs of disguised men threatened, beat, whipped, and killed the serious and sometimes not-so-serious offenders. In 1883, for example, "a pasteboard coffin was found on the doorstep" of a "gang of the very worst negro strumpets." The Atlanta *Constitution* did not explain in what sense they were the very worst, but someone in Walton County (about forty miles east of Atlanta) was apparently unhappy with their activities. A sign

27. Dawson *Weekly Journal*, September 30, 1880. See also, for example, *Emanuel Itemizer*, n.d., quoted in Atlanta *Constitution*, October 10, 1883; Gainesville *Eagle*, n.d., quoted in Atlanta *Constitution*, July 27, 1883.

warned the women "to leave town in 48 hours" or receive three hundred lashes. The following night "a quart of kerosene" was left "on top of the awning in front of Mr. O. E. Cutler's saloon." It seems Cutler had bailed one of the women out of jail. "The oil and the coffin . . . evidently means [sic] death" for the women and at least one of their friends, reported the newspaper. A few years later a similar incident took place in Carroll County on the Alabama border.[28]

White Caps or Ku Klux often punished those who offended their sexual or marital standards. Late one night in 1894, a group of "whitecaps well disguised" visited a man named King in south Georgia. They knew he had been abusing his wife, they said. They dragged him from his home into the woods, "tied and inhumanely whipped him," and warned him to leave the county or to expect another visit, which "would mean death." In Terrell, a black-belt county in southwest Georgia, vigilantes whipped a "respectable" white man who married "a notorious town 'scamp' only a few days after his previous wife died." Attacks like these continued in Georgia off and on into the 1950s and were an especially common activity for the "second" Ku Klux Klan, which grew large and powerful after World War I.[29]

Long before the rise of the second Klan, this pattern of coercion was not unusual to Georgia or even to the South. It was common in the Midwest, chronic on the frontier, and appeared even in New England.[30] Although the supposition might at first

28. Atlanta *Constitution*, June 1, 1883; "Those White Cap Cases" (Unascribed clippings, n.d., Scrapbook III, p. 71, in Northen Papers).

29. Americus *Times-Recorder*, October 12, 1894; Dawson *News*, April 1, 1891, cited in Albert Colby Smith, "Violence in Georgia's Black Belt: A Study of Crime in Baldwin and Terrell Counties, 1886–1899" (M.A. thesis, University of Georgia, 1974), 65; Augusta *Chronicle*, March 5, 1950 (Clipping in Ku Klux Klan File, Georgia Room, University of Georgia Libraries, Rare Books and Manuscript Department, Athens). Comments on the second Klan in Robert Maxwell Brown, "Historical Patterns of Violence in America," in Hugh D. Graham and Ted R. Gurr (eds.), *Violence in America: Historical and Comparative Perspectives. A Report to the National Commission on the Causes of Violence and Its Prevention* (Washington, D.C., 1969), 52.

30. On White Capping in Ohio and Indiana, see Americus *Weekly Recorder*, November 23, 1888, and comments on the Midwest in Edward P. Thompson, "'Rough Music': Le Charivari Anglais," *Annales: Economics; Sociétés; Civilization*, XXVII (March–April, 1972), 286–87. On Bold Knobbers in Missouri, see

seem farfetched, this illegal "justice" seems to be related to the "noisy masked demonstrations [used] to humiliate some wrong doer" in medieval and early modern Europe. The historian E. P. Thompson was the first, apparently, to make this connection. In France these demonstrations were called charivari; in England, rough music. Charivari were often associated with seasonal or religious festivals in which a community simultaneously mocked and affirmed its values. Lords of misrule dispensed justice in the inverted world of the carnival, but real offenders, whether wife beaters, shrews, submissive husbands, the sexually incontinent betrothed, or others who offended sexual or marital values were punished by the crowd.[31] The offenses included many of those punished by White Caps or Ku Klux in Georgia.

As part of the obscure symbolism of the festivals, men who punished offenders often dressed as women and wore paper masks or blackened their faces. Their victims would be led through the streets for public humiliation or "beaten with tripe, wooden sticks, knives, forks, spoons, frying pans, trenchers, and water pots." Beyond the ordinary benefits of disguise, historian Natalie Zemon Davis finds reasons for men to dress as women in the normative sex roles of the period: men drew upon the "sexual power and energy of unruly woman and her license . . . to defend the community's interest and to tell the truth about unjust rule."[32]

The relation of dress, morality, and charivari to the moral content of White Cap or Ku Klux violence is not the digression it may at first seem. Charivari persisted in attenuated form well into the twentieth century in the South and in sections of the Midwest where southerners settled. Even its name survived in the mutilated form "shivaree."[33] It is more than coincidence

---

Brown, "Historical Patterns of Violence in America," in Graham and Gurr (eds.), *Violence in America*, 50–51. For reports from Trumbell, Connecticut, see Atlanta *Constitution*, September 22, 1883.

31. Natalie Zemon Davis, "The Reasons of Misrule," in *Society and Culture in Early Modern France: Eight Essays by Natalie Zemon Davis* (Stanford, 1975), 97, 100; Edward P. Thompson, "'Rough Music,'" 287 n.

32. Davis, "Women on Top," 149–50 *et passim*, and "Reasons of Misrule," 100, both in Davis, *Society and Culture in Early Modern France*.

33. Edward P. Thompson, "'Rough Music,'" 286–87, 307–308. On southern culture in the Midwest, see Richard Lyle Power, *Planting Corn Belt Culture: The*

that blacks sometimes described Ku Klux disguises as dresses. "Some would be red and some black like a lady's dress," testified one freedman. "They all wore dresses," said another.[34] And it is certainly more than coincidence that "at the turn of the century" in Terrell County "masked men dressed in women's clothing took an accused arsonist from the custody of the sheriff and disappeared into the cypress swamps. A few days later the black man returned home severely beaten with a buggy trace."[35]

One may at least wonder why the Ku Klux or White Caps adopted full-length gowns to go along with their hoods or masks. Certainly gowns were not well suited to horse-borne troops. Some claimed the disguise made them look ghostly and helped frighten superstitious blacks. "They are men who rise from the dead . . . to protect their country," explained a planter to his former slave. But the freedmen were not, it seems, as foolish as this planter. "Master, do you believe there are men who rise from the dead and come Ku Klux a body up this way?" responded the freedman incredulously. "I studied it," he testified before a congressional committee in 1871, "but I did not believe it." Neither did any other freedman who testified. Because robed Klansmen often rode beside others who only blackened their faces, wore paper masks, or otherwise disguised themselves, the ghost explanation seems incomplete.[36]

Allen Trelease suggests that Klan regalia may have derived from that of other fraternal organizations, such as college fraternities, the Masons, or the Odd Fellows, which were especially popular in the nineteenth century.[37] This explanation pushes the origin of the feminine disguise back one step but does not explain what prompted the Odd Fellows to dress like Odd Fellows. It is possible that the long, impractical gowns were a stylized

Impress of the Upland Southerner and Yankee in the Old Northwest (Indianapolis, 1955).

34. H. Grady McWhitney and Francis B. Simkins, "The Ghostly Legend of the Ku-Klux Klan," *Negro History Bulletin*, XIV (February, 1951), 112.

35. Smith, "Violence in Georgia's Black Belt," 66.

36. Charles Smith, testimony, October 26, 1871, in *Joint Committee Report on the Ku Klux Klan*, VI, 599, VI and VII *passim*; McWhitney and Simkins, "The Ghostly Legend," *passim*. See also, Trelease, *White Terror*, 53.

37. Trelease, *White Terror*, 4–5.

anachronism, a symbol of fraternal, festival justice sapped of its former cultural significance. It is even possible that not all of the symbolism had been lost, for women remained the repository of society's moral values under the chivalric code of white south-erners. Like European peasants, who left no explanation for their actions and may have been unable to explain them com-pletely had they been asked, so too, white southerners may have been incompletely aware of the symbolic baggage of their own behavior.

Like the violence of Ku Klux or White Caps, charivari-related violence was not limited to enforcing sexual or marital values. In England, Ireland, and Scotland, bands of men dressed as women for vigilante activities with both moral and economic objects.[38] And during the mid-nineteenth century, French peas-ants in the foothills of the Pyrenees adopted the traditional femi-nine disguise associated with the cause of morality for a long, violent battle to preserve their customary right to pasture stock and gather wood in forests owned by local seigneurs and bour-geois.[39] This *Guerre des Demoiselles* was significantly similar to Ku Klux or White Cap efforts in mountainous, isolated sections of late nineteenth-century Georgia to protect moonshine from the impositions of federal tax officials—a latter-day version of the Whiskey Rebellion.[40]

In fact, after Reconstruction, even when one does not con-sider moonshine-related violence, economic "right" or economic "justice" was the only motive equal to racial norms and sexual purity in provoking the moral violence of vigilante bands. This association of property right with moral right was not linguistic happenstance or the fiction of some deft lawyer. "Thou shalt not steal" is, after all, one of the Ten Commandments. So while in late twentieth-century America crimes against property may seem of a lesser order than crimes against persons, that dis-tinction may be rooted in the luxury of a well-insured society

38. Davis, "Woman on Top," in Davis, *Society and Culture in Early Modern France*, 148–49.

39. John Merriman, "The Demoiselles of the Ariège, 1829–1831," in Merri-man (ed.), *1830 in France* (New York, 1975), *passim.*

40. Trelease, *White Terror*, 331; C. Mildred Thompson, *Reconstruction in Georgia*, 364.

now addicted to conspicuous consumption. The late nineteenth-century South was overwhelmingly poor. Even most planters may be described without exaggeration as "land poor." The poverty of southerners, both white and black, made them value what they had not only because they had so little but also because that little mattered a great deal to their livelihood. To attack a man's property was very often to attack his well-being. For most people, the punishment of an arsonist, a thief, or a swindler had as much moral justification as the punishment of a tart or wife-beater and was perhaps more common.[41] The fact that the same vigilante bands that punished sexual or marital offenders often punished thieves, swindlers, or insubordinate workers[42] suggests that the values they sought to protect, if not a systematic whole, were clustered together and defined as fundamental. Some things were simply right and others simply wrong. The pattern of 1880 was still apparent in some parts of the South in 1950, and entailed a consistent mentality.

White Capping, charivari, and the symbolism of moral conflict they shared with other forms of vigilante justice were products of the relative seclusion and intimacy of rural communities and reflected the weblike patterns of kinship and friendship that were a functional part of rural life.[43] In 1871, for example, Jackson County was in one of the most violent sections of the state. It was there that William Booth was visited by a Ku Klux band that included his brother-in-law. "It was said in the neighborhood" that Booth "and his wife did not well agree" because "he was pretty bad to drink." It was for his wife's sake and at the instigation of his brother-in-law that the Klan beat him for his

41. James Elbert Cutler, *Lynch-Law: An Investigation into the History of Lynchings in the United States* (London, 1905), 167, and Chart IX.

42. Where one type of offense was punished, several were punished. *Joint Committee Report on the Ku Klux Klan*, VI, VII, *passim*; Brown, "Historical Patterns of Violence in America," in Graham and Gurr (eds.), *Violence in America*, 50–54. See also Atlanta *Constitution*, May 27, 1883, and Gainesville *Eagle*, n.d., quoted in the *Constitution*, July 29, 1883.

43. This is also the conclusion of Edward Shorter, *The Making of the Modern Family* (New York, 1975), 218–17. Perhaps this may be analogous to the frontier tradition stressed in Brown, "Historical Patterns of Violence in America," and Joe B. Frantz, "The Frontier Tradition: An Invitation to Violence," both in Graham and Gurr (eds.), *Violence in America*, 35–64, 101–19, 121–50.

drunkenness and warned him of worse if he did not behave.[44] In nearby Gwinnett County that same year, a "white fellow" named Dougherty was whipped. He was a clerk in a local store and a Democrat but somewhat forward. "He tried to pull decent girls over the counter and screw them, saving your presence," testified Robert Bradford, with a halfhearted apology, before a congressional committee. Unaccustomed to being awakened during the soporific hearings, the committeemen showed unusual interest in Bradford's testimony. They were particularly concerned about Dougherty's *modus operandi* and its success (which was reputedly considerable). But Bradford was less forthcoming than they wished and kept reminding them of the righteousness of the whipping. Dougherty had managed to offend "the whole settlement," so the Klan got together and gave "him a pretty good whipping." He left the county soon after the incident. "Any man who acts like that ought to be whipped," repeated Bradford for the fourth time to his once again sleepy questioners.[45]

Although this kind of violence reflected the structure of rural communities, to distinguish between rural and village life in late nineteenth-century Georgia would be, at least for this purpose, somewhat meaningless. Except for about a half dozen cities, Georgia's towns and villages were small enough and still insular enough to share many of the attributes of the countryside. Like the *charivarieurs* of French villages, young men in late nineteenth-century Georgia would still stone an "outsider" who came courting a hometown girl—one of "our girls."[46] This method of dividing the world into "us" and "them," into familiar and unfamiliar, although as common as original sin, was a prerequisite of moral vigilantism. It became clearly and dangerously evident in the class and racial solipsism of the Ku Klux Klan. Some historians have restrospectively baptized the violent parochialism of idealized moonshiners or the *Demoiselles* as celebrations of democratic, egalitarian, or anticapitalistic values among "the people." Somehow, "the people" never appear

44. Susan Aaron, testimony, October 26, 1871, *Joint Committee Report on the Ku Klux Klan*, VI, 460, 590.

45. Robert H. Bradford, testimony, October 28, 1871, *ibid.*, VII, 710–11.

46. Herman Clarence Nixon, *Lower Piedmont Country* (New York, 1946), 88–89.

harsh. But it is now impossible to idealize the ignorance and cruelty of the Klan, and so historians have attributed Ku Klux violence to the planter elite alone. No matter how large or how popular the movement, the elite is always different from "the people," if in some ill-defined way.[47] Unfortunately, however, crowds, like kings, can be unpleasant. The folk can be despicable as well as right. And whether in the case of the moonshiners, the *Demoiselles*, or the Ku Klux Klan, the psychological and cultural mechanisms for bunching individuals into groups in order to organize and simplify the world remain the same.

The great majority, perhaps even all southern whites, drew a line between "us" and "them," between white and black, that both defined and justified what they considered appropriate social and economic roles. Individual definitions of those roles might vary in severity, but all were passionately committed to that line. And for that reason, a tradition of moral vigilantism offered many, perhaps even most white southerners—planters and yeomen—a culturally available alternative to watching their interconnected racial, economic, and moral caste-values shredded by northern free-labor ideology. They knew that their vigilantism was part of a broad tradition. John Christy of Athens, testified as much in 1871:

> Q. Did you know in your county of men in disguise going about before the war as they have since?
> A. In some rare instances.
> Q. Before the war?
> A. Yes, sir; there have been instances all over the Southern and Western states, as there used to be in California, where men used to set themselves up as regulators when they desired to get rid of some obnoxious person in the neighborhood. I have heard of disguised parties running off people in that way ever since I could recollect.
> Q. Did you ever hear of such cases in the state of Georgia?
> A. Yes, sir.[48]

47. See Merriman, "The Demoiselles of the Ariège," 88, 97, *et passim*; Vernon Burton, "Race and Reconstruction," 31–56; Edward P. Thompson, "'Rough Music,'" 308 n.

48. John Christy, testimony, July 24, 1871, in *Joint Committee Report on the Ku Klux Klan*, VI, 240.

It should be remembered, however, that southern employers did not turn to widespread vigilantism immediately after the war. Occasions for Klan violence between 1868 and 1871 were often the same as those that had led to charivari in Europe and to vigilantism in the South both before and after Reconstruction. The traditional pattern intensified as it crossed the racial boundary that divided southern society, and the social and economic companions of racial norms contributed their own opportunities for vigilantism. Theft, "insolence," insubordination on the part of a worker, teaching in schools for freedmen, and cohabitation or fornication of black men with white women were all occasions for whippings or even murder. But most common of all was the threatening, whipping, running-off, or even killing of politically active freedmen and Republicans.[49] Why?

The broad tradition of vigilantism provides a context in which to interpret these diverse elements of violence, which historians have singled out for attention. As a whole, the pattern of violence suggests that whites—planter and yeomen—found many things threatening, but it also suggests that their "vague notion" that the inviolable caste line was under attack was most compellingly symbolized in the politics of Reconstruction. This should hardly be surprising. After all, liberal historians have concentrated on Reconstruction politics for precisely the same reason. All whites had a relationship—however unfriendly— with their government. It disgusted them that prominent white men were being disfranchised while blacks (who were not even supposed to be a part of society) received the vote. It angered them that outsiders were turning their society upside down. And

49. E. H. Chambers, testimony, October 26, 1871, Nedan L. Argier, testimony, July 14, 1871, Charles Wallace Howard, testimony, October 31, 1871, Maria Carter, testimony, October 21, 1871, Linton Stephens, testimony, November 3, 1871, Charles Smith, testimony, October 26, 1871, all *ibid.*, VII, 602, VI, 172, VII, 839, VI, 413–14, VII, 983, 599, *et passim* VI, VII; H. D. F. Young to Captain M. Frank Gallagher, Clarke Raushenburg, report, John Emory Bryant, testimony, December 21, 1868, J. C. Norris to John Emory Bryant, November 28, 1868, all in "Conditions in Georgia," 60, 120–22, 28–29, 81, *et passim*; J. W. Alvord to O. O. Howard, January 20, 1871, in *Letters from the South Relating to the Condition of Freedmen Addressed to Major General O. O. Howard, Commissioner, Bureau, R., F., & A.L.* (Washington, D.C., 1870), 22; Memorandum in the Case of Perry Jeffreys, Col'd [November 1868?] (MS in Negro File, 1868–69, Georgia State Archives, Atlanta); Trelease, *White Terror*, xlvii.

whatever differences they had among themselves, they could gather together in a traditional way to protect the caste premises upon which they defined their society and to redeem their "white man's country" from alleged "black domination."

With this viciously parochial habit of mind, quite nearly all white southerners could join to protect something they thought was theirs. Just as moonshiners fought outsiders who threatened their livelihood, just as French peasants fought landowners who were attempting to foreclose a customary and economically important right, just as neighbors fought to protect their community against immoral influences, so now white Georgians, like other white southerners, saw themselves as protecting their society from outsiders (meaning blacks and Yankees) and traitors (meaning the small minority of southern whites who became Republicans).[50] South Carolina whites, in an often-quoted protest to Congress, succinctly summarized the position of most white southerners:

> Intelligence, virtue, and patriotism are to give place in all elections, to ignorance, stupidity and vice. The superior race is to be made subservient to the inferior. . . . They who own no property are to levy taxes and make all appropriations. . . . The consequences will be, in effect, confiscation. The appropriations to support free schools for the education of the negro children, for the support of old negroes in the poorhouse, and the vicious in the jails and penitentiary, together with a standing army of negro soldiers [militia], will be crushing and utterly ruinous to the State. Every man's property will have to be sold to pay his taxes. . . . The white people of our State will never quietly submit to negro rule. . . . We will keep up this contest until we have regained the heritage of political control handed down to us by honored ancestry. That is a duty we owe to the land that is ours, to the graves that it contains, and to the race of which you and we alike are members—the proud Caucasian race, whose sovereignty on earth God has ordained.[51]

50. Emphasis on outsiders in Davis, "The Reasons of Misrule," in Davis, *Society and Culture in Early Modern France, passim*; Merriman, "The Demoiselles of the Ariège," 88, 96–97, *et passim*.

51. Walter L. Fleming (ed.), *Documentary History of Reconstruction; Political,*

In a leap of faith as great as the one required to believe Saint Patrick sailed across the Irish Sea on altar stones, white southerners equated the division between white and black with a division between intelligence-virtue-wealth and poverty-ignorance-vice. In doing so they legitimized and made the relations between landowners and laborers dependent upon a larger, less overtly self-interested definition of race relations. This half-racial, half-economic dogma gave landless whites and small landowners who were not employers at least an emotional stake in the system of racially defined, economic subordination. But no clear division can be made between the economic stake of planters and the emotional stake of other whites. The noneconomic justifications for Klan violence offered by unapologetic, socially prominent whites and their vague sense of fear show that they had an emotional as well as economic stake in racial subordination. Their racially defined social cosmography was infused with moral value, which, while it was akin to economic self-interest, also had an independent life of its own.

Before the war, slavery had been a social as well as an economic institution. It affected almost every aspect of southern life. After the war, when northern Republicans tried to change the meaning of black labor for southern whites, they were faced with a challenge few of them completely understood. The definition of subordinate black labor was woven into the fabric of southern culture. Republicans attacked what they considered just a part of southern society, but their assumption was erroneous. As the violent reaction of a broad cross section of white southerners showed, the attack threatened the whole of the South's social system. It could not do otherwise. The whole depended on that part. On the other hand, white southerners had a limited tactical flexibility. They could alter this item or that without jeopardizing their system as a whole. The Georgia legislature showed as much when it chose not to enact a harsh black code. Whites found this flexibility adequate between 1865 and 1868, but when Congress moved forcefully to change the South's political and social system, southern whites successfully fought to protect their caste values and prevent a cultural revolution.

Military, Social, Religious, Educational, and Industrial, 1865 to the Present Time (2 vols.; Cleveland, 1906–1907), II, 455–56, quoted in Trelease, *White Terror*, xxxv.

Congressional Republicans forced large landowners into the position of political impotence characteristic of the less socially prominent and well-to-do. In order "to protect their society," upper-class southerners therefore resorted to vigilante behavior traditionally associated with the lower classes, with peasants in Europe and yeomen in America. Moral violence helped them "to redeem" their society. To those accustomed to political influence, Redemption (the ousting of Republicans from office) meant control. Once they were again in control of state and local government, they reasserted the value of law. Convenience and principle were one. Thus, in the black belt where planters and plantations were dominant, widespread Ku Kluxism died out in 1871, except where an occasional local government had yet to be redeemed.[52] But in the upper piedmont and other sections of Georgia where small landowners predominated, Klan violence continued after the state had been redeemed and planters withdrew their participation. Yeomen and poor white southerners without an obvious economic stake in the subordination of black labor were independently committed to maintaining the caste barrier. Their racism was not a simple function of planter interests. They did not simply defer. Once unleashed, their violence was difficult to control. This was particularly true because, no matter who held the positions of authority, a yeoman was unlikely to feel he had much influence, and the problems he saw remained unsolved.

After planters withdrew, Klan violence continued to reflect a mixture of racially defined social, economic, sexual, and political caste standards. Cohabitation and fornication of black males with white females continued to be severely punished; schools for the freedmen continued to be burned and their teachers whipped; theft continued to bring beatings; "insolence" continued to bring reprisals; Republicans continued to be abused. And significantly, black share hands and renters, who had a degree of autonomy greater than whites thought appropriate, were run off their lands. After widespread vigilantism burned itself out in Georgia during the early 1870s, this last form of violence di-

52. Trelease, *White Terror*, 235, 238, 318, 321–25. See also Thomas M. Allen, testimony, October 26, 1871, in *Joint Committee Report on the Ku Klux Klan*, VII, 611.

rected against share hands and renters would reappear across the South through the beginning of the twentieth century when new periods of economic crisis dramatically threatened the well-being of small-to-middling landowners and prompted them to action against violations of their caste standards.[53]

After Redemption, planters in areas in which Klan violence persisted loudly condemned it. Ku Kluxism was no longer necessary, they said. But most of all, they were upset because widespread vigilantism was disruptive of labor, including share hands and renters.[54] They had themselves been willing to "disorganize" labor in order to regain control, of course, but even then, in the black belt, where they were most dominant, they had tended to opt for the "Mississippi plan," which employed effective forms of intimidation and fraud that were less disruptive to labor than beatings, whippings, and murder.[55]

Disagreement among whites about Klan activity after Redemption reflects an important division among supposedly united whites. Small landowners and perhaps landless whites fought to maintain rigorously their idea of a proper social order. By running off black share hands and renters, poor-to-middling whites showed that they deeply resented any violation of the caste order that was supposed to relegate blacks to the position of abjectly subordinate and dependent labor. Planters certainly shared the racial faith of other white southerners but depended upon income from black workers and needed most of all a stable, year-round work force—whether wage hands, share hands, or renters. Just as their dedication to the law was tied to the in-

53. See C. Mildred Thompson, *Reconstruction in Georgia*, 364; Trelease, *White Terror*, 242; Young to Captain Gallagher, in "Conditions in Georgia," 364. Similar reports appear in Stagg, "The Problem of Klan Violence," and Vernon Burton, "Race and Reconstruction." Later, similar occurrences are described in Americus *Times-Recorder*, August 9, 1865; William F. Holmes, "Whitecapping: Agrarian Violence in Mississippi, 1902–1906," *Journal of Southern History*, XXXV, 165–85. Floyd County serves as an example. See planters' complaints in G. B. Burnett, testimony, November 2, 1871, and P. M. Sheibley, testimony, July 10, 1871, both in *Joint Committee Report on the Ku Klux Klan*, VII, 950, VI, 46, 55; Trelease, *White Terror*, 326, also xlvi–xlvii.

54. Floyd County serves as an example. See planters' complaints in G. B. Burnett, testimony, November 2, 1871, and P. M. Sheibley, testimony, July 10, 1871, both in *Joint Committee Report on the Ku Klux Klan*, VII, 950, VI, 46, 55; Trelease, *White Terror*, 326, also xlvi–xlvii.

55. Actually Trelease observed that the Mississippi plan was a development of techniques which first appeared in Georgia. Trelease, *White Terror*, 241–42. See also Stagg, "The Problem of Klan Violence," 312–13.

terests it served, their dedication to the absolute purity with which the caste line would be maintained was qualified by their stake in immediate profit from black labor. Oddly enough, their economic interests ended up competing ever so slightly with the racial doctrines upon which they predicated their economic order. Ironically, therefore, planters can be portrayed as simultaneously trying to exploit black labor and to protect it from disruptive abuse by others. Perhaps it is also ironic that small landowners, who persevered in trying to enforce rigid caste standards, were also the group from which the Republican party in Georgia and elsewhere in the South drew most of its white supporters. It might appear that small landowners were among those most committed to and also most willing to question the racial order. But just as the efforts of planters to protect their black workers from the interference of others in no way compromised their dedication to the subordination of black labor, so, too, white Republicans were just as dedicated to the caste system as other whites but were more worried about some other question.

Incompletely aware of divisions among themselves, white Georgians joined in a folk movement that was in many ways traditional, though of unprecedented scale, and redeemed their country in 1871. Poor-to-middling whites, like planters, showed themselves committed to a racial caste system. In doing so, they once again showed racism to be an independent force in southern society, but they also betrayed actual and potential divisions among whites that were not supposed to exist. Those divisions were not over the proper status of black labor. After Redemption, there was no dissent among whites when planters set out again, as they had with the black codes, to turn the state into the overseer of subordinate black labor. Yet planters would not fully succeed. The situation in 1871 was very different from that in 1865. Under the leaky umbrella of legal protection created by congressional action, the freedmen had permanently changed the plantation system. To appreciate the disparity between white ideology and practice and to understand the tensions among whites which that disparity exacerbated, requires, first, a familiarity with the postwar labor system.

Chapter III

THE PRIVILEGE OF PERSONAL INDEPENDENCE AND THE POSTBELLUM PLANTATION SYSTEM

Even under the best owners it was a hard, hard life: to toil six days out of seven, week after week, month after month, year after year, as long as life lasted; to be absolutely under the control of someone until the last breath was drawn; to win but the bare necessaries of life, no hope of more, no matter how hard the work, how long the toil; to know that nothing could change your lot. Obedience, submission, prayers—all were in vain. Waking sometimes in the night as I grew older and thinking over it all, I would grow sick with the misery of it all.

—Kate Holmes

SOME OF THEM go out to work very well," reported J. D. Collins, the overseer of Hurricane, a plantation that belonged to the brother of one of Georgia's most prominent politicians. That was all Collins would say about the few freedmen who satisfied him. Like Frances Butler and most other white Georgians in 1865, he was beside himself about the independence the freedmen showed: some "stay in thier houses until an hour by the sun [an hour after sunrise]; others go to thier houses an stay to an three days. Say ennything to them an the answer is I am sick but tha air drying fruit all the time. Tha take all day evry Satturday without my lief. . . . Some of them go when tha pleas an wher tha pleas an pay no attention to your orders or mine." Collins was disgusted enough to try to starve uncooperative freedmen into working as he wished. "I think I will get som of them by not feeding them which proses is now going on," he wrote. But he was still disconsolate as he tutored his employer in the illogic of free black labor: "You had as well sing Sams [Psalms] to a ded horse as tri to instruct a fool negrow."[1] Like other white southerners, Collins assumed that freed-

1. J. D. Collins to John A. Cobb, July 31, 1865, in C. Mildred Thompson, *Reconstruction in Georgia*, 71–72.

men should work as slaves had worked, that it was, for example, illegitimate for them to work at drying fruit for the winter, and that blacks as a caste should work to produce wealth for whites. He did not seem to understand that they could aspire to some different role.

Having defined absolute white control of black workers as ideal, natural, and inevitable, white employers like Frances Butler and overseers like Collins endured a postwar world that stubbornly refused to match their expectations. This was true while the Republican-dominated federal government "interfered" during Reconstruction. It was equally true after Redemption and, in fact, well into the twentieth century. The freedom that came with emancipation in 1865 released an often subtle but, as Collins reported, very real conflict between black workers and white landowners. That conflict built a new system of labor relations in the South.

The system began with innumerably various arrangements between landowners and laborers; yet by the 1870s, a hierarchy of four standard arrangements had emerged. Although there continued to be considerable variation in minor particulars, the usual basic arrangements for wage labor, sharecropping, share tenancy, and renting remained unchanged from the 1870s through the beginning of the twentieth century. To explain in detail the evolution of this elaborate system of labor relations and to describe even the most common variations on what quickly became standard arrangements would require the rewriting of pages that others have written many times before. However, a familiarity with the conflict between workers and landowners, with the market forces that influenced its outcome, and with the differences between wage laborers, sharecroppers, share tenants, and renters is a prerequisite to understanding the New South. An outline of the new plantation system in the black belt and its origins should suffice.

During Reconstruction, incidents of violence dramatized differences between landowners and freedmen. After Redemption, similar incidents occasionally did the same. But in both periods the strictures of racial etiquette meant that most conflict was masked in deferential politeness. The brutal repression of black organizations or even of individual "insolence" left freedmen only the meager advantage of competition for their labor in the marketplace as an effective means to improve the treatment they received. Many freedmen simply refused to work for those employers who would not agree to minimal requests.

The ability of blacks to take advantage of the market depended not only upon an unfilled demand for their labor but also upon their mobility—their right to stop working and leave harsh treatment. The right to move was, in fact, among the first rights that freedmen exercised. Soon after news of emancipation reached the plantations, many freedmen packed what little they had and left. Some sought reunion with mother, father, wife, husband, or child. Some sought opportunities in cities or on other plantations. But some moved simply because it felt pleasantly free. "Why didn't you stay on the old place," Sidney Andrews asked a freedman living in a hovel outside Macon. "Didn't you have a good master?" The freedman answered, "I'se has a berry good master, mass'r, but ye see I'se wanted to be a free man." Andrews did not understand. "But you were just as free there as you are here," he said. "P'r'aps I is," disagreed the former slave with well-practiced grace, "but I'se makes a livin up yer, I dun reckon, an' I likes ter be a free man wher I'se can go an' cum an' nobody say not'ing."[2]

In a recent study, historian Leon Litwack describes the going and coming of emancipated slaves as part of a testing of the "limits of freedom."[3] Newly freed blacks were testing a substantive right, for the immobility of slaves and of peons is a prerequisite to the coercion of their labor. As slaves, blacks had understood this well. They knew the obstacles to running away, the hopelessness of trying to escape the abuses of bondage.[4] Freedom meant they could decide for themselves whether or not they would work and where and when they would go. As Levi Pollard remembered, "Den us was us own boss, en could [come] and go like us any white, just so's us put in time dat us waz paid fo."[5]

Even before Union victory was complete, blacks in numerous

2. Andrews, *The South Since the War*, 351. See also Litwack, *Been in the Storm So Long*, 221–91. Paul D. Escott lists with percentages the motives of freedmen who moved in Escott, *Slavery Remembered*, 138, Table 5.3.

3. Litwack, *Been in the Storm So Long*, 227.

4. Escott, *Slavery Remembered*, 72–73.

5. Quoted in Litwack, *Been in the Storm So Long*, 327.

states quit work over such issues as who would be their overseers; whether or not they would have to work in gangs, on Saturdays, or under the threat of whipping; whether or not they
could have garden patches or keep hogs; and most frequently
they quit work to press for higher pay, whether in cash or shares.[6]
Their mobility and ability to find work elsewhere often forced
landowners to compromise on these and other issues. Contrary to
white assumptions about the proper role of black labor, freedmen
successfully pushed to moderate somewhat the long hours and
harsh treatment of slavery. As Whitelaw Reid reported, "Every
old slaveholder, I might say everybody in the old slavehold-
ing communities, vehemently argued that 'niggers wouldn't do
more'n half as much now that the lash was no longer behind
them.'" At the same time, Reid concluded from his own observations, although blacks had "worked more hours per day while in
slavery, . . . they were perfectly willing now to work as many
hours as any employer ought to ask."[7]

White employers disagreed. Consequently, in 1865 and 1866
the landowners who dominated southern legislatures adopted
black codes designed to end the mobility of freedmen. "Properly
controlled" black labor left no room for such "independence,"
"idleness," and "unreliability." But Congressional Reconstruction aborted the codes and brought constitutional amendments
that gutted analogous efforts after Redemption. Blacks retained
in both theory and practice their right to quit work and move
elsewhere. Gradually freedmen successfully used this right of
the marketplace to shorten their work week, escape whipping,
end most gang labor, and increase their pay from the wages as
low as a dollar a month and shares as small as a sixteenth of the
crop that were first offered them after emancipation.[8]

Freedmen used their right to withdraw their labor perhaps

6. Kolchin, *First Freedom*, 8–10, 22–23; Escott, *Slavery Remembered*, 119–42;
Litwack, *Been in the Storm So Long*, 393, for example, but Chaps. 4–8 *passim*;
Williamson, *After Slavery*, 44–46, 89, 91, 99–102, 114.

7. Reid, *After the War*, 503–504.

8. Collins to John A. Cobb, July 31, 1865, Howell Cobb to My Dear Wife, December, 1865, both in C. Mildred Thompson, *Reconstruction in Georgia*, 71–73;
Southern Cultivator, February, 1875; Williamson, *After Slavery*, 36, 45–46, 81, 89,
100, 102, 104, 107, 114; Litwack, *Been in the Storm So Long*, 227, 292–304, 329,
337, 340–46, 416–25, 432–37; Escott, *Slavery Remembered*, 148–58.

most dramatically as women and children adopted new economic roles. After emancipation, single black women and widows often worked as wage hands in cotton, but wives and children usually refused employment in the fields.[9] In part, this was because they adopted roles traditional among rural households. As one newspaperman explained, "after bearing and nursing children, cooking for the family, washing, making and mending clothes, etc.," black wives could "not earn much money."[10] However, this explanation was incomplete. In slavery, women worked as full-time field hands besides having responsibility for domestic chores.[11] After emancipation, the wives of many wage hands worked as cooks or maids or "took to the tub" and made money doing laundry. Like their children, they returned to the field to chop and pick cotton for the superior wages available during particularly busy times in the growing or harvesting season. And they sometimes even cultivated on shares a few acres of cotton and corn separate from the landowner's "general crops" and out from under his supervision.[12] Farther up the agricultural ladder, the wives of sharecroppers and renters regularly joined their husbands and children in the field after housework was finished for the day.[13] In fact, the regularity with which a freedman's family worked in the fields was, in general, inversely related to the close supervision of his white employer. Economic calculations, an aversion to being supervised by white employers, and a desire to lighten the heavy burdens of work that they had carried in slavery, all influenced blacks as they adopted new economic roles for women and children.

From the earliest days of Reconstruction, white landowners complained about the withdrawal of many women and children

9. Tenth Census, 1880, Population Schedules (microfilm).

10. Atlanta *Constitution*, October 15, 1883.

11. Stampp, *The Peculiar Institution*, 79–80.

12. *Henry Allen* v. *State*, Jones County, August, 1884, Supreme Court of the State of Georgia File No. A-13445, Georgia Department of Archives and History, Atlanta; Hammond, *The Cotton Industry*, 187; Milledgeville *Union and Recorder*, April 16, 1873; Atwater and Woods, "Dietary Studies," 26; Theodore Rosengarten, *All God's Dangers: The Life of Nate Shaw* (New York, 1975), 9–10, 127–28.

13. This was also true of white tenant women. See Margaret Jarmon Hagood, *Mothers of the South: Portraiture of White Tenant Farm Women* (New York, 1977), 83–84, Chap. 7.

from their supervision. Under slavery, planters had seldom allowed anything to interfere for long with the work in the fields; so even before the war was over, at least one group of planters complained that black women would "not work because they expect to get the money of the men." A scholarly apologist for slavery, writing in the 1890s, summarized with conviction the position of those postwar employers who remained incapable of seeing that freedmen had any legitimate interest or role that stretched beyond the employer's rows of cotton. "In the cultivation of cotton," he wrote, "the negro women seem to participate in a much less degree than they did in slavery days. They still form an important addition to the labor forces in picking time. But their evident desire to live as do the white women has generally caused them to shun outdoor employments, and the quality of their work has deteriorated even more than that of men."[14]

According to employers, black women were imitating their white betters and training their children solely for idleness. In 1883 the Atlanta *Constitution* repeated the usual refrain: "These black parents will only make vagrants and vagrants make thieves. If the leaders of the colored people would take the time to teach them that they are compelled to work now, just as they did when they were slaves, and that it is their duty to teach their children to work, it would be of much greater benefit" than anything else they could possibly do. A historian (reared in the planter class) left even less room for optimism: "Children born and raised under the influence of the new system are not so amenable to authority and are much less inclined to work" than their parents. But, he explained, this was to be expected. Black parents, "no longer supported by the power of the slaveholder," were unequal to the task of bringing up their children.[15]

One reason supervision was important in the redefinition of work roles was evident in outbursts of violence between workers and employers. In 1868, for example, "James Jester [black] was

14. Schurz, "Report of Carl Schurz," Accompanying Documents, No. 3, p. 84; Hammond, *The Cotton Industry*, 187.

15. Atlanta *Constitution*, July 21, 1883; Bruce, *The Plantation Negro as a Freeman*, 57, 3–6, 25–26. Similar complaints were common. See, for example, Hammond, *The Cotton Industry*, 186; *Cherokee Advance*, May 5, 1893; *Southern Cultivator*, February, 1884; Dawson *News*, February 19, 1890.

severely and cruelly beaten by James Porter (white) with the aid of James Witcomb and Calvin Curry, both white, for claiming the right of whipping his own child instead of allowing his employer and former master to do so." Even though the resistance of freedmen caused most employers reluctantly to abandon whipping, comparable incidents showed that much remained the same. In Schley County in 1872 a freedman named Allen Stallings burned the house of his employer at the insistence of his wife, who was infuriated that the landowner had whipped her "little son." She said that "the boy was not his" and that he "would be sorry for" what he had done. Similarly, in 1884 a freedman named Cook "struck [Roser] Wilson on the head with his hoe." A local newspaper reported that Wilson, the overseer of the plantation, had reprimanded Cook's "boy for his bad work." The boy retorted; Wilson slapped him; and Cook, who had been "working a few feet in advance, turned around and without warning, struck Wilson on the head." The overseer recovered from his "severe gash" as Cook fled.[16]

Historians have long recognized the frustration of a slave who watched impotently as his owner or overseer beat his spouse or child. As former slaves, Jester, Stallings, and Cook illustrated something more than the affection of parents when they reacted furiously to the abuse of their children. Their reactions, like the new work roles of wives and children, were part of the irreconcilable difference between landowners and laborers over the practical meaning of free labor over the limits of white supervision or control.

Freedom from abusive supervision was a goal to which most freedmen applied whatever leverage they could derive from the market demand for their labor—a demand perhaps enhanced by the new work roles of wives and children.[17] The end of whipping was one reward. Because most blacks simply refused to work for employers who would not abandon the practice, it be-

16. "Report on Murder and Assaults with Intent to Kill Committed upon Freed People in the State of Georgia from January 1, 1868, to November 15, 1868," in "Conditions in Georgia," p. 129, case no. 95; *Allen Stallings* v. *State*, Schley County, December, 1872, Supreme Court File No. A-6062; Americus *Weekly Recorder*, July 24, 1884.

17. Ransom and Sutch, *One Kind of Freedom*, 44–48, App. C.

came increasingly rare. Of course, abusive supervision was not limited to physical cruelty. The severity of a freedman's employer or landlord, as well as the freedman's nominal position on the agricultural ladder, could be an important measure of his economic well-being. During Reconstruction, as freedmen bargained over the terms of contracts, they helped to create a system of labor that, within the limited options available to them, reflected calculations of economic self-interest as well as personal dignity. But because whites defined the proper role of black labor as abject subordination, blacks most often found both economic self-interest and personal dignity where whites were absent.

The ownership of land provided an economic and personal independence more complete than any other and was the goal of most blacks. Northerners and southerners alike were unanimous in reporting the freedman's ambition. Those to whom Union soldiers had promised farms during the war were disappointed from the start, and rumors of "forty acres and a mule" raised hopes that died hard. As a south Georgia newspaper explained as early as July, 1865, the freedmen could not see why the redistribution of land "should not be done. . . . to convince them that it will not be done and at the same time . . . show them that they must continue to labor will be to convince the Negro that he is not free." The comments of blacks confirm the newspaper report. "Me tort when de Yankees come, dey gib us all dis country," said one freedman. "An now dat man [an officer of the Freedmen's Bureau] say we git nuffin' 'cept we work." Others bristled, "Damn such freedom as that" and "We will still be slaves." [18]

Denied help from the government, freedmen tried to purchase land despite their own poverty and intense opposition from whites. When Frances Butler's hands gathered enough money to attempt purchases, they traveled to the nearby port of Darien. As their mistress explained, "lands were sold to them [only] by a common class of men, principally small shop keepers and Jews

18. Thomasville *Enterprise*, n.d., *Southern Cultivator*, XXII (1865), Augusta *Constitutionalist*, May 9, 1865 (rpr. from New York *Times*), and *Southern Cultivator*, XXIII (1865), all quoted in Manuel Gottlieb, "The Land Question in Georgia During Reconstruction," *Science and Society*, III, 361.

(the gentlemen refusing to sell land to the negroes, although they occasionally rented it to them)." Because planters refused to sell, Butler's hands "paid forty, fifty and even more for an acre" of land "either within the town limits," for which they got no titles, and from which they were soon turned off, or out in the piney woods, where the land was so poor they could not raise a peck of corn to the acre."[19]

Immediately following the war, opposition to black land-ownership was indeed intense, and it continued. In 1896 and, for that matter, 1936, most white landowners still opposed the selling of land to blacks. But as historian Vernon Wharton concluded, this attitude gradually became "less effective" after Reconstruction.[20] The steady if slow advance of landowning among blacks through the end of the century testifies both to their undiminished desire for independence and to the inability of whites to prohibit legally (hence absolutely) the freedmen's right to buy. Yet discrimination exacted a high price. Even an unsympathetic newspaperman could report in 1889 that those blacks who bought land had to "pay very high prices, . . . buying it on time at almost any figure asked."[21] The farm lands available to blacks were usually small plots of inferior soil. In Georgia black landownership was heavily concentrated in a band of infertile, often swampy, and rather isolated piney woods near the coast. Elsewhere in the state, those few freedmen who were able to buy land could often purchase only lots large enough for a house and garden, so many black landowners still had to farm a white man's land as croppers or renters. But despite racial discrimination, despite enforced poverty, blacks by 1891 owned more than a million mostly thin and sandy acres in Georgia.[22]

The increase in landownership among blacks in the nine-

19. Leigh, *Ten Years on a Georgia Plantation*, 78–79.
20. *House Reports*, 39th Cong., 1st Sess., No. 30, Pt. 3, p. 101; Wharton, *The Negro in Mississippi*, 60–61; Gottlieb, "The Land Question in Georgia During Reconstruction," 383; Frederick L. Hoffman, *Race Traits and Tendencies of the American Negro* (New York, 1896), 269; S. H. Bassett, address to the Georgia State Agricultural Society, in *Southern Cultivator*, November, 1884; Arthur F. Raper, *Preface to Peasantry: A Tale of Two Black Belt Counties* (Chapel Hill, 1936), 22, 121–22.
21. Covington *Georgia Enterprise*, June 13, 1889.
22. On the quality and size of landholdings, see William Edward Burghardt

teenth century was an achievement that can be described without exaggeration as heroic. Yet black landowners remained a very tiny fraction of blacks and a very tiny fraction of landowners. In the plantation belt, where most blacks lived, the ownership of land remained overwhelmingly concentrated in the hands of planters.[23] At the end of the century, whites could assure themselves that "it is not to be regretted that the majority of negroes, in their present state of inefficiency, have not acquired ownership of land." Blacks had been kept part of the labor system as wage hands, sharecroppers, share tenants, and renters. There, whites said, blacks could best add "to the aggregate wealth of the community"—meaning, of course, the white community.[24] It was on these lower rungs of the agricultural ladder that most blacks had to seek economic self-interest and personal dignity.

Wage labor stood on the bottom rung of the agricultural ladder.[25] Except for casual employees, wage laborers were usually paid by the month and employed by the year. Historians have tended to dismiss the wage system as a passing experiment of Reconstruction eclipsed by the rise of sharecropping.[26] In one sense they have been right. Planters complained loudly that blacks refused to work for wages. One wrote, for example, that

---

Du Bois, "The Negro Landholder of Georgia," U.S. Department of Labor *Bulletin*, No. 35 (July, 1901), 647–777, esp. 665; Oscar Zeichner, "The Transition from Slave to Free Agricultural Labor in the Southern States," *Agricultural History*, XIII (January, 1939), 30; Leigh, *Ten Years on a Georgia Plantation*, 78–79; Hoffman, *Race Traits and Tendencies of the American Negro*, 269; George Brown Tindall, *South Carolina Negroes, 1877–1900* (Columbia, 1952), 95–96; Raper, *Preface to Peasantry*, 22.

23. Banks, *The Economics of Land Tenure in Georgia* (New York, 1905), 37, 40–42; Roger Shugg, "Survival of the Plantation System in Louisiana," *Journal of Southern History*, III, 311–25; Wiener, *Social Origins of the New South*, 16–34; Ransom and Sutch, *One Kind of Freedom*, 78–80.

24. Hammond, *The Cotton Industry*, 189; Hoffman, *Race Traits and Tendencies of the American Negro*, 269.

25. Because whites were sometimes inexact in their references to various categories of labor, the labels of wage laborer, sharecropper, share tenant, and renter used in the following discussion are anachronistically precise.

26. Brooks, *Agrarian Revolution in Georgia*, 25–26ff; Ransom and Sutch, *One Kind of Freedom*, 68–70; Tindall, *South Carolina Negroes*, 93; Wharton, *The Negro in Mississippi*, 70.

freedmen would "starve and go naked" before they would work as wage hands "for a white man." They all wanted "to get a patch of ground to live on and get out from under" white control. A few planters were more precise. One from Oglethorpe County explained, "the Negro became less willing to work in large bodies on large plantation's [sic]; they became harder to manage and many began to get off to themselves and run one and two horse farms." [27]

Large planters like these resented the hesitancy of blacks to work as wage hands in gangs. Planters preferred the wage system because its discipline could resemble that of slavery. [28] Wage laborers still lived in what had been the quarters; a horn or bell still summoned them to the fields at dawn and home at dusk; work still filled five and a half long days a week; and a captain or driver still oversaw the pace and performance of gangs, an arrangement blacks found particularly distasteful. [29] The refusal of most blacks to work in gangs under the supervision of an overseer made the running of large farms with wage labor increasingly rare during and after Reconstruction. Unable to find wage hands enough to work their lands with gangs, planters one by one decentralized their plantations with the share and renting systems.

Although most freedmen refused to work in gangs, a majority did work for wages. In fact, in 1880 over 280,000 Georgians, most of them black males, worked as wage hands on farms, and in 1890 over 210,000. The census does not seem to have exaggerated their number, or at least not significantly, for in a category

27. Letter from Warren County, in *Southern Cultivator*, March 1867, quoted in Brooks, *Agrarian Revolution in Georgia*, 23 n; A. Stevens (Questionnaire, "Inquiries I," 1912, in Brooks Papers).

28. W. B. Hill, "Rural Survey of Clarke County, Georgia, with Special Reference to the Negroes," *Bulletin of the University of Georgia*, XV, No. 3 (March, 1915), 18, 20. See also O. B. Stevens, W. L. Peck, and J. E. Nunnally, testimony, all in Industrial Commission, *Report of the Industrial Commission on Agriculture and Agricultural Labor, House Reports*, 57th Cong., 1st Sess., No. 179, pp. 907, 911, 455–56, 459–60, hereinafter cited as *Report on Agricultural Labor*; Eugene W. Hilgard, *Report on Cotton Production in the United States; Also Embracing Agricultural and Physio-Geographical Descriptions of Several Cotton States and California* (2 vols.; Washington, D.C., 1884), II, 172–73.

29. Atlanta *Journal*, n.d., quoted in Dawson *News*, March 20, 1889. See also "Inquiries I," 1912, Brooks Papers.

separate from wage laborers, the census in both 1880 and 1890 counted more "planters, farmers and overseers" than there were farm units. This shows that sharecroppers were counted as tenant farmers (though legally they were employees), in accordance with the policy of the census office to count the land assigned to each sharecropper as a separate farm. Wives and children were occasionally reported as farmers and, presumably, farm laborers, but since approximately two-thirds of those listed as agricultural laborers were male and since the practice occurred in reporting both farmers and laborers, it is questionable how much it skewed the results.[30] Even a casual glance at the manuscript schedules of the 1880 census shows that enumerators in most Georgia counties carefully distinguished among farmers (including renters, share tenants, and sharecroppers), farm laborers, and family members who helped on the farm.

Patterns of employment among black wage hands confirm the relative freedom of the labor market. Planters could not hire gangs because blacks did not want to work in gangs and had sufficient economic leverage to enforce their choice. A farmer could, however, readily employ several wage hands to work beside him in his fields, while letting out the balance of his land to sharehands and renters. As one farmer explained, "landowners and their families" worked their own fields with the aid of "1 or 2 hands," while "the greater portion of" their land was worked "on the share plan."[31] Many resident landowners, therefore, worked their farms under several different arrangements. Reserving their best land to themselves, they farmed it with the help of wage labor and rented or hired sharehands to farm their lesser lands. A planter in Sumter County was unusual only in that he tried to practice the latest techniques of scientific agriculture. "He manages everything in a most systematic way," reported a local newspaper, "and superintends the work himself. He divides the labor—some for wages, others croppers, all negroes."[32] The preferences of blacks evident in this pattern of employment sug-

30. *Tenth Census, 1880: Agriculture*, 110, *Population*, 760, 818; *Eleventh Census, 1890: Agriculture*, 202, *Population*, Pt. 2, pp. 312, 304.
31. J. E. Nunnally, testimony, and see O. B. Stevens, testimony, both in Industrial Commission, *Report on Agricultural Labor*, 455, 909.
32. Americus *Weekly Recorder*, July 11, 1884; Herman Clarence Nixon, *Possum Trot: Rural Community, South* (Norman, Okla., 1941), 49–51.

gest a postwar corollary to what some scholars have suspected but been unable to prove about the antebellum South. It seems likely that on small farms where landowners and workers toiled side by side, supervision was less likely to be harsh than on large units where relationships were less personal and employers did not have to share the burdens of their own demands. Supervision could be tolerable or onerous. A foreman can, with little effort, make otherwise tolerable work unbearable. The son of a planter explained his father's successful handling of wage hands in precisely these terms: "He nearly always got the maximum production from hired labor, mainly by staying with his workers and himself setting the work pace, whether with a plow gang, a crowd of cotton choppers, or the gin workers."[33]

This explanation for the willingness of many blacks to work for wages but not in gangs also allows for those unusual cases in which large plantations continued to be run on the old system, for there were a few plantations still run with gang labor as late as the early twentieth century.[34] Where a paternalistic planter allowed hands to have garden patches, pigs, chickens, and small fields in which their families could raise cotton while they worked for wages, and where hands did not have to work all day on Saturdays, fear whipping, or endure severe demands and degrading treatment, the wage system might survive. One planter in Baldwin County, for example, explained his successful management of wage labor by citing the differences between his policies and the practices of his white neighbors. "I have no negro tenants," he wrote; "all my negroes are laborers who work under my orders, or those of my managers, and as I treat them fairly, pay them fully all that is due them, and feed them abundantly, I get along smoothly." While the women "do not engage to work in the general crop," he continued, they cultivate family plots of cotton and corn "and do it well. . . . I also allow them to keep cows, hogs, and chickens, and to have gardens. . . . Disobedience, idleness, dishonesty, neglect, or insolence, I punish on the spot with dismissal."[35]

33. Nixon, *Possum Trot*, 51.

34. Thomas Jackson Woofter, Jr., *Negro Migration: Changes in Rural Organization and Population in the Cotton Belt* (New York, 1920), 49; David Barrow, "A Georgia Plantation," *Scribner's Monthly*, XXI, 831.

35. Milledgeville *Union and Recorder*, April 16, 1873.

Few planters were as "generous" as this one, and both he and his workers knew it. John Dent constantly felt the urge to limit even his share hands in almost every way. "Negroes and Patches," one of many cathartic essays he scribbled into his endless journal, offers a fair example. Dent exclaimed with annoyance that his croppers wanted to use his mules to break ground for their vegetables: "They do not want patches but plantations and expect the teams you furnish them to attend the regular crops to do all the extra work." Four years later he was angry again. "This letting hands have patches independent of the crops is not a good system and don't work at all. They neglect their crops for their patches and the proprietor is greatly the loser—in future I shall never agree to such terms again." As with most of Dent's resolutions, there is no evidence he carried through on this one; however, other landowners did deny their hands the right to have gardens and other simple privileges.[36] A harsh employer might pay his hands as much as a paternalistic one, but he could degrade them by his manner and deny them important economic privileges.

As R. J. Smith of Jones County discovered, wage hands knew they might force a change when an employer demanded or denied too much. Smith still employed gang labor as late as 1884, but then he overstepped his bounds. Although he could describe his employees as good workers, he decided one week to withhold their pay because he was dissatisfied with their performance. "They looked like they were mad," he said. He was right. While he was fixing his plantation bell, a spokesman for his workers announced that he need not bother; he would have "no use for" it. Next year he would have to "rent the place."[37] When farmers like Smith found themselves unable to maintain the gang system, they farmed what they could with the help of wage hands and resorted to sharecropping, share tenancy, and renting arrangements to farm the balance of their land.

By the 1870s, a sharecropper worked for a half or, less commonly, a third of all he grew. The share depended upon whether the cropper or the employer paid for rations; croppers generally

36. Mathis, Mathis, and Purcell (eds.), *Dent Journals*, X, March 9, 1872, XII, July 6, 1876; Atwater and Woods, "Dietary Studies," 28; Otken, *The Ills of the South*, 48; Nixon, *Forty Acres and Steel Mules*, 40.
37. *Henry Allen* v. *State.*

preferred to choose their own food and pay for it ("on time," of course). The cropper's only asset was his labor. His employer supplied a plow, a mule, and land for him to farm. The usual cropper working on halves paid for half the fertilizer bill, food, and all other personal expenses out of his share. A share tenant differed from a cropper in that he owned a mule or horse and often a plow. Because he supplied these important assets in addition to his labor, he received a greater share of the crop—two-thirds of the cotton and three-fourths of the corn—and paid a proportionately greater share of the fertilizer bill. A renter paid a fixed amount of cotton for his use of the land—whether a fixed number of bales (usually two) or a fixed dollar's worth of lint. He almost always supplied everything except the land, but occasionally he hired a mule from his landlord for an additional twenty-five or thirty dollars per year (the value of 80 to 90 percent of a four-hundred-pound bale of cotton selling at eight cents a pound).[38]

These arrangements can best be understood as degrees of compromise between landowners and landless laborers. During Reconstruction and in lean years thereafter, some resident land owners resorted to share arrangements for lack of cash with which to pay wages. During the depression of the late 1870s, for example, a planter reported that "more farmers are farming on the share system" this year because "money is scarce." A few planters also seem to have opted for the share system voluntarily, but as R. J. Smith learned while he was repairing his plantation bell, both the lack of money and the voluntary choices of planters can easily be overrated as causes for the rise of share and renting arrangements. Lack of cash does not explain why, in good years, when planters wished to return to the wage system, they were unable to do so. "I see this Rental and partnership system is becoming unpopular," wrote one planter; "there is a desire to stop it on the part of the Farmers. But not so with the Negroes as they tested the privileges of extreme latitude." The system would not change "where labor is very scarce."[39]

38. The names used for these anachronistically precise categories are found in Banks, *The Economics of Land Tenure in Georgia, passim*; Nixon, *Possum Trot*, 53; Hill, "Rural Survey of Clarke County, Georgia," 17–19, 58; Hilgard, *Report on Cotton Production in the United States*, 172–73—and elsewhere.
39. Mathis, Mathis, and Purcell (eds.), *Dent Journals*, XIII, Introduction, January 1, 1878, IX, February 4, 1875, and see XIII, February 5, 1878.

Blacks did prefer the share system because of the relative latitude it allowed. It was a decentralized form of plantation agriculture. Each share hand, his family, and sometimes other relatives lived in a cabin in or near the field he worked. This pattern of residence reflected the end of gang labor, the end of moment-by-moment supervision by the landowner.[40] The landowner still had authority to make all the major decisions. He could decide what would be planted or done, when, where, and how. And he could visit as often as he liked to make sure that his hand kept him satisfied. Yet the decentralized system freed blacks to pace their own work, to tend their gardens (when they were allowed to have them), or to hunt for food, as they judged best.

Planters repeatedly explained that they dropped the gang system because "sharecropping seemed to suit our labor better."[41] It did. But obviously it was not the delicate sensitivity of white employers to the preferences of their black workers that brought the change. Most employers adopted the share system only when they had no real choice. As a merchant from Columbus explained, blacks increased their independence of white supervision only when they could enforce their demands.[42] What exactly did the merchant mean? How did the market allow freedmen to make the landowners change their system?

From the perspective of white landowners, the late nineteenth-century South was suffering a severe labor shortage. Planters wanted more black laborers than they could find, and they wanted them cheaper than they came. They blamed the "shortage" on any movement of blacks outside the narrowly defined role of dependent agricultural labor. White landowners complained about the withdrawal of women and children from their fields, the movement of relatively insignificant numbers of blacks to cities, the enticing pay offered by lumbermen and railroad contractors, the influence of immigration agents who encouraged blacks to move to richer lands in Arkansas and the

40. Barrow, "A Georgia Plantation," 830–36. See also O. B. Stevens, testimony, in Industrial Commission, *Report on Agricultural Labor*, 909.

41. No name, Bulloch County (Questionnaire, "Inquiries I," 1912, in Brooks Papers). Other comments on these questionnaires were similar.

42. John D. Pou to Robert Preston Brooks, February 15, 1912, *ibid.* Other questionnaires support this claim.

Mississippi Delta; they also blamed simple idleness and the rise of the share and renting system itself.[43] It is difficult, however, to give credence to complaints about a shortage of labor. Labor was certainly plentiful enough to be cheap, and so mechanized farming remained rare. Blacks could command only a bare subsistence wage. From their standpoint, the "shortage" looked like a surplus that limited the cash value of their labor.[44]

But ironically, perhaps, the cheapness of black labor helped to increase the demand for it and allowed freedmen some leverage in the marketplace. Land was plentiful enough, labor cheap enough, and cotton profitable enough so that inefficient methods of farming remained profitable for landowners. Despite poor methods and the low price of cotton, landlords still received a tolerable, though by no means sumptuous income from their lands.[45] Even during the severe depression of the 1890s, when cotton prices hit their lowest point in the century, a planter in north Georgia estimated that "the land devoted to cotton-growing would be increased 33.3 percent if labor could be had." [46] As a transplanted northern farmer observed, southerners were tempted "to ignore the best methods of farming" because labor "only cost 50 or 60 cents a day." The "abundance of cheap labor in the South is" rather a curse than a blessing, he concluded. It

43. Woofter, *Black Migration*, 36. Complaints about turpentine works in, for example, Albany *News*, n.d., quoted in Atlanta *Constitution*, June 13, 1883. Complaints about "high-wage" truck farms in, for example, Robert Preston Brooks, "Economic Conditions" (MS dated 1911, in Brooks Papers), II, 4–5. See also Milledgeville *Union and Recorder*, January 22, 1873; *Pike County News*, n.d., quoted in Atlanta *Constitution*, January 16, 1883; Mathis, Mathis, and Purcell (eds.), *Dent Journals*, XII, December 31, 1877, XIII, January 5, 1878; letter from Burke County, in *Southern Cultivator*, February, 1869.

44. P. H. Lovejoy, testimony, in Industrial Commission, *Report on Agricultural Labor*, 75.

45. Industrial Commission, *Report of the Industrial Commission on Agriculture and on Taxation in Various States*, House Reports, 57th Cong., 1st Sess., No. 180, pp. 135–36, hereinafter cited as *Report on Agriculture and Taxation*.

46. T. R. Jones to Committee on Agriculture and Forestry, August 15, 1893, in "Letters from Cotton Growers," *Report of the Committee on Agriculture and Forestry on the Condition of Cotton Growers and the Remedy; and on Cotton Consumption and Production, February 3, 1895*, Senate Reports, 53rd Cong., 3rd Sess., No. 986, Pt. I, 306. See also Hart, *The Southern South*, 121; Otken, *The Ills of the South*, 43; *Southern Cultivator*, February, 1869, quoted in Brooks, *Agrarian Revolution in Georgia*, 25.

is "against the success of agriculture. If we [landowners] could not get a living so easily, we could make more money out of it. That may be a peculiar statement," he admitted, "but it is warranted by the facts." The prosperity of those exceptional planters who employed scientific techniques and sought to maximize productivity lends credence to this northerner's claims.[47]

Except in years of unusually low prices, landowners seemed assured of their share or rent, and they seemed assured of being paid for what they had furnished their share hands or renters, but they still made less and their tenants made less than scientific agriculture would have allowed. Thus, landlords engaged in a system under which they profited but did not prosper. And thus, in order to increase their incomes, they hired as many hands as possible. This demand for labor, which provided blacks some small leverage over the terms of their employment, resulted in the systems of sharecropping, share tenancy, and renting. These arrangements reflected the constraints upon blacks trapped in poverty but also, by their very existence, the limited freedom that the market afforded. Like the new work roles of women and children, the share and renting systems provided blacks with ways to maintain personal dignity while acting in their own economic interest.

Calculations of economic self-interest were reflected in the negotiations that produced these systems during the half-dozen years after the end of the Civil War. From the first days of Reconstruction, freedmen pressed for the best deals they could get. Soon employers were submitting to share arrangements. "Whether or not it is a good policy is not the question," wrote one planter. Landowners could not hire enough hands any other way. One man, he said, had let out two thousand acres to sharecroppers, "and a great many others had let out more or less."[48] In early share agreements, landowners offered workers as little as an eighth or even a sixteenth of the crop, but slowly employees used their right to refuse to work and the force of the market to compel more equitable arrangements. "Nothing satis-

47. Industrial Commission, *Report on Agriculture and Taxation*, 136.
48. Letter from Warren County, in *Southern Cultivator*, March, 1867, quoted in Brooks, *Agrarian Revolution in Georgia*, 23 n. At least fourteen of twenty respondents to one survey changed from wage labor to the share system because they had no choice. "Inquiries I," 1912, in Brooks Papers.

fied them," complained a planter forced in 1866 to increase his workers' shares to a third (without rations). "Grant them one thing," he complained, "and they demand something more. . . . there is no telling where they would stop. The truth is I am disgusted with free negro labor."[49]

The freedmen did not stop at a third. "The negroes hold a camp meeting this week," wrote John Dent in 1873. "It is held as a Religious meeting. But their intentions are to hold a consultation as to getting higher wages—more privileges—and greater liberties. Their strike will be for half of all that is made by farmers this year." Although by 1873 half shares were already standard across much of the South, to Dent a strike meant that blacks in his neighborhood would refuse to contract for less—they had been getting a third plus rations. They are putting farmers "on the road to ruin," exclaimed the ever irritable planter. "They are not satisfied to leave well enough alone." The problem, thought Dent, was that freedmen "consult each other so much about their plans and arrangements, that they hear too much advice and it confuses them."[50]

Share tenancy and renting, still further advances toward relative independence, appeared shortly after sharecropping. A year with good prices and abundant crops gave some sharecroppers the chance to advance. "The idea with the laborer now is to try to buy some old horse or mule" in order to claim "two thirds of all the grain he makes and three fourths of all the cotton," reported one planter. As always, whites resisted. "The laborer on such terms makes all—as he is at no expense but to feed himself and horses" and, the planter neglected to mention, to pay the larger part of the fertilizer and seed bills. "It is certainly better than owning a farm. It already shows that the laborer is the master and the landowner, the poor dependent."[51] It also took little capital to rent land for a fixed amount of cotton, whether in bales or dollar value.[52] Like so many other landowners, John Dent complained about these share tenancy and renting arrange-

49. Howell Cobb to [?], December, 1866, quoted in Brooks, *Agrarian Revolution in Georgia*, 21–22.

50. Mathis, Mathis, and Purcell (eds.), *Dent Journals*, X, September 11–12, 1873, December 23, 1873, XII, November 13, 1876, X, January 19, 1872.

51. *Ibid.*, X, August 8, 1872.

52. Woofter, *Negro Migration*, 64, 80; Nixon, *Forty Acres and Steel Mules*, 19.

ments, just as he did about sharecropping. In fact, he vowed to resist them all and yet had no choice but to submit to all three.

If profits from good years allowed some blacks a chance to become share tenants or renters, losses from bad years were equally common, and the crucial asset of a mule was easily lost to unpaid debts. Thus, Nate Shaw, like his father before him, climbed both up and down the agricultural ladder. At one point he even put a down payment on a piece of property only to lose it to a capricious harvest the following year.[53] Those who worked hard to become renters could easily find themselves croppers or even wage hands a year later.[54] Although the hierarchy of arrangements between landowners and laborers had, by the early 1870s, assumed the form it would hold for the rest of the century, there continued each year to be a great deal of movement on the rungs of the agricultural ladder: a sign of both continued poverty and continued freedom in the marketplace.

As an uneasy, unwelcome compromise between the expectations of whites and the aspirations of blacks, the decentralized plantation system did not end disagreement between landowners and freedmen over the practical meaning of free labor. The end of moment-by-moment supervision of gang labor merely lessened opportunities for overt conflict. Landowners continued to assume prerogatives that blacks resented. The Dawson *Journal* reported one incident that typified the feelings of the two groups. Colonel John R. Jones rode out to visit "a negro to whom he had rented land and furnished . . . a mule." When the colonel "came in sight of this negro he was sitting on the fence and the mule standing still. The Col. remarked to the boy [*i.e.*, black man] that this kind of proceeding would not do, and ordered him to go to plowing. The negro responded that he was waiting for a plow, the one he had on his stock being too dull. The Col. commanded him to plow with the one he had until the one sent for came, . . . [and] the negro reluctantly started to plow, Col. Jones following to the end of the row." One can almost hear the colonel as "he remarked that the plow . . . did very well." It is easy, more than a hundred years later, to empathize with the enraged freedman, "who said he did not want a white man to fol-

53. Rosengarten, *All God's Dangers*, 243.
54. Dawson *Journal*, January 10, 1884.

low after him and stand over him" anymore, but Colonel Jones could not. The response startled him. "If he could not control his own farm he would abandon it," he said. "Those employed there must submit to his government or leave." The colonel kicked his tenant off the plantation, and the newspaper editor showed that the planter's assumptions were by no means unique: "We trust this negro may not be able to secure employment in this section. He is a dangerous character."[55]

Because the caste assumptions of whites had remained fundamentally unchanged since the days of slavery, supervision remained the major point of conflict between white employers and their black workers. The need to supervise black workers closely, and the frequent difficulty of doing so, were major premises of virtually all white criticism of the postwar labor system. From the inception of the decentralized plantation through the end of the century, whites engaged in a tedious debate over which labor arrangement was most profitable. It was an unresolvable debate because the relative profits from different labor arrangements varied as the price of cotton varied, but it reveals much about the operation of the complex labor system.

Whether on large farms or small, whites assumed a connection between a landowner's profit and close supervision of black workers. They saw great benefits in the system of wage labor because it implied constant close supervision. They stressed this point again and again.[56] And except when there was a bad crop or the price of cotton fell especially low, many whites also believed that wage labor was the cheapest form of labor. A share hand received as pay a portion of all he grew; he shared the profits or, in a bad year, the losses. But no matter what the price of cotton, no matter how large or small the landowner's profits, a wage hand received only a fixed sum—by 1870 and throughout the late nineteenth century, usually five to eight dollars a month

55. *Ibid.*, May 14, 1874.

56. Robert Somers, *The Southern States Since the War*, 60; "Farming with Labor or on Shares," in Mathis, Mathis, and Purcell (eds.), *Dent Journals*, XII, November 17–18, 1876; Letter from Burke County, in *Southern Cultivator*, February, 1869, quoted in Brooks, *Agrarian Revolution in Georgia*, 25; Otken, *The Ills of the South*, 35–36; Atlanta *Constitution*, July 7, 1883; *Southern Cultivator*, November, 1890.

plus rations.[57] Rations consisted of about three and a half pounds of fatback and a peck of cornmeal a week, the same amounts that had been given slaves.[58]

In addition to pay, however, one very important difference for both workers and employers distinguished free from slave labor. A disgruntled hand could leave a farm with crops standing in the field and the planter's profit threatened. John Dent recorded his frustration after he spoke to one of his hands about "his idleness" in 1883; "his reply was 'I can leave and I will do so.'—and such all do who are hired for wages, leaving you at a time when their services are most needed."[59] Because cotton required a year-round work force, employers tried to bind wage hands by withholding their pay until the end of the year. However, wages were too small and the price of goods charged against them too great for these efforts to succeed completely.[60] From the perspective of some employers, wage labor was too unreliable.

For this reason, a few white landowners preferred share arrangements. Because a share hand received as pay a proportion of all he grew, self-interest bound him to the land more securely than the wage hand. "He was interested in his crop," and so whites thought him likely to stay a whole year and to work well.[61] Since landowners could supervise share hands closely and because the fragile margin of relative profit between share and wage labor depended upon the unpredictable price of cotton, a few whites claimed that share arrangements had the advantage of the wage system and more.

With every participant in the debate advocating close supervision, it may seem odd that actual supervision varied a great deal. Legally, a renter was a tenant, but he could be supervised as if he were an employee. Legally, a sharecropper was an em-

57. Hilgard, *Report on Cotton Production in the United States*, II, 172; Atlanta *Journal*, n.d., quoted in Dawson *News*, March 20, 1889.

58. Nixon, *Lower Piedmont Country*, 15.

59. Mathis, Mathis, and Purcell (eds.), *Dent Journals*, XV, March 3, 1883. See also Hill, "Rural Survey of Clarke County, Georgia," 22–24.

60. I. W. Avery, letter, in *Southern Cultivator*, November, 1890; Ransom and Sutch, *One Kind of Freedom*, 60, 66.

61. Mathis, Mathis, and Purcell (eds.), *Dent Journals*, XV, March 30, 1883. Hilgard, *Report on Cotton Production in the United States*, II, 172–73; Somers, *The Southern States Since the War*, 60.

ployee, but he could be left alone as if he were a tenant. Legally, a share tenant could be either an employee or a tenant, but he might be supervised closely or not at all. Supervision was not a function of legal status; yet patterns did exist.[62] Those landowners who did supervise closely tended to direct croppers more than share tenants and renters less than both. This was logical enough. As one explained, he supervised croppers "more than renters" because he "had more at stake." The size of his profit or loss from a cropper depended upon the size of the crop, whereas he received a fixed amount from the renter in any case.[63]

A more important pattern resulted from the size of landholdings. The smaller a proprietor's estate, the more he tended to supervise. This was not a function of available time. The income of the small-to-middling employer depended almost entirely upon his share of the crops raised by his hands plus whatever he raised himself. The large landowner, on the other hand, had an important additional source of income: the interest he charged his hands for provisions advanced to them against their pay (if they worked on shares) or crops (if they were renters). Planters, absentee landowners, and planter-merchants could thus ignore their hands and interfere, in the words of one planter, only "far enough to see that sufficient cotton is made to pay."[64] Without supervision, their hands were less productive even when farming superior land, but as the Georgia commissioner of agriculture admitted, inattentive landlords "recouped to a great extent by trafficking and trading" what they lost through lack of supervision.[65] All landlords could "farm" their share hands and renters as well as their land. If they were not merchants themselves, they could, and usually did, exact a percentage fee (a kickback) for assigning the accounts of their share hands and

62. Arnett, *The Populist Movement in Georgia*, 53; "Inquiries I," 1912, in Brooks Papers; Hill, "Rural Survey of Clarke County, Georgia," 53; O. B. Stevens, testimony, in Industrial Commission, *Report on Agricultural Labor*, 911.

63. No name, Bulloch County (Questionnaire, "Inquiries I," 1912, in Brooks Papers).

64. Barrow, "A Georgia Plantation," 833.

65. O. B. Stevens, testimony, in Industrial Commission, *Report on Agricultural Labor*, 907–908. See also T. R. Jones, letter, August 15, 1893, in "Letters from Cotton Growers," *Report of the Committee on Agriculture and Forestry*, Pt. I, 305–306.

renters to a local merchant.[66] As the commissioner of agriculture, the transplanted northern farmer, future governor William Northen, Nate Shaw, and many, many others explained, satisfaction with these profits was common among large and absentee black belt landowners.[67]

The lack of onerous supervision made large farms and absentee owners particularly attractive to blacks. Whether or not a freedman owned a mule, whether he was a cropper, share tenant, or renter, he could find day-to-day freedom from abusive supervision on these lands. Inattentive landowners therefore found it easier to secure tenants than their more watchful colleagues. Some whites thought blacks were attracted to these lands by the "glamour associated with the town or city dweller, particularly the merchant who was always thought to be exceedingly rich and hence quite superior to the resident farmer."[68] Blacks were not nearly so foolish. On such farms not only were they free from an overlord's daily arrogance, but they were also in many ways economically better off.

By any purely statistical measure, the claim that blacks gained from lack of supervision would seem to be wrong. Sympathetic observers admitted and statistical studies confirm that plantation belt blacks, farming superior lands but trapped in enforced ignorance, were less productive than whites farming inferior soil.[69] Even W. E. B. Du Bois called typical, unsupervised black share hands and renters a "degraded set." But perhaps Du Bois was so obsessed with the drive for "uplift" that he failed to recognize the ways in which the lives of unsupervised hands were qualitatively superior to those of closely supervised blacks, who were commonly denied basic economic privileges. Unsupervised families usually owned "a mule or two and sometimes a cow"; grew almost everything they ate, including "corn, wheat,

66. Hill, "Rural Survey of Clarke County, Georgia," 27.
67. J. H. Hale, testimony, in Industrial Commission, *Report on Agricultural Labor*, 379; "Semi-Annual Address Delivered by Col. W. J. Northen, President, Georgia State Agricultural Society, at Brunswick, February 12, 1889," Scrapbook, 1887–1889, pp. 1–4, in Northen Papers; Rosengarten, *All God's Dangers*, 114.
68. Arnett, *The Populist Movement in Georgia*, 53.
69. Hart, *The Southern South*, 121; DeCanio, *Agriculture in the Postbellum South*; Woodward, *Origins of the New South*, 208; Brooks, "Economic Conditions."

pork, and molasses"; and raised "chickens and eggs" both as food and to be "used as currency at the country store to purchase cloth, tobacco, coffee, etc."[70] According to a study by the Department of Agriculture, this group also tended to have vegetable gardens whereas only a few closely supervised croppers had very small garden patches, and most had none. Typical was a "small patch of collards" tucked into the corner of a farm "planted entirely with cotton," but just as likely was the cropper with "cotton cultivated close up to the cabin door" and a landlord who allowed room only for "a small patch of sugar cane," from which to make molasses, and no vegetable garden at all. Diets were so limited that some freedmen called fatback meat and knew it "by no other name," nor "did they seem to know of any other kind of meat except of oppossum and rabbits which they occasionally hunted and of chickens which they raised to a limited extent."[71]

With meager gardens (if any) and insufficient crops of corn (or none at all), croppers who worked for severe landowners ate provisions usually purchased on credit and supplemented their diet as best they could. J. W. Hoffman of Tuskegee Institute described their cuisine: "Corn meal is mixed with water and baked on the flat surface of a hoe or griddle. The salt pork is sliced thin and fried until very brown and much of the grease is fried out. Molasses from cane or sorghum is added to the fat, making what is known as 'sap,' which is eaten with the corn bread. Hot water sweetened with molasses is used as a beverage. This is the bill of fare of most cabins on the plantations of the 'black belt' three times a day during the year."[72] This diet resulted from the racial beliefs widely shared by white southerners. As one put it, "The Nigger, when poverty stricken . . . will work well for you—but as soon as you get him up and he begins to be prosperous, he becomes impudent and unmanageable" and is no longer a good worker.[73]

70. William Edward Burghardt Du Bois, "The Negro in the Cotton Belt: Some Social Sketches," U.S. Department of Labor *Bulletin*, No. 22 (May, 1899), 402.

71. Atwater and Woods, "Dietary Studies," 17, 35, 28, 19.

72. *Ibid.*, 21. Some whites claimed blacks preferred a poor diet. See, for example, Moses W. Harris (Questionnaire, "Inquiries I," 1912, in Brooks Papers).

73. Mathis, Mathis, and Purcell (eds.), *Dent Journals*, XV, May 24, 1882.

It was unsupervised blacks about whom future governor Northen, Charles Otken, U. B. Phillips, and innumerable middling proprietors complained most bitterly. They complained because unsupervised lands were an escape hatch from abject subordination and therefore helped to keep alive the bargaining power of even those blacks who remained under the watch of their employers. Unsupervised lands contributed to the competition for labor that kept the black caste more free and independent than whites believed appropriate. Whites therefore blamed these unsupervised farms for southern poverty, not so much because these farms were less productive than they could have been, but because they were responsible for "idle," "unreliable," "independent," black labor that could not be exploited as thoroughly as whites wished.

No group was content with this postwar labor system. Very different experiences governed the expectations that each brought to the free-labor system. Many large landowners, unable to hire gang labor and despairing of the possibility of rigorous discipline and control, sought to recoup the lost income of slavery through profits from trading with their hands; yet in supervising their hands loosely or not at all, these landowners decreased their own and their workers' incomes. Most blacks remained in some form of dependency moderated somewhat by negotiations in the marketplace. Some improved the quality of their lives in important ways as they advanced to relative independence and escaped regular, often abusive, supervision; yet their escape also decreased productivity and perpetuated extreme poverty. And many middling white proprietors, unable to gain much by trading with their few workers, continued to be frustrated because blacks were able to use the marketplace to protect themselves, to moderate the severity of white supervision or sometimes to escape it entirely.

One must understand this background of pervasive discontent to understand the New South. But since whites effectively monopolized power in Georgia by 1871 and in all other southern states after Redemption and since law governed the relations between capital and labor, one must also understand why the law supported a plantation system with which whites were so

very discontented through the beginning of the following century. Why did ideology and practice continue to diverge after
Redemption in 1871? Why were whites unable to subordinate
black labor as thoroughly as they wished?

Chapter IV

THE PLANTERS' LEGAL AGGRESSION AND THE FREEDMEN'S DEFENSE

The negro to be made a useful citizen or of benefit to himself must be governed. Without government and discipline they become a nuisance to themselves and society. . . . taking a Christian and humane view of the matter, for the benefit of the negro race as a whole, it would be best for them to be retained among the whites, that is, among the intelligent classes, with such laws for their proper government and discipline as would promote their good and welfare. The 'Nigger Shriekers' may say that we would be carrying them back to slavery. We may ask, are not laws formed for the general good even if they are oppressive in their tendencies. When they are for the general good of society they must be forced and submitted to. Hence it is necessary to make such laws as are best suited to their conditions and circumstances.

—John H. Dent

BEFORE PROMINENT white Georgians were expelled from state government and again after they redeemed it for themselves, they adopted new statutes and wrote court decisions that invariably drove the freedmen back toward dependent subordination. These sometimes intricate changes in law reflected, as historians have stressed, the abuse of blacks at the hands of whites. They also showed, however, the continuing limits that the constitutional amendments adopted during Reconstruction placed on that abuse—the reasons why blacks were not as thoroughly subordinated as whites wished. In the law, therefore, can be found a primary source of the disparity between the rigid caste norms of whites and the actual, less simply defined mechanics of late nineteenth-century southern society.

Even before Redemption, the legal maneuvers of white Georgians included far more than the invalidated black codes. In 1866, for example, the legislature tried to cut opportunities for blacks and guarantee planters a stable work force by restricting competition for labor. It outlawed the hiring of "any servant whatever during his term of service" under a contract with someone else, and it forbade the use of any such low tactic as "offering higher wages" to "entice, persuade, or decoy" away any worker. This law was not affected by the civil rights legislation of Congressional Reconstruction because it drew no explicit distinction between white and black workers. Nor was it repealed during the Republican interregnum in Georgia. In fact, in 1883 the general assembly tightened its wording by "inserting after the word 'servant' . . . the words 'cropper or farm laborer . . . whether under written or parole contract.'"[1]

The change suggests an ambiguity in the status of many freedmen. Was the addition of croppers and farm laborers meant to expand or clarify the original statute? Whites seem to have considered it a mere clarification. After all, as early as 1866 the head of the Freedmen's Bureau in Georgia reported the jailing of people attempting to hire away black farm laborers.[2] Those who considered the amendment a mere clarification were right. But they were right only because the amendment was added in 1883 and not 1866. During the intervening years, politically powerful white landowning employers had changed the legal definition of sharecroppers from tenants to farm workers in order to match their definition of proper relations between blacks and whites and between labor and capital.

Before the war, sharecropping was not common, but where it existed, croppers were considered the tenant-partners of landowners.[3] One partner contributed the asset of his labor; the other, the assets of his land and equipment. The assumption of tenant-partnership lingered on into Reconstruction. A planter named Robert Couper said, for example, that he had dropped a successful experiment with sharecropping soon after the war "on account of a prejudice by my neighbors against hiring slaves

1. *Acts of the General Assembly of the State of Georgia* (Milledgeville and Atlanta, 1866–96), 1866 (No. 217), 153–54, 1882–83 (No. 355), 60–61, hereinafter cited as *Acts*.

2. Davis Tillson to O. O. Howard, November 1, 1866, in Stanton, "Letter of the Secretary of War," 50.

3. Frank Reinhart Diary, 1840, quoted in Lloyd G. Marlin, *A History of Cherokee County* (Atlanta, 1932), 151. The rarity of antebellum sharecropping is discussed in Banks, *The Economics of Land Tenure in Georgia*, 82.

as partners."[4] Although the relations between antebellum land-owner and cropper were not spelled out in any statute, the assumption of tenant-partnership had common-law standing in court. This assumption continued in law for a short time after the war. It applied in 1869 when Lymus Holloway (a freedman) and Franklin Brinkley (white) "made an agreement to farm together." Holloway "was to have half the crop." Brinkley "was to furnish the stock and the land." During the year, Brinkley also furnished Holloway "One hundred and thirty pounds of bacon," but that was all. "Even though there was six bags of long cotton made," Holloway got nothing at the end of the year because Brinkley stole the crop. When Holloway brought charges against him in the city court of Savannah, however, the legal tradition of tenant-partnership gave Brinkley victory. The court, a criminal court, decided it lacked jurisdiction. "A suit brought to settle partnership matters" should be heard in a "court of equity," said the judge.[5]

The definition of sharecroppers as tenant-partners did not long survive emancipation. As blacks in the late 1860s began to work their way up the agricultural ladder, whites were determined to keep them "properly subordinate." If freedom to take advantage of the marketplace, hard work, and the occasionally favorable price of cotton allowed blacks some opportunity for independence, landowners would minimize it all they could through manipulation of the law. Sharecroppers lost their status as tenant-partners and became employees paid in kind.

Phrases like "whites were determined" and "manipulation of the law" are perhaps deceptive. They portray the behavior of whites as rather deliberate, and in a sense it had to be. It is possible to trace clear changes in the law; one can say that they were significant. But the logic of the changes, the way whites understood and justified what they were doing, is less clear. This lack of clarity is undoubtedly due to the racial antipathy that underlay their understanding of the relations between labor and capital. *Black* meant labor. Even while the law defined black croppers as tenant-partners, whites often referred to them as la-

4. Robert Couper (Questionnaire, "Inquiries I," 1912, in Brooks Papers).
5. *Lymus Holloway* v. *Franklin Brinkley*, Chatham County, August, 1870, Supreme Court File No. A-4933.

borers, hands, servants, workers, or even as slaves. Landowners were determined to preserve as best they could relatively traditional relations between black workers and themselves. They believed they were preserving the good, right, natural, and God-given, that they were maintaining their own rightful place, but they left no evidence that they thought in terms of making changes in order to reverse the upward mobility of blacks. They described upwardly mobile blacks, not as improving their position, but as destroying the proper social order. Obviously, maintaining the social order and reversing the upward mobility of blacks were synonymous. However, these two phrases reflect very different ways of viewing the world, in fact, two contradictory assumptions about justice. Although some late nineteenth-century white southerners could claim it was a blessing to be rid of slavery, few ever said slavery was wrong.[6] Their definition of justice had not changed after emancipation, nor had their definition of self-interest.

The change in the legal status of croppers came by way of the lien law—the indefatigable companion of share arrangements and the major legal means by which landowners sought to exploit black labor. Historians have long recognized the burdens that the lien law and "time prices" placed upon farmers. Crop liens applied differently, however, to landowners, renters, share tenants, and sharecroppers. These differences were created by laws that defined who owned the crop and thus who could give a lien upon it.

In 1866 the Georgia legislature adopted its first crop-lien law. It allowed landowners to have liens "upon the growing crops of their tenants" in return for "stock, farming utensils, and provisions furnished . . . for the purpose of making the crop." Factors and merchants could have liens upon "the growing crops of farmers"—*farmers* meaning only landowners.[7] The law seems straightforward enough. If anything, it codified the intention of landed whites to force the freedmen to remain dependent and subservient. Even blacks who were able to demand share agreements would have to mortgage their crops to their landlords in order to buy provisions "on time." But the apparent clarity is an

6. Gaston, *The New South Creed*, 128–29, 181–84, 224–25.
7. *Acts*, 1866 (No. 196), 141.

illusion. In 1872 the state supreme court decided that the statute did not mean what it seemed to say. "There is an obvious distinction between a cropper and a tenant," said the court. A tenant has "possession of the premises exclusive of the landlord" and owns his crop, but where the landlord furnishes a share hand supplies and equipment with which to farm, that hand is a cropper and his share "is rather a mode of paying wages than a tenancy." According to the court, therefore, a cropper did not own a share of the crop until after he had settled his account with his employer. A tenant owned his crop and could give his landlord a lien upon it. A cropper did not own his crop or even his share and therefore could not give a lien.[8]

What the court called an "obvious distinction" had not been obvious twenty years before. Nor was there any reason for it to be obvious in 1872. Previous usage, court decisions, and even the lien statute of 1866 described sharecroppers as tenants, but by some curious logic the court suddenly decided sharecroppers were laborers. The court narrowed the definition of tenants to include only those few share hands who did not receive supplies or equipment on credit and those who paid a fixed amount rather than a proportion of the crops to their landlords. And even though tenants were legally "in possession" of their leased land and the owners of their crops, under the statute of 1866 they still could not give crop liens to anyone except their landlords.

The legal conversion of sharecropping into a form of wage labor was no accident. When in 1873 the general assembly passed a new, more comprehensive, crop-lien law, it adopted the term *laborers* to describe sharecroppers. In the same statute, it also made an informative slip. It failed to distinguish between tenants and farmers when it allowed merchants to receive liens.[9] Merchants quickly began to supply renters without the approval of landlords and nudged the landlords out of a chance to increase their share of their tenants' crops through interest charges on supplies. It should be remembered that some landlords had regularly assigned to merchants responsibility for furnishing supplies to their croppers, share tenants, and renters.

8. *Appling* v. *Odum*, 46 *Georgia Reports* 587, quoted in Banks, *The Economics of Land Tenure in Georgia*, 81.
9. *Acts*, 1873 (No. 315), 42–47.

Sometimes this was merely bookkeeping practice or a convenience for absentee landowners, but when landowners assigned an account, they retained the power to limit its size and to profit from it. Under the new law, merchants were undermining the planters' authority over their renters, ending both their power to limit the size of debts secured with the crop and the renters' dependence upon them for supplies. Even though the law stipulated that a landlord's lien upon the property of his tenant was superior to all other liens except those for taxes, attentive planters were unhappy to lose opportunitites for profit. "The very men whose liens are entitled to the highest place . . . are entirely cut out," complained a black belt editor. "This view of the matter if no other, should cause a change in the law" back to the exclusive landlord's lien.[10]

The landowners who dominated the general assembly quickly agreed. After but one harvest, a year almost to the day after they had adopted the new lien law, they repealed it for everyone "except landlords."[11] From 1874 through the end of the nineteenth century, therefore, merchants could receive crop liens only from landowners or, of course, their own tenants. Landowners supplied both their cropper-employees and their tenants either directly or by assigning their accounts to a merchant. While renters owned their crops, they did not have the full authority of ownership and could not decide where they wished to do business. And croppers had no authority at all, for they were laborers who, like tailors in a sweatshop, did not own the goods they produced even though they received part of them as payment for their work.

So in 1888 a judge in Coweta County could quite un-self-consciously charge a jury with the peculiar terminology handed down by the state supreme court and general assembly years before: "This is not a case of partnership, but a case between landlord and cropper. The law of partnership does not apply. This being a case between landlord and cropper, the law of mortgages does not apply. If Mr. Wood had leased or rented the land

10. *Chronicle and Herald*, n.d., quoted in Dawson *Weekly Journal*, February 5, 1874.

11. *Acts*, 1874 (No. 28), 18. On a landlord's liability after endorsing his tenant's debt, see Banks, *The Economics of Land Tenure in Georgia*, 49.

in question," the case would be different. But where there is a case of a landlord and cropper "the title of the crop is in the landlord, until he has retained his part of the crop and [enough to pay] for all advances made out of the cropper's part and has turned the cropper's part to the cropper, and the cropper has no right or title to the crop until the landlord has got his part of the crop and all advances made."[12] This was confusion, indeed. The poor judge had to talk about a landlord who had no tenant and a cropper's part that was not really his part until it was part of the landlord's part first.

The judge can be excused for sounding silly. He needed more precise words than he found in colloquial usage. Yet the judge probably made perfect sense to his fellow whites because they, like him, freely mixed terms reflecting their normative assumptions about the proper role of blacks with more traditional and, in a sense, more accurate terms for the relationship between landowners and sharecroppers. They spoke of *employing* tenants, of *hiring* partners, and they referred to sharecroppers as workers, laborers, and hands. White legislators and jurists shared the fundamental assumptions of the class from which they came. They based the law upon those assumptions. In that white Georgians were by no means unique. Between 1839 and 1874, the Supreme Court of North Carolina also rewrote the law. Before the war, it decided that "a landlord had no right to the crop before the tenant actually gave the landlord his share." In other words, it defined croppers as tenants who pay a proportion of their crops as rent. But in 1874 the court reversed itself—a confession of error of which most judges are constitutionally incapable. The cropper became "only a laborer receiving pay in a share of the crop." In 1884 the Supreme Court of Tennessee followed suit: "The payment of a certain portion of the crop to the laborer is the same as a payment of so much money, and constitutes him as a hired hand just the same as if he receives wages."[13]

Why were these changes made? Normative assumptions may

12. *M.A. Padgett v. State*, Coweta County, May, 1888, Supreme Court File No. A-15302.

13. *Deaver v. Rice*, 20 N. Car. 431 (1839), *Harrison v. Ricks*, 71 N. Car. 7 (1874), both cited in Lawrence M. Friedman, *A History of American Law* (New York, 1973), 373; *Southern Cultivator*, March 3, 1884.

have cleared away the obstacles of a few antebellum precedents and occasional usage, but they provided little motivation. One historian called the development of lien law an enactment of custom, but the custom being enacted was not that of sharecropping but of white attitudes toward black labor, the definition of blacks as a subordinate laboring caste. Another historian has written, "the legal attributes of sharecropping" developed "along with its changing social meaning." That is as safe as it is uninformative. Whites were not waiting for society to evolve and then changing the law to match the practice.[14] Landowners were using law to change social relationships, to force even upwardly mobile blacks to remain subordinate to them, exploitable by them. If the legal logic was elusive, its effects were clear. These changes in law, deliberate and unquestioned, can be explained only as they increased the authority of the landowners and protected their profits.

While crop liens arose out of necessity as well as the greed of white landowners, the legal maneuvers turned on questions of power alone. The definition of sharecroppers as employees had obvious implications for the relative authority of the landowner and the relative independence of the cropper. First, this change, not the crop lien itself, was the means through which landowners obtained the power to decide what and how much would be planted, and when, where, and how the planting would be done. It meant landowners could decide, for example, whether or not croppers could have kitchen gardens. And it meant that the landowners controlled when, where, and to whom the crops would be sold. It legally made the planter once again the overseer of a factory scattered among his fields, for it gave him the power of any employer over an employee—much more power than a landlord had over a tenant.

Second, even if a landlord assigned a merchant responsibility for furnishing a cropper, the landowner had to give a lien on *his* crop to secure his employee's debt. Although this made the landowner's share vulnerable to the debts of the cropper, it provided him much in return. The landowner could charge a fee for the

14. Banks, *The Economics of Land Tenure in Georgia*, 48; Friedman, *A History of American Law*, 373.

merchant's service.[15] He could also limit the size of the cropper's debt and keep the cropper dependent solely upon him. Thus landowners assured themselves the opportunity to profit from their employees' debts, kept the power to protect their own shares, and increased their authority over their croppers. Thus, also, landowners created the fine legal distinction between a share tenant who was a tenant and a share tenant who was an employee. If a share tenant did not receive supplies on credit, the landowner's profit remained invulnerable, and the share tenant was a tenant. But if the tenant did receive supplies or any other form of credit (as almost all of them did), he was considered, under the court's definition, an employee. As the landlord's share became vulnerable, his authority increased markedly. A similar principle applied to renters, despite the voluminous protection in Anglo-Saxon law and usage that kept them from being officially classified as employees. A renter could not use his crops to secure a loan except through his landlord. In theory, the landlord could be bypassed if the renter had sufficient assets other than crops to secure the loan, and some renters, particularly white renters, may have been able to remain independent of their landlords. But most renters, like most croppers, had nothing of value but their crops, and if they received credit, it had to be from or through their landlords. In all three cases—croppers, share tenants and renters—landowners reserved to themselves the authority to limit debts and the opportunity to profit either as the supplier of credit or as the go-between to a merchant. This was the crux of subordination. The landowner, his authority, and his profit were the primary, if not the only, concerns.

Third, the definition of sharecroppers as employees made other instruments of law—both criminal law and police powers—more accessible to the landowner in his effort to control his workers. A cropper could hardly be accused of stealing a crop if he owned it, for example, but he could be charged with theft if he sold what the law defined as the landowner's crop. In this and other cases, as the general assembly fattened its statute books with new laws for the control of labor, it showed how

15. Hill, "Rural Survey of Clarke County, Georgia," 27.

emancipation had left much the same despite the changed relationship between planter and worker. The state merely assumed responsibilities previously left in the arbitrary hands of masters.

Some new laws simply catalogued the fears of whites. In response to a panicky rumor that the freedmen would rebel on Christmas day, 1865, for example, the assembly adopted the death penalty for insurrection ("any combined resistance to the lawful authority of the state") and mandated five to twenty years in prison for anyone circulating printed materials inciting "riot, conspiracy, or resistance."[16] The rumor and the law were reminiscent of the periodic fear of slave rebellions and consequent constraints upon antislavery activity in the antebellum South. They reflected the same inability to adjust to free and willful labor that an overseer showed as he explained to a northern traveler the imminent "danger of a negro insurrection." The southerner claimed, "It is not half an hour since four negroes raised their axes against me," but when asked exactly what had happened, he continued, "I told old ——— to go out into the field and bring up the cattle, and he said he would not do it. I took up an axe (admitting that he was the first to do so) and as soon as I did it his daughter, who was there, took up an axe. There were others present and they picked up axes, and I had to run for my life."[17]

Other laws can also be traced to the enigmatic experience of slavery. A master might have ignored the disappearance of a hog, though iron bars on storehouse windows suggest otherwise, but he would certainly have punished habitual or large-scale theft. What self-interest, however, would encourage the postbellum landlord to tolerate the loss of even one pig? And what planter before or after the war could tolerate the abuse of work animals? From the worker's point of view, why should an exploited freedman be any less tempted than he was as an exploited slave to steal one of his employer's hogs for food or to avenge the injustice he felt when his employer seriously violated the expectations he and other blacks had built upon their past experience? The criminal law mapped this large territory on

16. *Acts*, 1866 (No. 214), 152–53. On rumors, see Trelease, *White Terror*, xii.

17. Albert Warren Kelsey, testimony, January 22, 1866, in *House Reports*, 39th Cong., 1st Sess., No. 30, Pt. 2, p. 3. See also Williamson, *After Slavery*, 103–104.

which blacks and whites fought for their interests. Of course, whites wrote only one perspective into the law, but blacks by the crimes they committed showed that they were not resigned to the material deprivation to which they were condemned. The direct if covert conflict between planter and worker did not disappear after emancipation any faster than the masters' assumptions about the rightful subordination of black labor. And so, soon after the war, the general assembly began to write new laws for the punishment of cruelty to animals, theft, and arson.[18]

Just as theft was a defense against the hardships of slavery, it was an illegal defense against the hardships of freedom. The code of the slave quarters encouraged theft from masters to help oneself or even to help slaves on other plantations. "Some [masters] wouldn't give their slaves enough to eat," recalled one freedman, "but we had plenty, and my folks would steal meat and give it to . . . those half-starved slaves who would slip over for something to eat." It was "just natural for Negroes to steal."[19] After the war blacks had no particular reason to change their view of the relationship between their plight and the property of whites.

Planters certainly did nothing to encourage a new set of values. They did, however, replace their lost power to police the slave quarters with somewhat ineffectual criminal statutes. These laws, passed by the general assembly, applied to individual counties or groups of counties in behalf of local planters without troubling farmers in other parts of the state, such as the mountain and upper piedmont counties where yeoman farming prevailed. The first law, adopted in 1872, prohibited "buying, selling, receiving, or delivering . . . between sunset and sunrise . . . cotton, corn, wheat, cow peas, oats, rye, barley" or any other farm product without the permission of the owner or renter of the land upon which it was grown. The law applied only to forty-

18. *Acts*, 1875 (No. 192), 101 (tightened 1878–79 [No. 312], 183–84); *The Code of the State of Georgia* (Atlanta and Macon, 1867, 1873), 890; *Acts*, 1871 (No. 26), 72–73, 1874 (No. 38), 21, 1875 (No. 379), 104, 1878–79 (Nos. 217, 223), 61–62, 165–66.

19. *Unwritten History of Slavery*, 11–12, 95, 137–38, 148–49. See also Escott, *Slavery Remembered*, 65–66, 76–77, 114–15, 166–67; Eugene Genovese, *Roll, Jordan, Roll: The World the Slaves Made* (New York, 1974), 599–609; Stampp, *The Peculiar Institution*, 198, 258.

two counties along the coast or in the black belt where most blacks lived. During the following four years, the prohibition was extended to nineteen additional counties in the same areas, which brought the total to almost half the counties in Georgia.[20]

More interesting were innovations in the use of state police powers. The theft of grain was serious, but the theft of seed cotton was especially costly. Cotton was the most valuable crop and was easily stolen right from the field. Immediately after the war, its theft was most prevalent in southwest Georgia, still a fast-growing, frontierlike part of the black belt. Some plantations there had "lost 25 percent of their crops for the past several years," claimed one farmer in 1875. "Thieving negroes . . . carry their stolen produce to . . . 'dead falls' . . . and sell it for a mere pittance," he said. These "'dead falls,' scattered all over, have become so bold as to send out drummers for their illicit trade and have guards around their stores and pickets out at considerable distances . . . to prevent detection; and it is next to impossible to get negroes to inform or give evidence against them." The farmer complained, "Who ever heard of night watchmen being required on a plantation before." (Evidently he forgot the slave patrols.) "Farmers are compelled to sit up night after night to guard not merely their produce in the barns and ginhouses—but even in the *fields*—for they [blacks] gather corn and pick cotton at night . . . by the sack or basket and carry [them] to these places."[21]

And so, counties in southwest Georgia (Thomas, Randolph, Lee, Calhoun, Decatur, and Baker) led in innovations. Outspoken grand juries, composed, as usual, of prominent landowners, persuaded the general assembly to pass special acts to help them end the illicit trade. It was hard to prove theft. The corn or cotton in one sack looked pretty much like the corn or cotton in another; so landowners decided to regulate the entire business. In 1876 two counties began to charge $500 for a license to trade in seed cotton to guarantee that merchants would not mistake stolen cotton for honestly traded goods. During the following

20. *Acts*, 1872 (Nos. 318, 172), 484, 1873 (No. 133), 290, 1875 (No. 284), 301–302, 1876 (Nos. 112, 218, 10, 71, 101), 320, 331, 332, 339, 340.

21. "A Farmer of Lee [County]" to *Sumter Republican*, n.d., quoted in Dawson *Weekly Journal*, November 25, 1875.

two years, these regulations were extended to four other counties, and Thomas County got its own rigorously effective law. Besides requiring a license and fee, it required an application setting forth the place of business, the products to be traded, and "the written consent of three-fourths of the freeholders living within three miles" of the business. If shady merchants could not be punished for receiving stolen goods, they could be prevented from doing business at all. During the 1880s the problem, though less severe, appeared elsewhere, and regulation tagged along. And in 1889 the "Farmers' Legislature," herald of the "Alliance Legislature" elected the following year, completely prohibited trade in seed cotton in thirteen black belt counties from August through December, which was, of course, picking time.[22]

As usual, when a thief stole something he had to sell, he gained less than did his "fence." But other kinds of theft were more common and offered blacks more immediate relief from the extreme poverty to which they were banished by whites. All kinds of food were vulnerable, but hogs most of all. In most counties, the law required farmers to enclose crops and allowed animals to roam, graze, and root in woods and along roads. Night often found hogs far from any watchful eyes at the planters' house—particularly in the hard winter months when fields were empty and provisions most scarce. In 1875 the general assembly upgraded the crime of hog stealing from a misdemeanor to a felony in an effort to repress it.[23] The statute did not work. The training of slavery was too appropriate for penurious freedom. Whites were so troubled by the incessant and costly thievery of blacks that some could point to it as an explanation for the rise of the Klan. As in the case of crops, where the problem of stolen animals became especially severe, local regulation of the sale of meat joined statewide criminal statutes in the effort to control theft.[24]

The free-handed discipline of an antebellum plantation in the

22. *Acts*, 1876 (No. 368), 343–44, 1877 (No. 252), 301, 1878–79 (Nos. 296, 298), 399–400, 1882–83 (No. 242), 660–61, 1884–85 (Nos. 67, 369), 634, 651–52, 1889 (Nos. 238, 239, 265, 342 348, 371, 521, 635, 647, 708, 717, 845), 1387–95.

23. *Acts*, 1875 (No. 29), 26, cited in Daniel A. Novak, *The Wheel of Servitude: Black Forced Labor After Slavery* (Lexington, 1978), 32.

24. For example, *Acts*, 1871 (No. 65), 120.

postbellum South, the motives of a former slave, and the continuing problem of disappearing hogs can all be seen in the typical case of Henry Rivers. Rivers was a sharecropper in Lee County, and John Moreland was his overseer. One Sunday evening late in November when Moreland "called up the hogs" to slop them as usual, one was missing: "It was black and worth four or five dollars." Going "out to hunt for it," he "was informed" (by whom he did not say) that "it was in Henry Rivers' Crib." The hog was found, "buried deep under shuck and fodder," but Rivers "got a good sound thrashing before he said anything about it." Moreland testified, "I took a big switch to him and gave him a good whipping" and "made him find the hog's head and hide" to serve as evidence that it was the missing animal. Rivers, of course, remembered the whipping well. "He and his son took me down and beat me and strapped me. . . . He told me he was going to make me find the hog or kill me." Henry Rivers got two years at hard labor for stealing five dollars worth of food.[25]

Whites knew why blacks were stealing, but the rights of property and the procedures of law legitimized severity. "Now that the cotton crop is gathered, and nearly all other crops, the average day hand finds but little work, and possum and hog hunting is the order of the night," reported one newspaper indifferently. "We hear of some success in the hog catch . . . and the hunters jugged, which gives employment to the county court." Another paper reported in 1883 that "the negroes . . . have been badly demoralized by the failure of last year's crop and many have gone to stealing." Their plight brought little sympathy; rather, the editor instructed planters that "hogs can eat arsenic with impunity, but the flesh of a hog that has been fed on the poison will produce death when eaten." A third newspaper added to a report that Calvin Carter, Jr., had chased, shot, and killed a black corn thief named Sam Ingraham the coldly moral declaration: "He deserves his fate."[26] But to whites the legitimizing authority of

25. *Henry Rivers* v. *State*, Lee County, November, 1875, Supreme Court File No. A-8838. See also *Jule Greene* v. *State*, Wilkes County, December, 1894, Supreme Court File No. A-19173.

26. Americus *Weekly Recorder*, October 24, 1884; *News and Advertiser*, n.d., quoted *ibid.*, December 14, 1883; *Sumter Republican*, n.d., quoted in Dawson *Weekly Journal*, May 4, 1876.

law was secondary to the moral rights of property. The punishment of theft remained a major object of the Klan during Reconstruction and of White Cap, Klan, and unsystematic vigilantism after Redemption.

Like theft, arson continued to play its antebellum role. Before the war slaves struck back at or punished their masters with fire. After the war freedmen continued the pattern. Almost invariably arsonists were employees or former employees of their victims. Emanuel Murry in Lee County was typical. In 1870 he fired the ginhouse of Thomas Bryan, for whom he had worked the year before. In this case, as in others, the distinction between an employee and former employee was purposeless, for arsonists (including Murry) usually struck out of anger following a settlement—which meant at the end of one year or beginning of the next when croppers or wage hands (particularly unhappy ones) were most likely to change employers. If an arsonist was not an employee and had never been one, he acted on behalf of an employee. Wiley Smith, for example, fired the cornhouse of John Dye in 1879, not because of a personal grudge, but at the insistence of his father, who had worked for Dye.[27]

One case adequately illustrates the general pattern. Stephen Brooks worked for Colonel Hawkins Price of Barton County the year Price's barn burned. "It was just before daylight that it caught," testified Charles Jones, another black sharecropper on the place. The night of the burning, Brooks, his wife Topsey, and at least four other freedmen who lived nearby had gone to Jones's cabin for a prayer meeting—a regular event for them. That night "Prince Crawford and Ed Clark carried our meeting," remembered Jones. We all "heard Prince preach and Ed exhort a little," but Brooks "went out before we broke up." That he had "something against Price" was commonly known, for several witnesses testified to remarks he had made about the landowner. He had been working on the colonel's place for two years when "at corn gathering time they fell out." The "burning occurred [that] same

27. Stampp, *The Peculiar Institution*, 127–28; *Emanuel Murry* v. *State*, Lee County, September, 1870, Supreme Court File No. A-5190; *Wiley Smith* v. *State*, Monroe County, December, 1879, Supreme Court File No. A-1039. See also *Allen Stallings* v. *State*, Schley County, December, 1872, Supreme Court File No. A-6062.

fall." Brooks did not stay another year; he left to work on a nearby plantation. But before he left he was indiscreet. "I know he abused Col. Price some," said Prince Crawford. "He said he was a D——d rascal that he had wronged him out of all he'd made and that he would have his rights out of him if he could get them." To a cotton picker named William Washington, Brooks said he planned to make Colonel Price "lose more than he had gained" by cheating him "out of his crop 2 years." Brooks's big mouth more than his pyromania got him five years at hard labor.[28]

The same pattern of employees believing themselves cheated and resorting to arson appeared in case after case, for arson made effective revenge.[29] It was safer than outright resistance to an employer because it was anonymous, difficult to prove, and thus difficult to punish. In fact, the planter was more vulnerable to arson after the war than before. With the freedmen's cabins now scattered among his fields, he could not monitor his hands at night any better than he could all day. And there were now, perhaps, more numerous occasions for arson because the new financial dealings between planter and worker encouraged particular economic grievances, the feeling of being cheated. It is, therefore, important to remember that arson was an economic weapon in an economic war. It could seem morally justified because its perpetrator believed he was repaying one economic hurt with another. Ginhouses, barns, and stables were the most frequent targets. One historian, in a study of two black belt counties, concluded that "slightly over seventy-five percent of all instances of arson involved destruction of objects directly connected with economic activity." Even this large estimate understates the case, however, for this historian inexplicably excluded such things as stacks of fodder and farm fences (a major investment where crops instead of stock were enclosed) from the economic category. In proclamations offering rewards for the arrest of arsonists between 1883 and 1889, governors of Georgia noted

28. *Stephen Brooks* v. *State*, Bartow County, September, 1873, Supreme Court File No. A-6058.

29. *Charles Jones* v. *State*, Cobb County, April 1879, Supreme Court File No. A-10551; Leigh, *Ten Years on a Georgia Plantation*, 200; Atlanta *Constitution*, October 20, 1883. Examples filled the newspapers of the period each fall and winter.

the object burned in fifty-four cases. Thirty-four were ginhouses; ten were barns and/or stables; and three were commission-merchant buildings. These cases accounted for 87 percent of the total.[30]

The pattern of arson is not surprising, though its frequency may be. Burnings in Georgia added up to well over a hundred per season for ginhouses alone.[31] And whites understood what was going on. Perhaps they did not go as far as William Faulkner's Jody Varner, who, for fear of a burned barn, hired Flem Snopes to work in his store, but a planter did well to hesitate at least before he acted against a hand. John Dent, for example, had more bravado than Varner. In 1884 he discharged Lem Carroll, his son Jourdan, his daughter Tish, and his son-in-law Jack Mosley. "I get rid of the most Rascally, thievish, insolent negroes that dwell in the county," wrote Dent in his journal. "*Jourdan* and *Tish* I'll stake against any thing in nigger shape." But all was not relief. "I fear them as characters that would apply the Incendiary torch. But I will risk that rather than keep such a set of Devils on my place." The roles of Dent and Tish were ancient ones, having been played for centuries by landowners and peasants.[32]

Sporadic covert revenge and theft reflect a mentality and a relationship between landowner and dependent laborer fundamentally unchanged from slavery. Like most groups trapped in an unenviable position, blacks before and after emancipation continued to recognize and reconcile themselves to their limited options in dealing with whites.[33] But if revenge was understandable, it was not necessarily well directed. Like the thievery of poverty, burnings became more numerous as the price of cotton fell and less frequent when it rose.[34] This reflected, perhaps, a moral sense on the freedman's part that he deserved a "just" return for his labor. Encouraged by a long-standing sense of collec-

30. Smith, "Violence in Georgia's Black Belt," 40; Executive Rewards, 1883–1889, Georgia State Archives, Atlanta.

31. Atlanta *Constitution*, October 20, 1883.

32. William Faulkner, *The Hamlet* (New York, 1940), 20–29, 76; Mathis, Mathis, and Purcell (eds.), *Dent Journals*, XVI, November [?], 1884; Barbara W. Tuchman, *A Distant Mirror: The Calamitous 14th Century* (New York, 1978), 41.

33. Escott, *Slavery Remembered*, 18–35.

34. Atlanta *Constitution*, October 20, 1883; Smith, "Violence in Georgia's Black Belt," 31.

tive injustice, he tended to blame the nearest authority for both a failure to receive a just income and any especially hard times that followed. In 1867, for example, Frances Butler's hands were convinced she had cheated them. They worked for shares, and the low price of cotton that year did not allow them to be paid well. Butler "was so anxious . . . they should see that they had been fairly dealt with, that" she "went over and over again each man's account with him." Although the hands acknowledged each yard of homespun and each dollar they had received, the accounts did not convince them that they should not receive more than only "dis much." They lamented the death of her father despite the fact that she was using his accounts: "No, no, missus, massa not treat us so."[35] Their expectations and their definitions of justice were based, like those of nearly everyone, upon experience and its repository in intuition.

Black workers not only took revenge when they believed themselves especially abused but also repeatedly showed a stillborn collective awareness of the injustice of their status as an exploited, racially defined, working caste. This awareness was not new.[36] No great theorist had to point out the obvious racial and economic order to either slave or freedman. Caste to them was not a theory; it was a shared experience. Nevertheless, leaders were necessary to call upon their preexisting awareness and inspire each small outburst of labor unionism. In these outbursts of frustration, freedmen allowed themselves to ignore the certain futility of their cause and assert their "natural right" to economic and civil equality.

Tidbits of union sentiment appeared regularly, but three major incidents in 1875, 1884, and 1887 are more informative than most.[37] These incidents were not important because of any chance of success, for they had none, but because they involved

35. Leigh, *Ten Years on a Georgia Plantation*, 75–76.
36. Escott, *Slavery Remembered*, 71–94.
37. Americus *Weekly Recorder*, May 30, 1884; Atlanta *Constitution*, October 10, 1883, April 2, 1884; Mathis, Mathis, and Purcell (eds.), *Dent Journals*, X, November 12, 1873; Waynesboro *True Citizen*, September 1, 1882; Roger W. Shugg, *Origins of Class Struggle in Louisiana: A Social History of White Farmers and Laborers During Slavery and After, 1840–1875* (Baton Rouge, 1972), 253–54; Roger W. Shugg, "The New Orleans General Strike of 1892," *Louisiana Historical Quarterly*, XXI, 550.

more people than usual and received more than a contemptuous dismissal from whites. All three incidents took place in the oldest and poorest section of the black belt and followed a brief, almost ritualistic course to failure or, put more accurately, white repression.

On July 24, 1875, with Georgia redeemed but national Reconstruction not yet over, Cordy Harris led a procession of fellow blacks to the courthouse in Washington County. He demanded the right to meet there and was emphatically refused. The confrontation must have been fairly tense, for Harris turned on the courthouse steps and "advised" his followers "to go home, to avoid . . . violence, to drink no liquor and to behave quietly and peacefully." [38] It hardly seems likely that a black insurrectionary in Georgia would want to meet his troops in a public courthouse to plan their war, but that is the way whites interpreted the forcefulness of Harris. His ideas on both economic and political "Equal Rights," which were reported in capital letters but without specifics by a local newspaper, his "irritating harangues," and his willingness to organize blacks in several counties into what whites interpreted as military companies, all seemed frightening indeed. [39]

Captain J. R. Murphy of the Jefferson Dragoons sent first word of the coming insurrection to Democratic governor James Milton Smith three days after the courthouse confrontation. The captain asked for arms to help protect Jefferson, Johnson, Washington, and Burke counties. [40] By early August, the reports of local whites to the governor sounded (in retrospect, at least) hysterical: "They have been meeting in various parts of the county [Johnson County] at night organizing and drilling (all done secretly) and wearing badges of different colors some saying they mean one thing and others another." The air is full of "their threats . . . to the effect that in a short time they intend to march into this place (Wrightsville), murder the inhabitants burn and pillage the place [and] 'divide the lands and personality [sic]

38. Milledgeville *Union and Recorder*, September 7, 1875.
39. Salem Dutcher to James M. Smith, September 6, 1875, in James M. Smith, Governor's Incoming Correspondence, Georgia Department of Archives and History, Atlanta.
40. J. R. Murphy, to James M. Smith, July 28, 1875, *ibid.*

which was left public & government property since the passage of the enemy through the State.'" The report continued: "The whites . . . organized two companies one foot the other cavalry, but having no arms . . . leaves us, Governor, in an awkward and to say the least of it helpless and defenseless condition. Exposing our homes and all most dear to us (our wives and children) to any brutal outrage that their ignorant, savage and brute nature may see fit to visit upon us. What are we to do?"[41]

By August 18, "negro drums were heard all . . . night" and "leading citizens" picketed bridges and roads leading toward town. "Armed bodies of Negroes made some public manifestations along the roads" in Burke County, and whites "sent to every Negro . . . to borrow his gun or pistol." With whites expecting something like Toussaint L'Ouverture, even freedmen with no connection to Harris began to get nervous.[42] But before a shot was fired, Harris "surrendered himself voluntarily to the sheriff & demand[ed an] investigation of the charges against him." Other supposed leaders were pursued but not caught. "All quiet with us," was the report to Governor Smith from Washington County, while rumors of impending insurrections and requests to arm new militia companies flowed in from whites across the black belt.[43]

Harris was lucky. His judge had unusual dedication to procedural exactitude and the rules of evidence; so the verdict was not guilty. Some whites were angry that there was insufficient evidence to convict, but their purpose was achieved.[44] The movement was dead.

A century later there is not enough evidence to judge what happened. It is not possible to determine what Harris and his followers believed or even whether or not they intended violence. The report that blacks believed all property had become

41. M. H. Mason to James M. Smith, August 5, 1875, *ibid.*

42. Murphy to James M. Smith, August 19, 21, 1875, T. J. Smith to James M. Smith, August 21, 1875, all *ibid.*

43. John W. Gilmore to James M. Smith, August 8, 1875, letters from Appling County, September 11, 1875, Putnam, Jones, Baldwin, and Meriwether counties, September 24, 1875, John H. Baker to James M. Smith, October 2, 1875, all *ibid.*

44. Milledgeville *Union and Recorder*, August 31, September 7, 1875; Dutcher to James M. Smith, September 6, 1875, in Smith, Governor's Incoming Correspondence.

public property at the end of the war and that they deserved a share has overtones of the rumors of confiscation and redistribution of land that whites so feared and in which the freedmen placed great hope. In general, this "insurrectionary movement" does seem to have had more direct political origins and content than subsequent ones. But even if a host of other influences were at work, the incident suggests much. At the very least the receptivity of blacks to the leadership of Cordy Harris, the threat to property that whites perceived in the assertiveness of their black employees, and the fearful images in which whites wrapped the danger they saw—all reflected a relationship between the racial and economic order that both blacks and whites acknowledged and that racism had infused with inflexible moral value for whites. Where whites saw a conflict between land and labor in the politics of Reconstruction, they saw it again after Redemption in any renewed assertiveness among blacks.

An incident in 1884 took a similar course in counties near but, with one exception, different from the first. On March 20 a flippant blurb in The Sandersville *Herald* in Washington County reported, "a sable crank . . . making inflamatory speeches to our colored population, attempting to get up a feeling of hostility between white and black by preaching communism, etc." Whites became more concerned during the next several days. The "sable crank" was identified as John F. Clarke, "A Black John Brown," and newspapers printed reports of his speeches embroidered with improbability. Clarke was said to advocate murder and rape. A white farmer named Dave Hill claimed to have heard one speech which became so "offensive" that "he interrupted him and protested against any such talk to the negroes, but . . . Clarke kept right on, and advised them to rise to a man and kill all the white men outrage the women, and slay all the male children." The costs of the violence were supposedly to be borne by General Grant.[45]

The chief of police in Milledgeville, Baldwin County, sent to Savannah for three thousand cartridges, and police as far as fifty miles away in Macon "kept a strict lookout for" the "incendiary"

45. Sandersville *Herald*, March 20, 1884; Sandersville *Mercury*, March 25, 1884.

black preacher from Cincinnati: "He is described as being of medium height, mulatto, with a black mustache. He has many friends among the ignorant who harbor him." The Atlanta *Constitution* ran the headline, "RIOTOUS NEGROES of Whose Incendiarism Sandersville Stands in Fear," and called Clarke "a lunatic . . . more furious and fanatical than a sheik of the desert." His speeches are "calculated to exercise an undue influence over evil minded and ignorant negroes." He says, "We [freedmen] are going to have our rights if we have to wade in blood waist deep."[46]

Such reports seem especially improbable because they included news that "some of the negroes who were looked upon as the best and most peaceable in the county, have joined Clarke's forces and quit work." Clarke was encouraging them, not to kill the whites and to pillage the countryside, it seems, but to organize. The newspaper mentioned in passing the less sensational facts of the case: "farm hands have struck for two dollars per day and are insulting in their demands."[47] Clarke claimed to represent a labor union headquartered in Louisville, Kentucky. "What are you getting per day, month or year?" he asked his crowds. "Some of you say forty, fifty, or seventy-five cents per day. Gentlemen, do you know the meaning of a labor reform society? I'll tell you what it means. It means that you will stop working for nothing for 'Mars' John. Farm hands' wages shall be raised to $2 for men; boys of fifteen years $1.50 and women $1.25 per day, washerwomen $1 per dozen garments, big, little, great or small, the price shall remain the same." Pointing to a man in the audience, he shouted, "you are as good as any white man that ever made track upon this earth." "And so are you," he shouted to another. "The money is in the country and we must have it for our labor. Then you [too] can [have] fine horses and buggies to ride in and fine houses to live in—in other words, be boss some ourselves."[48]

Reports of insurrection and union activity were intermingled as if they were one, but the threats of violence seem to be incongruous fabrications tacked onto Clarke's words and the ac-

46. Sandersville *Mercury*, March 25, 1884; Atlanta *Constitution*, March 31, April 1, 1884.
47. Sandersville *Mercury*, March 25, 1884.
48. Atlanta *Constitution*, March 31, 1884.

tions of his followers. If insurrection was justified, it was still a fiction written in the minds of whites. But the fears of whites were in no way remarkable or insincere. The association of union activity with insurrection was quite consistent with their definition of appropriate social roles. Even the first flippant reports of Clarke's activism described him as promoting "hostility between white and black by preaching communism, etc." The causality was clear. To whites the unionization of blacks really was insurrectionary because it threatened the racially defined economic and social order. Many southern whites may have been hostile to white unions, too, but the different degree of hostility was great enough to be a difference in kind. Black assertiveness threatened to undermine absolute white domination of southern society. Where whites perceived this great threat, rumors of other culturally encouraged fears crept among them.

The convictions of whites were deeply felt. On the A. J. Kingry plantation in Wilkinson County, one of Kingry's sons got into "some controversy" with a black laborer named Sidney Wright. As the Atlanta *Constitution* reported it, the fight was about "the colored crank Clarke" who was "figuring so largely in the surrounding counties. . . . Wright, inclining to favor the course of Clarke, caused young Kingry to resent his presence about the white people." The solution was simple and from all appearances both unsurprising and unobjectionable to the *Constitution*'s reporter and editor. "The young man," sought Wright during the night following their argument and "fired at him with a No. 2 revolver, which took effect somewhere under the chin." So much for the annoying presence. Wright was dead.[49]

The reaction of whites was so extreme—so predictably extreme—that "a number of negro . . . property owners . . . vainly protested Clarke's incendiarism." Whether employers themselves or, as was far more likely, merely fearing for what little they had, these men were caught in the middle. The union movement was a certain failure. They would gain nothing from supporting it and might lose everything that was theirs to the anger of whites. Yet if they opposed it, they earned the anger of other blacks who expected their support. The second course was easiest but had

49. *Ibid.*, April 11, 1884.

its own costs. Soon after the movement died "a church was . . . destroyed on the property of Henry Dickinson, colored, because he would not allow Clarke to hold his meetings" there. Another church was also burned in Baldwin County for the same reason.[50] Whites were not alone in expecting racial solidarity.

In one of the last incidents of Clarke's campaign, a sheriff tried to arrest him "at a speech in the woods near Pitt's Chapel in Jones County." He saw the sheriff coming, "leaped from the stump on which he had been standing and ran. The sheriff fired at him but failed to hit him" and killed someone standing in the crowd.[51] Faced with constant police harassment and probable death, Clarke slipped away carrying his movement with him.

A third incident, better known than these, has been covered elsewhere in the little detail available.[52] During the fall of 1886, Georgians heard that blacks were "forming Knights of Labor organizations in the South." John Dent, at least, was sanguine: "Should they get up strikes, they can hold out only so long as their Brother Knights in the North can feed and maintain them in idleness. . . . [As] long as food comes free, they will make no effort to work." During the following spring, Hiram F. Hoover, an agent of the Knights, traveled through black-belt counties in South Carolina and Georgia trying to organize black agricultural workers. Because "in many places a member [of the Knights] was discharged as soon as his connection . . . was discovered," Hoover, like other agents of the brotherhood, adopted a pseudonym for his union, the Co-operative Workers of America.[53]

Hoover's organizing activities did not last long in Georgia. By the time the first reports of his speeches appeared in local news-

50. Sandersville *Herald*, March 27, 1884; Atlanta *Constitution*, March 31, April 18, 1884.
51. Sandersville *Mercury*, March 25, 1884; Atlanta *Constitution*, April 4, 1884.
52. Sidney Kessler, "The Organization of Negroes in the Knights of Labor," *Journal of Negro History*, XXXVII, 248–76; Kenneth Kann, "The Knights of Labor and the Southern Black Worker," *Labor History*, XVIII (Winter, 1977), 49–70; Tindall, *South Carolina Negroes*, 114–16. See also Robert C. McMath, "Southern White Farmers and the Organization of Black Farm Workers: A North Carolina Document," *Labor History*, XVIII (Winter, 1977), 115–19; Frederic Meyers, "The Knights of Labor in the South," *Southern Economic Journal*, VI, 479–87.
53. Mathis, Mathis, and Purcell (eds.), *Dent Journals*, XVIII, October 28, 1866; Kessler, "Organization of Negroes in the Knights of Labor," 267–68.

papers, he had already been shot and lay critically ill. "His addresses were of such a character as to excite feelings of bitter hostility on the part of blacks against the whites," was the familiar refrain. "He is said to have persuaded the negroes that they had been cheated out of a fair return for their labor by the whites and that they should demand a dollar and a half a day for their work and if their demands should be refused, he advised his hearers to enforce them by using the torch and even the shedding of blood. . . . The effect upon some of the negroes was very bad and no one could doubt that there would be a bitter state of feeling here between the two races where peace and good will have heretofore prevailed, if such a firebrand as Hoover were given liberty to sow the seeds of hostility and bitterness." In Milledgeville, Hoover had been warned to leave and then run out of his hotel. Not taking the hint, he "proceeded to Warrenton, where while making a speech to the negroes in one of the colored churches," he indulged "in language of so despicable and dangerous a nature . . . that he was shot" from a window, his face and shoulders "plentifully sprinkled with birdshot," an eye ruptured. Critically wounded, he escaped to Augusta where he was allowed to stay only until he was able to travel out of the state. Like the two earlier movements, this one died leaderless under the threat of violence.[54]

Claims that Hoover or his followers intended violence are absurd. Evidence from South Carolina shows that they wanted "more wages and easier rents," that they contemplated a strike, and that they hoped to set up a cooperative store in order to lower the cost of provisions. But even in South Carolina, after planters assured themselves that their workers planned no violence, the landowners told the "Hoover Clubs" that they "would not tolerate them" and forced disbandment.[55] No evidence shows that Hoover changed his program as he crossed the Savannah River into Georgia.

These three similar incidents show both a frustrated readiness on the part of blacks to resist exploitation and their impotence to do so. Overt resistance by blacks was not responsible for

54. Milledgeville *Union and Recorder*, May 24, 31, June 7, 1887. See also Sandersville *Herald*, June 2, 1887.
55. Kessler, "Organization of Negroes in the Knights of Labor," 267–68.

the measure of freedom they retained. Any threat to the economic interests of employers was interpreted (perhaps accurately) and crushed as a threat to the caste system. With equal clarity these incidents again show the hybrid of law and illegal violence with which whites protected the meat and bone of their social system. Law legitimized much repression. (Doubtless, Cordy Harris would not have surrendered himself to the Klan.) And wrapped in abstract robes of procedure and impartiality, law also enhanced the conviction with which whites defined their social order as just. But after Reconstruction, whites were still willing to act as vigilantes when a threat to their moral system, including racially defined economic roles, seemed dramatically immediate and the law seemed inadequate or perhaps just cumbersome. The system they defended in 1887 was quite different from the one that existed in 1865. Sharecropping and renting had become common in the black belt well before 1887. But these changes had come without the threatening appearance of a fundamental change in the authority of whites in general over blacks in general. Whites remained convinced of the rightness of their social and economic position and their unqualified right to uphold it.

It also seems clear, however, that the law was as much a liability as a tool to Georgia's white landowners. As the rise and persistence of the share and rental system reflects, the legal cage in which landowners sought to trap black labor was far less confining than they wished. In fact, it was a feeble imitation of the intentions with which they had begun Reconstruction. Lien law and criminal law were not nearly as severe as the peonage mandated in black codes. This is no small point. Whites had not changed their views after 1865. The complaints of landowners about idle and unreliable black labor testify that their definition of control was still more hope than reality. Farmers from John Dent to future governor William J. Northen called for laws ensuring effective control of black labor. The complaints of 1865 were the complaints of 1900. And yet, although blacks were unable to resist oppression effectively, whites could not solve their "labor problems" as they wished because the law limited as well as served them.

The only substantive protection blacks had was the constitutional bequest of Reconstruction. The prohibition of involuntary servitude in the Thirteenth Amendment and the definition of citizenship and the equal protection clause in the Fourteenth were their great shields. Warped interpretations of these amendments allowed practices that they had been meant to preclude, but these legal fictions were still required to maintain the ostensible appearance of equality. Even the doctrine of separate but equal, although the weapon of measureless injustice, applied, on its face, equally to blacks and whites. As bad as this doctrine was, it would have been far worse without this proviso, which prevented whites from legally defining blacks as a separate laboring class. Anyone even remotely familiar with South African apartheid cannot deny that, even during the worst of segregation, the constitution protected American blacks from significantly more severe oppression. The Thirteenth and Fourteenth Amendments assured that peonage would be illegal for blacks and, indeed, for whites, though they were not in danger of being subjugated to that extent.[56] Try as the white landowning class might to exploit black labor, oppress blacks as it did, after Reconstruction it was never again able to subordinate blacks as thoroughly as it wished. The legal impediments to the coercion of labor were never completely circumvented.

Some recent scholars have described peonage among late nineteenth-century blacks as if it were the general rule rather than the exception.[57] As evidence, they cite the expressed desires of whites, vagrancy laws, lien laws, and court records from peonage cases in the early twentieth century. There were undoubtedly cases of peonage. In 1910 after a rise in cotton prices and a consequent rise in demand for labor, Albert Bushnell Hart estimated that cases might even number in the thousands.[58] But to exaggerate these exceptions into a general description of the

56. See Hart, *The Southern South*, 280–83; Novak, *The Wheel of Servitude*, 46–47.

57. Including William Cohen, "Negro Involuntary Servitude in the South, 1865–1940: A Preliminary Analysis," *Journal of Southern History*, XLII, 31–60; Novak, *The Wheel of Servitude*, his disclaimer notwithstanding; and Wiener, *Social Origins of the New South*, 107–108; Pete Daniel, "The Metamorphosis of Slavery, 1865–1900," *Journal of American History*, LXVI (June, 1976), 88–99.

58. Hart, *The Southern South*, 280.

southern social and economic order is to distort a complex history and requires inattention to much evidence.

It is important to listen to whites who wanted a form of black peonage and who incessantly complained that the law did not meet their needs. In 1888, for example, a planter named E. M. Clarkson, called on lawmakers "to employ their brains and the people's time in devising a law by which small debts would be collected. . . . The advancing of small amounts of money or provisions to laborers during the year in order to secure their labor in the crops when needed, is an imperative custom. And in very many instances, . . . neither the labor nor the money is paid when due."[59] But such laws proved impossible to devise in the late nineteenth century. From the 1860s until the early twentieth century, "a score of bills were attempted" in Georgia's general assembly "to penalize breach of contract or failure to refund the amount advanced." The bills "failed on the rock of unconstitutionality."[60] Late nineteenth-century whites could not devise a legal means to bind blacks to their land.[61] This was true not only in law but in fact. The substantial migration of blacks from farm to farm within neighborhoods and among southern states testifies that peonage was anything but the rule. In fact, patterns of migration show that blacks were highly mobile, even though trapped in a low social stratum without opportunity to advance. There was not even a demand for their labor in the fast-growing North, which only proves the national pervasiveness of racism and the national responsibility for their plight. Blacks were kept down in the South and out of the North. Racism did what the law alone could not do, but racism alone could not do everything whites wished.

Even in the early twentieth century, as Judge Thomas Norwood of Savannah retired from the bench, he could denounce

59. Americus *Weekly Recorder*, February 2, 1888.

60. [Mohr?], "Labor History of Georgia" (MS in University of Georgia Libraries, Rare Books and Manuscript Department, Athens), Pt. 3, pp. 2–3.

61. Following the turn of the century, means were found to temporarily circumvent the restriction. See Hart, *The Southern South*, 278–87; [Mohr?], "Labor History of Georgia," Pt. 3, pp. 2–3; Novak, *The Wheel of Servitude*, Chap. 5 *passim*.

the requirement of legal equality. A former United States senator and unsuccessful challenger to the reelection of Governor Alfred Colquitt in 1880, Norwood reflected the propensities of his class as he passionately reiterated the position of planters since long before the Civil War. Years of experience had supposedly taught him that a black "never works except from necessity or compulsion, has no incentive, is brutal to his family, recognizes no government except force, knows neither ambition, honor nor shame, possesses no morals." Norwood protested "the insanity of putting millions of semi-savages under white men's laws for their government."[62] As severe as the laws that applied to blacks may have been, as poor as blacks may have been kept, men like Norwood, Clarkson, Dent, and Northen were unsatisfied.

To understand the uses and limits of law for white southerners, one must examine its effects. Although there is consistency between the mentality that produced the black codes and the mentality that produced the laws that replaced them, one should not fail to recognize differences in substance as well as form. The rise of sharecropping and renting arrangements and the persistence of the decentralized plantation system after Redemption, both of which dissatisfied so many whites, show that the law did not re-create slavery in a different form. Since blacks could not be defined in law as a separate laboring group, attentive landowners could not stop their absent or indifferent neighbors or the planter-merchants from allowing blacks an escape into forms of tenancy available to whites. There was, therefore, a stalemate over the economic and social status of blacks. The stalemate was not between southern whites and blacks but between southern whites and the mandates of federal law. Despite the way southern whites wrote lien and labor law, despite the way southern whites defined the value of black labor, federal laws that were foreign to their values and yet were to an important degree invulnerable to their attack had been forcibly imposed during Reconstruction. Thus, federal law created the nineteenth-century tension between the kind of black labor whites wanted and the kind they got.

The legal system also pulled powerful whites into a second

62. Quoted in Hart, *The Southern South*, 93.

form of tension. Because of the constraints of federal law and participation in the political system, landowners who wielded political power and who wanted to exploit black workers ever more effectively also had the contradictory task of acting as their protectors. Like the judge who presided over the trial of Cordy Harris and perhaps even like Thomas Norwood as he sat on the bench, they could be as bigoted as the other members of their class but had to be dedicated to the legal system that legitimized their rule while remaining only semipervious to their deeply held caste values. For this reason every governor of Georgia actively if ineffectively fought lynching. For this reason Salem Dutcher, the prosecutor in the case of Cordy Harris, could agonize over the refusal of a grand jury to indict several lynchers in Burke County. "I cannot but think that it would be a mockery of justice not to take further steps on evidence so positive, direct and unimpeachable," he wrote to the governor, beseeching advice. For this reason, John B. Gordon, Georgia's most prominent professional Civil War hero, Redeemer extraordinary, nominal head of the state's Ku Klux Klan, and politician of convenient ethics, vetoed in 1888 a bill that mandated discrimination against "negro schools" in the allocation of state funds "on the ground that it was against sound policy and a violation of the constitution of the state and the United States." For this reason William Fleming, James C. C. Black, and other Democratic, rabidly anti-Populist politicians could appeal to blacks on the basis of their party's "progressive" racial policy.[63] And for this reason, Georgia's Democratic regime was not unique in receiving the support of black voters against insurgents who challenged it. The oppressors, the political insiders, could more convincingly claim that they would defend the rights of blacks than could challengers like Norwood, playing insurgent, or even the Populists. Politicians from both groups might come from the

63. Dutcher to James M. Smith, June 16, 1877, in Smith, Governor's Incoming Correspondence; William H. Fleming, *Slavery and the Race Problem in the South, with Special Reference to the State of Georgia: Address of Hon. William H. Fleming Before the Alumni Society of the State University, Athens, June 19, 1906* (Augusta, 1906), 15–16; Robert Saunders, "Southern Populists and the Negro, 1893–1895," *Journal of Negro History*, LIV, 240–61; Randolph Dennis Werner, "Hegemony and Conflict: The Political Economy of a Southern Region, Augusta, Georgia, 1865–1895" (Ph.D. dissertation, University of Virginia, 1977), 409.

same class and share the same values, but insiders gained advantages simply from doing their job.

The constraints of federal law had one other important implication. They increased opportunities for tension between poor whites and the caste system. Federal law required that the traps designed around lien law in the early 1870s for the subordination of the black laboring caste and the criminal statutes that helped control black labor also applied to the white agricultural laboring class, which grew rapidly after Reconstruction. Efforts to make blacks conform as closely as possible to expectations born of slavery defined the status of white as well as black workers. At the same time as federal law prevented landowners from pushing blacks down as far as they wished, it served to push white laborers downward in contradiction to the racially defined social cosmography of southern whites.

So, despite the landowners' successful resort to moral violence in order to regain control of government and to redeem the racial order, which they defined with religious conviction, neither the government nor the society turned out to be theirs alone. A foreign system of values constrained them. They sought to exploit yet, within limits, were bound to protect their black workers. The legal system and thus the economy of the New South failed in substantial ways to match the severity of persistent antebellum social dogma. As the incessant complaints of whites showed, ideology and practice diverged discomfortingly. Blacks could be upwardly mobile. Resident white landowners could be frustrated. And the yeomanry, which had shown in Ku Klux Klan violence that it was independently committed to the subordination of black labor, was quickly giving birth to an ever larger white laboring class that had no place in the social cosmography of whites and that could feel more than a little put upon. In a sense, white southerners lived in a society at odds with itself.

Chapter V

THE PRIVILEGES OF PROPERTY

Not every man that is poor in purse is poor in mind. . . .
[Many have] more genuine love of country at heart than a
thousand such puppets as would attempt to abuse a poor
man for his poverty by classing him with a "nigger". . . . If the
capitalists of the country are determined to crush out every
poor man, rest assured the day is not far distant when he will
have great cause to regret it.

—"Zoilus," Sparta *Ishmaelite*

L IKE THE LAWS that defined the position of labor, the laws
that defined the rights of landownership established the
power and privileges of employers. As landowners sought
changes in law to regain coercive authority over emancipated
workers, they also increasingly defined their property rights as
absolute. There was a clear relationship between the two sets of
changes. Through law, employers transferred to property-in-
land some of the authority they had once had over property-
in-labor. But the constitutional amendments adopted during
Congressional Reconstruction assured that these changes, like
postbellum labor laws, affected landless whites as well as freedmen. Landless whites, like blacks, resisted abuse at the hands of
the relatively well-to-do, but they were freer to be vocal in their
resistance. As they protested changes in property law, they re-
vealed their attitudes both toward those more prosperous than
themselves and toward their landless black counterparts. These
fights can, therefore, help to untangle the complexity of the
South's social system—to map the area that whites said was not
supposed to exist: where class divisions among whites overlap-
ped the caste barrier dividing whites and blacks.

The intent behind changes in property laws was apparent in
early postwar enactments governing hunting, fishing, and trespassing. In early 1866 the Georgia legislature outlawed hunting
on Sundays "with firearms, dog, or dogs" in some seventy-two
counties, the overwhelming majority of which were in the black

belt or along the coast. The penalty for offenders was severe: fifty dollars, ten days in prison, or both. The assembly also adopted restrictions on fishing.[1] Since the new system of decentralized plantations was just starting to emerge in 1866, planters still expected blacks to work six days a week as laborers in gangs. Employers were using legislation to tighten their authority over free labor by outlawing the efforts of freedmen on their one day off to supplement monotonous and inadequate diets.

In 1866 the general assembly also enacted laws against squatting and against collecting timber, fruit, honey, berries, or anything else "of any value whatever" without the consent of the owner of the land, whether it was "enclosed or unenclosed," meaning whether fenced or not.[2] Squatters were not to escape their supposedly rightful position as laborers. Laborers were not to escape complete dependence upon their employers.

Perhaps the assembly best illustrated the relationship between the privileges of property and the well-being of labor as it adopted a special law for three counties along the coast. There, landowners like Pierce Butler and his daughter Frances were struggling to reestablish their rice and long-staple cotton plantations. To help them, the legislature empowered county governments to "collect a tax of two dollars per head on each and every dog over the number of three, and a dollar a piece on every gun or pistol, musket or rifle over the number of three kept any plantation." Effectively exempting the dogs and guns of the planter and, at the same time, making him "responsible for the tax imposed," the assembly was helping to enforce the dependence and subservice of labor.[3] While one- and two-dollar taxes may seem minimal, they would be as difficult for poor laborers to pay as the one-dollar poll tax imposed later. Without guns and dogs, a major source of food would be denied.

These new laws were part of the response of landowners to the freedmen's pursuit of self-interest and independence. Not only did blacks seek to escape specific hardships of slavery; they

1. *Acts*, 1866 (Nos. 219, 69), 154–55, 39; *Code of the State of Georgia*, Secs. 4532, 4533 (both adopted in 1866), 892.
2. *Acts*, 1866 (No. 248), 237–38; *Code of the State of Georgia*, Sec. 4528 (adopted in 1866), 892.
3. *Acts*, 1866 (No. 41), 27.

also sought to expand privileges that slaveholders had sometimes allowed out of either humane concern or enlightened self-
interest. Hunting, fishing, lumbering, vegetable gardening, picking wild fruits and berries, making baskets, raising a few swine,
cattle, or chickens, and other activities typical of the lives of yeomen farmers had sometimes been allowed slaves not only to improve their lives directly but also to enable them, within narrow
limits, to earn a little money with which to buy modest ameni-
ties. "Most of the white folks would let niggers" do something to
make money, remembered one freedman whose parents had
been allowed to grow tobacco and corn for their own use and to
sell. They also were allowed to "cook ginger cakes and take"
them to local "dances, and make money." Slaves "used to bootleg, yes, sell whiskey just like they do now," the freedman continued. "They always had money; they would get it some way or
'nother." Another former slave remembered that her "pa" had
been allowed to raise chickens and vegetables to sell to his master and his master's uncle. Pa was even more enterprising than
his master thought. The uncle ran a hotel. "He would buy anything my pa brought to him; and many times he was buying his
own stuff or his nephew's stuff," which pa had stolen. Pa also ran
a secret catering business. Slaves and "free Negroes would steal
to" his cabin "at a specified time to buy a chicken or barbecue
dinner." Pa's master "allowed his slaves to earn any money they
could for their own use," but, chuckled pa's daughter, he did not
"know about the little restaurant we had in our cabin."[4]

Pa was an unusual entrepreneur. The privileges allowed most
slaves were quite restricted in both law and practice. After the
war, employers lost the power to limit privileges, with important consequences for themselves and their workers. Hunting
serves as one example. Among the earliest legal restrictions on
slaves was, for obvious reasons, a ban on the possession of firearms.[5] And masters had, of course, absolute authority to limit

4. *Unwritten History of Slavery*, 36, 285–86, 107; William Freehling, *Prelude to
Civil War: The Nullification Crisis in South Carolina* (New York, 1968), 56; William E. Dodd, *The Cotton Kingdom: A Chronicle of the Old South* (New Haven,
1919), 74–75, 91–95; Herman Clarence Nixon, *Lower Piedmont County*, 15–18;
Wharton, *The Negro in Mississippi*, 15.

5. Winthrop D. Jordan, *White over Black: American Attitudes Toward the
Negro, 1550–1812* (New York, 1977), 78.

hunting or any other privilege they allowed. After emancipation, employers lacked the absolute authority of masters but were by no means resigned to this fate. Ku Klux Klansmen seized firearms from former slaves, and in some southern states, black codes included attempts to prohibit all blacks from owning guns.[6] As had been the case during slavery, the chronic fear of insurrection was one concern. The abject dependence of labor was another. Since freedom, like slavery, provided blacks a bare subsistence, employers, like masters, tried to use food to coerce recalcitrant workers. Thus capital responded to the emancipation of labor in a near endless series of local statutes that redefined the rights of property, penalized trespassing, and restricted or altogether prohibited hunting, fishing, and gathering.[7]

Alternative sources of food and income threatened the power of employers. But landowners found that statutory enactments worked less well than had the absolute authority of bondage. Like J. D. Collins on Hurricane Plantation, Frances Butler complained that she could not starve uncooperative freedmen into working as she wished. It was impossible to force them to work, she said, and "as for starving them, . . . that is impossible too, for it is a well-known fact that you can't starve a negro." She explained her trying experience: "At the moment there are about a dozen on Butler's Island who do not work, consequently get no food, and I see no difference whatever in their condition and [that of] those who get twelve dollars a month and full rations. They all raise a little corn and sweet potatoes and with their facility for catching fish and oysters, and shooting wild game, they have as much to eat as they want, and are quite satisfied with that." She considered their behavior ignorant: they had not yet "learned to want the things that money can buy."[8]

Butler's conviction that "her" freedmen's proper role was to work as laborers in her cotton distorted her view of their actions. She attributed their "idleness" to ignorance and lack of ambition, but she un-self-consciously admitted that those freed-

6. James Wilford Garner, *Reconstruction in Mississippi* (1901; rpr. Baton Rouge, 1968), 113–16.
7. The decades following emancipation brought scores of statutes similar to those cited above. See any year of *Acts*.
8. Leigh, *Ten Years on a Georgia Plantation*, 124.

men who attempted to live off the land and those who worked long hours as laborers in her fields fared at least about the same. Her misjudgment was not uncommon. Members of her class would long claim that blacks were averse to raising cotton, that they were satisfied with a bare subsistence, and that they would work only if hungry. In fact, blacks responded to the opportunities and dangers of the market economy with rational sensitivity. If Frances Butler's hands had not learned of everything that money could buy, they did know that it could buy land, and they wanted that badly enough to disgust her.[9]

The ideal of most freedmen in seeking independence of whites seems to have been a yeomanlike self-sufficiency supplemented by a cash crop.[10] This path promised both security and profit and was analogous to the program of "diversified agriculture" advocated by preachers of the New South creed. The rise of share and renting arrangements speaks in part of the landless freedmen's desire for as much autonomy as they could get. Even if a landowner closely supervised his share hands and renters, their work was organized by tasks rather than by the time spent at them. Thus, these freedmen, to a degree greater than wage hands, were free to pursue self-interest defined more broadly than employers hoped to allow. When federal Department of Agriculture researchers noted that "but few families [of black sharecroppers and renters] were not supplied" with dogs "living in the open space between" their cabin floors and the ground, the agents were remarking on valuable assets, not pets.[11] Dogs were as valuable for hunting as guns, and it was an unusual cropper or renter who did not hunt, fish, and take odd jobs to supplement his family's income. Nate Shaw and his father, both as croppers and as renters, did a bit of each. For them hunting, fishing, lumbering, making baskets, and hiring out to do hard labor were all important sources of income.[12] Women and children did likewise: "Every Nigger woman, Girl, and Boy have

9. *Ibid.*, 155–56.

10. This was reflected in the behavior of proprietors and in the tendency of renters and proprietors to have gardens. See also Thomas J. Woofter, Jr., *Black Yeomanry: Life on St. Helena Island* (New York, 1930).

11. Atwater and Woods, "Dietary Studies," 16.

12. Theodore Rosengarten, *All God's Dangers*, 9, 14, 17, 18, 32, 85, 119.

thrown down their hoes and quit the fields and gone to picking Black Berry's to sell in Cave Spring," complained a landowner about his croppers' families. "Good fruit years demoralize the Negro more than anything else. To get the Nigger right, let corn, bacon, and fruit be scarce and they are compelled to work for their bellies. Let him fill his belly easily and there is no work from him."[13]

Like this planter, whites regularly complained about the "idleness" of blacks who spent time gathering fruit, hunting, and fishing. Some whites were indignant that blacks presumed to practice a white man's sport, for employers considered these activities to be mere pleasures.[14] To work meant to work for them, and it meant fieldwork in their cotton. Even middle-class black observers failed to admit the important economic role of these yeoman pursuits. Two students of W. E. B. Du Bois, traveling from the Georgia coast inland along "low and sandy roads . . . all under water," arrived at an isolated community of black proprietors farming poor soil. The students reported disparagingly that these "people were poorer and more ignorant than those nearer the coast and many constantly rove about leaving their farms unattended, and spend their time idling, fishing, and lumbering." One student wrote, "It seems to me as though they are very indolent and lazy. One man who owns 50 acres of land told me that he did not have any anxiety whatever to raise a large crop—no more than sufficient to support himself and his family—that if he raised a larger crop, he couldn't get a price on the market sufficient to pay for the labor; therefore, he did not have any desire to keep apace with the world and . . . would be content with a small crop. All of them seemed to have this idea in their heads, and therefore did not care whether they worked or not."[15]

There was nothing unusual about these farmers. There was no distinctive black economics. No doubt blacks in the backwaters of McIntosh and other coastal counties were not knowledgeable about the most modern methods of farming or business, but they adopted patterns of agriculture typical among poor and

13. Mathis, Mathis, and Purcell (eds.), *Dent Journals*, XVI, June 20, 1884.
14. Williamson, *After Slavery*, 47.
15. Du Bois, "The Negro Landholder of Georgia," 739–40.

Average Proportion of Cotton Acreage to Total Crop Acreage in Sample Census Districts

	Owners		Renters		Share Hands	
	White	Black	White	Black	White	Black
Black Belt						
Baldwin (District 5)	.36	.67	—	.74	.61	.67
Greene (District 33)	.46	.52	.58	.57	.55	.56
Quitman (District 95)	.44	.45	.49	.58	.52	.74
Sumter (District 72)	.46	.53	.47	—	.52	.59
Upson (District 137)	.40	.38	.47	.50	.38	.58
Upper Piedmont						
Floyd (Districts 71 and 62)	.47	.52	.52	.50	.46	.55
Gwinnett (District 115)	.27	.42	.28	—	.31	.18
Haralson (District 141)	.23	—	.33	—	.27	—

SOURCES: Eighth Census, 1880: Agricultural Schedules, William R. Perkins Library, Duke University, Durham, N.C., and Eighth Census, 1880: Population Schedules (microfilm).
NOTE: The smaller numbers reflect the greater likelihood of self-sufficiency.

isolated people, patterns long identified with white southern mountaineers and "poor whites" living in the infertile corners of the plantation belt, pine barrens, and coastal counties. Physically isolated black and white proprietors alike pursued patterns of subsistence agriculture, raising a little for cash or bartering for those things they could not raise. When not isolated, despite the claim of whites that blacks refused to raise cotton on their own, black and white proprietors planted cotton and corn in about the same proportions. In fact, because black proprietors usually owned fewer acres and had fewer animals to feed, they averaged a slightly greater proportion of cotton to corn than did white proprietors as a whole.[16]

Whether landowners or not, isolated or not, blacks exploited woodlands for both subsistence and commercial gain. Women and children picking blackberries to sell in Cave Spring offered a minor illustration of this pattern, which appeared immediately after the end of the war. Not long before Frances Butler

16. Timothy Thomas Fortune, *Black and White: Land, Labor, and Politics in the South* (1884; rpr. Chicago, 1970), 121–22.

and her father returned to their Sea Island plantations to be troubled by willful former slaves, an officer of the Freedmen's Bureau reported angrily on the business activities of blacks on St. Simon's Island. "The freedmen were armed," he wrote. They "would not allow any white person to land. They were mostly fed on government rations, and, with very few exceptions, were spending their time in fishing, hunting, and destroying the cattle, large numbers of which had been left on the islands by the former owners. It was found that, while the government was sending them rations, they were slaughtering the deer which abound upon the islands, and selling the venison at high prices in Savannah." Other freedmen busily cut wood to sell to passing steamers.[17]

On the frontier, as in most of the antebellum South, there were no restrictions on hunting, fishing, lumbering, or gathering by any freeman. Farmers on the frontier and in many upper piedmont and mountainous areas of the South, isolated from markets, tended to exploit local resources for subsistence only. With resources apparently plentiful, the small, scattered population had a legal and practical right to all they could use. In Georgia and across the South, emancipation broke the bonds that had preserved a certain frontierlike quality of life for southern whites even in well-developed plantation districts. "The country was full of varmints—just full," exclaimed a former slave as he described the neighborhood of his master's plantation immediately after the war. "A man could go out and kill a dozen squirrels, they was that thick. Pigeons were thick too, thicker than hens and chickens. . . . Wild ducks were numerous, wild ducks came in droves."[18]

Such plenty did not last long. Because of a relatively large rural population and because of commercial possibilities unavailable on a true frontier, emancipation released demands on game, forests, fish, and fowl that nature could not meet. Rapid population growth also added to demand. Between 1860 and

17. Davis Tillson to O. O. Howard, October 25, 1865, in Stanton, "Letter of the Secretary of War," 52–53.
18. *Unwritten History of Slavery*, 95. See also Somers, *The Southern States Since the War*, 69–71, 92; Mary (McDowell) Duffus Hardy, *Down South* (London, 1883), 256–57.

POPULATION DENSITY OF GEORGIA BLACK BELT, 1890

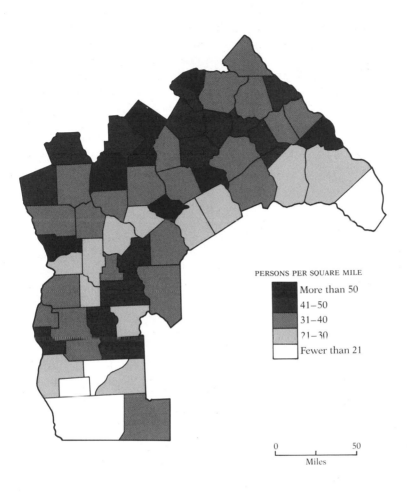

PERSONS PER SQUARE MILE

More than 50
41–50
31–40
21–30
Fewer than 21

0   50
        Miles

1890, Georgia's population increased about 75 percent, and population density nearly doubled (going from about eighteen to over thirty-one people per square mile). Of course, population was not evenly distributed, and long before 1890, most of the plantation belt, particularly its older section, had a population density well above the state average.[19]

Most blacks lived in this region, and their demands upon woodlands were great at the same time as woodlands were disappearing. Cheap land, cheap labor, and cotton prices encouraged the inefficiency of the decentralized plantation system. The more croppers and renters a landowner hired, the more land brought under cultivation—no matter how poor the techniques—the greater his income would be from his shares, rent, and the sale of supplies to hands. The poorly cultivated fields of inefficiently run plantations consequently engrossed more and more land at the expense of woods. Between 1880 and 1890 alone, the area of farms devoted to fields and (less important) pastures, meadows, orchards, and vineyards, increased rapidly in black belt counties—more rapidly, in fact, than population. Thus, as demands on nature increased, the woodlands available to fill them were disappearing.

The increasingly severe limitations upon hunting, fishing, trespassing, and gathering that the Georgia legislature adopted at the behest of landowners in county after county reflected, therefore, more than one motive. Conservation was one intent. Statutes did try to protect animals during breeding season. One, adopted in 1873, is an adequate example: "whereas, a continued wholesale and ill-seasoned destruction of deer, partridges, and wild turkey . . . has threatened to exterminate" them "in the counties of Chatham and Bryan," the legislature prohibited "killing, shooting or trapping" those species in those counties between April and September. Other local statutes made it illegal to fish with anything other than a hook and lines or outlawed practices such as seining and using poison or explosives to catch large numbers of fish. One act made its intent explicit as it prohibited the use of any "contrivance for catching fish for sale"

19. Overall population density is from U.S. Department of Commerce, Bureau of the Census, *Historical Statistics of the United States, Colonial Times to 1970* (2 vols.; Washington, D.C., 1975), I, 26.

without the "written consent of the owner of the land."[20] To prohibit commercial exploitation would help to preserve the property of the landowner and the internal frontier.

Conservation was, then, not a subterfuge, or at least not always. Natural resources were being depleted. A black belt editor could tell his readers that "it is unlawful to shoot deer" at "this time of year," but he admitted, "this law does not trouble the hunters of this section" because "there are few deer left to shoot." And it was presumably to meet some need that the legislature empowered the state commissioner of agriculture to restock and "secure the artificial propagation . . . of food-fish" in the rivers and lakes of the state.[21]

But if conservation was a noble cause, it also bore a price. It placed a burden upon black labor that, while not necessarily intentional, at least signaled the indifference of white landowners to the poverty that surrounded them. Whites complained, for example, that blacks destroyed singing birds, which "have claims upon human sympathy, and are besides unfit for food." The legislature made it a misdemeanor to kill any "whippoorwill, sparrow, thrush, mockingbird, finch, martin, chimney-swallow, barn swallow, flicker, oriole, red bird, cedar-bird, yannager, cat-bird, blue bird, or any other insectiverous bird" or to "rob or destroy the nest of any such bird." Whites did not acknowledge or perhaps did not know that birds they regarded as uneatable supplemented the diets of desperately poor black workers.[22]

Some statutes aimed at conservation, but in doing so, many clearly aimed at preserving the internal frontier for landowners alone. When the legislature adopted laws for black belt counties,

20. *Acts*, 1873 (No. 190), 235, 1875 (No. 277), 296, 1876 (No. 365), 296, 1877 (No. 139), 322, 1880–81 (No. 149), 135, 1875 (No. 210), 113, and see 1872 (Nos. 346, 281), 469, 1872 (Nos. 311, 300), 432, 1875 (No. 285), 302–303, 1877 (No. 23), 321, 1878–79 (No. 82), 375.

21. Milledgeville *Union and Recorder*, March 19, 1895; *Acts*, 1896 (No. 518), 20–21. Additional evidence includes a few acts passed for especially densely populated counties before the war. In 1886, for example, the legislature repealed an act that it had adopted in 1859. *Acts*, 1886 (No. 108), 285.

22. *Southern Cultivator*, September 1884; *Acts*, 1874 (No. 95), 400–401. In its session of 1878–79, the general assembly adopted two more statutes making it illegal to kill any "insectiverous, or singing bird." *Acts*, 1878–79 (Nos. 330, 118), 376–77.

IMPROVED FARMLANDS IN GEORGIA BLACK BELT, 1880

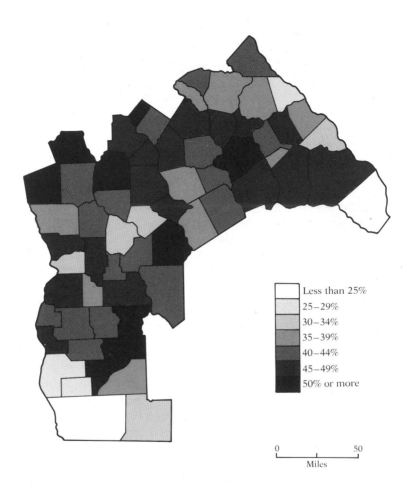

Less than 25%
25–29%
30–34%
35–39%
40–44%
45–49%
50% or more

0   50
     Miles

IMPROVED FARMLANDS IN GEORGIA BLACK BELT, 1890

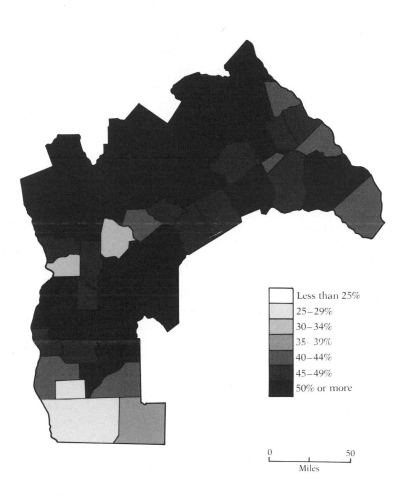

Less than 25%
25–29%
30–34%
35–39%
40–44%
45–49%
50% or more

0   50
Miles

it did not expect restrictions on Sunday hunting and fishing, rigorous definitions of trespassing, and the taxation of dogs to be equally borne.[23] But because of the "foreign," or nationally imposed, system of values that, through Congressional Reconstruction and the Fourteenth Amendment, constrained white southerners, laws that redefined the rights of property, like those that defined the position of labor, applied to white as well as black workers. As was the case with labor law, the attempts in southern legislatures to limit privilege along racial lines through the black codes gave way to restrictions based purely on class. The practice of adopting county-by-county statutes muted or dispersed the political effects of this violation of the white social cosmography. Law reflected the distribution of power in each county. But within a neighborhood, in the life of individual black and white laborers, the effects of restrictions remained great.

In the plantation belt, where most labor was black, landowners quickly exchanged customary usage for absolute property rights. In the upper piedmont, where white labor was increasingly common in the late nineteenth century and where the internal frontier was quickly breaking down, statutory changes in the rights of property lagged somewhat behind increasing social distance between landowners and white landless laborers.

The burden of all this legislation was partially relieved by the difficulty of enforcing it. As was generally true of government regulation in the late nineteenth century, enforcement was left in private hands.[24] Lawsuits initiated by landowners played the role later given to policemen. Landowners would have to have been incessantly vigilant to police their lands adequately, and on large holdings that was impossible.[25] However, this practical problem of enforcement was not the case for all new land laws, and the major exception—fence laws—created the bitterest political issue in Georgia politics between Redemption and the Populist Revolt of the 1890s. Vigilantism and incendiarism perversely reflected the moral conviction of the antagonists, who

23. For statutes on weekend fishing, see *Acts*, 1872 (Nos. 366, 104), 483, 1875 (No. 86), 357, 1876 (No. 518), 20–21.

24. Friedman, *A History of American Law*, 165.

25. Thomas P. Janes, *A Manual of Georgia for the Use of Immigrants and Capitalists* (Atlanta, 1878), 104.

fought in elections and occasionally used all the corrupt techniques that Redeemers had made acceptable for "righteous" causes. Most important, however, the fence-law controversy illustrated the intersecting class and racial division in the life of the New South.

At the close of the Civil War, as throughout the South since colonial times, Georgia farmers fenced in their crops and allowed swine and cattle to root and range freely in surrounding woodlands. When whites first invaded the South, land was so relatively plentiful that there was little reason for them to go to the expense or trouble of making pastures and tending their large herds. Rather, they burned over unfenced land, forcing tender grass to sprout for their cattle. This technique was reminiscent of the practice of Indians, whose burning of undergrowth had promoted the forest-garden and abundant game so astounding to the first white southerners.[26]

The practice of southern frontiersmen continued unchanged, and in the late nineteenth century, zig-zag, or worm, fences with rails spaced close enough to keep out hogs and stacked high enough to keep out cattle still snaked around fields of cotton and grain. Fires, too, still burned, often causing serious damage as the countryside became increasingly developed.[27] As population grew, as whites and blacks settled more densely, as the area under cultivation expanded and woodlands shrank, as freedmen began to own stock and to farm as sharehands and renters—the practices of the frontier became burdensome for many landlords. Of course, these changes affected neighborhoods at different rates. Conditions at one end of a county could be quite different from those at the other. But where pressure was greatest, landowners—most frequently resident landowning employers— sought to change the law and require cattle and swine to be kept in pastures and pens. For employers, the "no-fence" or stock law requiring that cows and hogs be fenced in would mean less work

26. James C. Bonner, *A History of Georgia Agriculture, 1732–1860* (Athens, 1964), 25–31; Edmund S. Morgan, *American Slavery—American Freedom: The Ordeal of Colonial Virginia* (New York, 1975), 52–56.

27. See comments by C. R. Pringle to the Georgia State Agricultural Society, Athens, Georgia, August 12, 1891, in *Southern Cultivator*, December, 1891; Atlanta *Constitution*, April 4, 5, 1884.

maintaining fences, fewer rails, less expense. For landless laborers and small landowners, it had very different implications.[28]

The battle began in 1872 after the general assembly adopted "An act relating to fences and stock, and for the protection of crops." Under the provisions of the act, if fifty freeholders petitioned to close the open range and adopt the no-fence system, the county was required to hold an election to decide the issue. Opponents could forestall the election by presenting a counter-petition by fifty other freeholders, but this could be overridden by an additional twenty-five signatures on the original no-fence petition.[29] Proponents of no-fence argued that the open range should be abandoned because timber was increasingly scarce, because the time, labor, and rails necessary to build fences around crops were too costly, because the breeding of freely ranging animals was uncontrolled and stock was of poor quality, because the old fence rows took up too much cultivatable space, and because wandering stock were easy prey for theft. "When our fathers first settled this county and when our range was good and when the acreage in cultivation was small the present system of fencing was proper," wrote a proponent of no-fence in Carroll County, "but now we have no range, and our cows are hungry, . . . hence the necessity for a change."[30]

The no-fence arguments had validity. There is, for example, substantial evidence that timber was increasingly scarce and fencing an increasingly costly burden. In 1879 the assembly legalized wire fencing, but it, too, was expensive and failed to keep hogs out of cornfields.[31] Some farmers in counties without the new stock law tried board and post-and-rail fences, which

28. For a compact, if technical, discussion of no-fence from the period, see *The Fence Question in the Southern States as Related to General Husbandry and Sheep Raising, with a History of Fence Customs, and Laws Pertaining Thereto: and a View of the Farm System of the South, as Shown in the Census of 1880* (Worcester, Mass., 1881). See also J. Crawford King, Jr., "The Closing of the Southern Range: An Exploratory Study," *Journal of Southern History*, XLVIII, 53–70.

29. *Acts*, 1872 (Nos. 30, 329), 34–36.

30. "School Boy," letter, in *Carroll County Times*, September 1, 1882. One or several of these arguments appeared in every statement by proponents of the stock law, but they are all summarized in the Sparta *Mercury*, November 1, 1881.

31. *Acts*, 1878–79 (No. 304), 165. Expense discussed in *Southern Cultivator*, March, 1883.

took less wood and space but even more labor than a traditional worm fence. Farmers who found timber especially scarce planted quick-growing black locusts on spots of worn-out land to supply fence posts, while others who owned fields on both sides of a road put up a gate at each end to avoid fencing the roadsides in between. Soon tin roofs on tenant cabins would testify to "the exhaustion of local forests from which shingles were once rived."[32]

Opponents of no-fence had their own valid and self-interested arguments. The no-fence men "are determined to 'rule or ruin' our country . . . and oppress the laboring men around them," wrote a landless farmer from Hancock County in 1883. "Within the last year or two," he claimed, tenants had done well enough to keep a little corn on hand and buy "a milk cow, a few pigs, etc., and because the prospects are that they will not be quite as dependent as before, these *charitable christian* men," who push for the no-fence system, are making every effort to force their tenants' "downfall." With the new stock law, he complained, "no poor man not a landowner could raise stock of any kind" except "at the mercy of the landlord." Another tenant farmer wrote, "This law will simply take rights away from the poor man and give them to the rich." It would deny poor men "the liberty that our forefathers fought for."[33]

Whether landless opponents of the new system accurately described the motives of no-fence men or not, they did accurately describe the effects of the system. Proponents were at least indifferent to the burdens that the change placed upon the poor. As one tenant farmer caustically observed, proponents of no-fence were saying that "there never was any thing that brought more relief to the tenant and laborer than the stock law." Landless men could not disagree with that, he wrote. They would be "relieved of the privileges our fathers established." They would "be relieved of the care and use of the cow, the hog, and in short, all the necessities" of life except "as they are furnished by the landholder." In threatening the right of tenants, laborers, and all

32. Milledgeville *Union and Recorder*, November 9, 1875, May 9, 1877; *Southern Cultivator*, March, 1883, and see January, August, 1888; Arthur F. Raper and Ira De A. Reid, *Sharecroppers All* (Chapel Hill, 1941), vii.

33. "Zoilus," letter, in Sparta *Ishmaelite*, June 20, 1883, emphasis in the original; "Plow Boy," letter, in *Southwestern News* (Dawson), May 4, 1887.

other landless men to own livestock, the law threatened not only those who had taken a few steps toward independence but also the hopes of even those who had not. "If you will show me one man who owns no land and never expects to," said one opponent of no-fence, "I say don't let him vote [on the stock law] for he cannot be found."[34] The customary right to graze stock was as substantive a property right as any other.

Proponents of no-fence answered these attacks by claiming that landlords would have to provide pastures for stock that belonged to tenants and laborers or else be unable to rent their lands or hire hands.[35] To this claim, the experience of landless men was answer enough. They knew that they paid for all they got and that many landowners begrudged any time or energy devoted to anything besides cash crops. To landless men, wrote one, this law "is bread and meat out of their children's mouths. Who does it benefit? Nobody but the landowners. There is not one man out of them that will let them [tenants, croppers, and wage hands] have pasture room free from rent."[36] Experience in counties subject to the law confirmed the fears of opponents. Tenants with stock moved away from counties with the new law.[37]

Of course class lines were not rigid. Some landlords held tradition-bound views not uncommon in agricultural societies. Others from neighborhoods not densely populated or from the relatively new plantation districts in southwest Georgia where forests were not yet depleted were at first prone to oppose change. In 1878, for example, several planters from southwest Georgia attending a convention of the state agricultural society supported the position of tenants and laborers in older sections

34. *Carroll County Times*, September 8, 1882.

35. Examples include *Southern Cultivator*, May, 1876; G. G. Flynt, letter, to Monroe *Advertiser*, n.d., quoted in Dawson *Journal*, February 9, 1882; Sandersville *Herald*, January 15, 1891; F. L. G., letter, in *Cherokee Advance*, June 9, 1881; *Transactions of the Georgia State Agricultural Society from August, 1876, to February, 1878* (Atlanta, 1878), 412. Some even erroneously claimed that landowners were legally required to make free pastures available. See, for example, I. H. P. Beck, letter, in *Carroll Free Press*, May 15, 1885.

36. *Carroll Free Press*, May 15, 1885.

37. Proponents and opponents agreed that this happened. See "School Boy," letter, in *Carroll County Times*, September 1, 1882; J. M. P., letter, in Dawson *Journal*, August 9, 1883.

of the black belt where the stock law was already an issue. No matter what the claims of proponents, said one planter, "This stock law does oppress the poor." Similarly, in wiregrass counties, where cattle raising was a major business, local observers could report that "the no fence law . . . never entered into the mind of man." Landowners in these counties were content with laws that prohibited residents of Florida from grazing herds on Georgia land. And in isolated, mountainous, and heavily wooded counties at the northern end of the state, other observers reported that everyone was "satisfied to let . . . cattle run at large."[38]

These quiet districts would eventually join the bitter battle first witnessed in middle Georgia. Within only ten years after southwestern planters spoke out against the stock law, most were on the other side of the fight. Like other black belt employers, they often found electoral contests futile. Electoral frauds sometimes produced victory for no-fence, but it was far more common for the votes of black tenants and laborers to prevail. "Whites favored it, negroes opposed to it" was the common explanation for defeat.[39]

Proponents of the new stock law argued, in the words of one farmer, that "the non-landholding class have no right to vote on this subject. . . . None should be allowed to vote on this question except landholders." Only two years after Georgia's general assembly passed the county-option stock law bill, members of the state grange demanded that the legislature limit the franchise. "The *land owners* of each County" should have the power "to adopt such a stock law as they desire," read their memorial. "It is the right peculiarly of the *owners* of the land to decide . . . the question." Four years later members of the state agricultural society applauded enthusiastically as a planter from Sumter County voiced the same opinion: "The men who own the land are the men who ought to vote upon this question, and not the men who own the stock. I am willing to leave the question to

38. *Transactions of the Georgia State Agricultural Society*, 412, 418, and see 416–17, 422; Atlanta *Constitution*, September 11, 1883; *Acts*, 1876 (No. 79), 316, 1876 (No. 161), 351, 1877 (No. 268), 395, 1882–83 (No. 334), 129.

39. Sparta *Ishmaelite*, November 21, 1883. Numerous frauds appear in contested election results. See, for example, Atlanta *Constitution*, May 2, 4, 5, July 12, August 30, October 4, 9, 1883.

the land-holders, and abide the decision. That is just; that is right."[40]

Black belt legislators regularly introduced legislation to change the franchise, but a de facto disfranchisement of landless blacks took place instead. Whenever most landowners in a black belt county favored the no-fence system, the general assembly overrode the opposition of local poor and enacted it by special statute. Clay County in southwest Georgia offers an example. In 1889 at the request of local white landowners, the legislature imposed the stock law on the 431st and one other of Clay's three militia districts.[41] One hundred adult black males who lived in the 431st district had either signed a petition opposing the statute or, because of illiteracy, had had someone sign for them. No white man signed the petition. The division was not, however, purely racial. Blacks seem to have divided along rough class lines of their own. The petitioners sought support among freeholders and carefully noted those who signed. Eight black landholders opposed the stock law. All of them lived on property they owned in the town of Fort Gaines and would not have been affected by the law. Of the thirteen local black landowners who did not sign, all owned land outside the town.[42]

Clay was a county of large plantations in which rural whites were, almost without exception, landowners or members of landowning families. Two other petitions came from Baldwin County in an older section of the black belt. In Baldwin, as in Clay, most labor was black, but in 1890 a number of landless whites worked as sharehands or laborers in the county. Only whites signed the two petitions in Baldwin, one opposing and one favoring the stock law. Eleven of the thirty-five opponents of the law owned land, but eight of them owned very little—thirty-five acres or less. Eighty-eight whites signed the petition in favor of the law.

40. *Carroll County Times*, May 3, 1878; "Memorial from State Grange of Patrons of Husbandry," February 7, 1874, in Petitions and Memorials, Record of the House and Senate, Georgia Department of Archives and History, Atlanta; *Transactions of the Georgia State Agricultural Society*, 420. See also Milledgeville *Union and Recorder*, April 10, 1883.

41. *Acts*, 1889 (No. 202), 1259–60, 1889 (No. 326), 1267–68.

42. Stock Law Petition, Clay County, 1889, in Petitions and Memorials; Clay County Tax Digest, 1889, Georgia County Property Tax Digests, Georgia Department of Archives and History, Atlanta.

Like most adult white males in rural Baldwin, nearly all were landowners, and of those who were not, surnames identify most as members of landowning families. The holdings of these men were considerably larger than those of opponents. Only seven owned fewer than a hundred acres; none owned fewer than fifty; and while holdings of several hundred acres were most common, a half-dozen owned more than a thousand. The size of these holdings indicates that nearly all of these men certainly employed wage hands and croppers.[43]

It is notable that proponents of no-fence in the black belt seldom mentioned the opposition of landless whites. Rather they tended to describe the division as if it were a purely racial one. Landless white renters, sharehands, and laborers were such a small minority in most black belt counties that proponents of no-fence could easily ignore them. Landless whites were, however, occasionally mentioned in passing. A proponent of no-fence in Sumter County typified these instances as he lumped landless whites with blacks in a division he incongruously described as racial. "I hope they will inaugurate some plan by which we can have a fair election," he wrote. "They will have to disfranchise all but freeholders, which in this case would be strictly justice. For a negro that isn't worth a copper to say (by his ballot) that I must keep up my five miles of fence so his pig, that isn't worth a quarter, can run at large is not only injustice but insulting. So disfranchise the negro and white man that hasn't any land and let us have a fair election."[44]

The response of "several non-freeholders" to this planter was also typical. They were concerned about themselves as white equals and did not identify with their more numerous black counterparts, for they wrote, "There are a few of us in this district . . . who do not own any land, . . . but we feel like we are

43. Petitions, in Milledgeville *Union and Recorder*, July 20, 1890. Baldwin County Tax Digest, 1890, Georgia County Property Tax Digests. That these landowners signed the petition indicates that they were more likely to be interested in the management of their land than were absent or indifferent landowners. Since, in 1890, over 50 percent of the farm units in Baldwin County were tilled by share hands, it is likely that for the most part these landowners farmed with a few wage hands and let out the balance of their lands under the share system.

44. "Simeon," letter, in Americus *Weekly Recorder*, March 22, 1889.

citizens with clean hands." They accused the planter of being willing to sell "his weaker and less fortunate brother into degradation and bondage, by taking his franchise away." Bondage was an interesting metaphor, for theirs was an appeal to white democracy. They reminded the landowners that in the Civil War it was men like them "who gave their lives defending the property of their more affluent countrymen." They insisted that if the stock law passed in a free election they would "have not one word to say, but pass it through the circuitous and often rascally channels of the legislature and we will be found raising our voice in opposition to it all the time." The response was eloquent but ineffective. There were too few landless whites to matter. The legislature imposed the stock law on Sumter County the same year they wrote their letter.[45]

Legislative fiat worked well for planters in counties besides Clay and Sumter. By 1889 all or part of at least forty-four of the sixty-four counties in Georgia's black belt had the stock law. The general assembly had imposed no-fence on over half of these. But the legislature, so willing to intervene where blacks were a majority, was willing to impose the stock law on only three counties outside the black belt. The politics of no-fence assumed a different character where whites were a majority. Such was the case in the upper piedmont.

The upper piedmont witnessed the bitterest conflicts over no-fence. In the late nineteenth century, rapid changes in its economy had effects more comprehensive than, but in some ways comparable to, the effects of emancipation on the internal frontier of the plantation belt. These changes began before the Civil War with the construction of two railroads through upper Georgia. One ran from Chattanooga, Tennessee, south to Atlanta and then through the black belt and wiregrass to the coast at Savannah. The other began at the Alabama border, ran east through Atlanta to Augusta and then continued on through South Carolina to Charleston. After the war, new railroads rapidly crisscrossed the state and by 1890 passed through most counties in the upper piedmont and several mountain counties as well.

45. "Several Non-Freeholders," letter, *ibid.*, April 5, 1889; *Acts*, 1889 (No. [?]), 1269–70.

The upper piedmont was hilly, broken country, a prelude to the mountains to its north. Before the arrival of railroads, its terrain had kept communities socially and economically isolated. In patterns that were typical of towns on the frontier and isolated rural areas before the intrusion of railroads and canals, subsistence agriculture and "home manufacturing" were economic necessities.[46] Artisans performed their crafts using local materials for local markets. Yeomen, so often idealized by writers, tended to live in poverty and filth, but few were likely to go hungry. Although they often raised a bit of cotton, this was solely for home use. Their wives and daughters spun, wove, and sewed the family's clothes. Yeomen mostly raised grain, often using poor techniques and getting low yields even from rich soil, and they raised large numbers of swine and stock in wooded hills about their farms. The size of these farms differed, as did degrees of wealth, but this economy did not create the demand for or the wealth to buy great numbers of slaves; thus, there were very few major slaveholders in the upper piedmont.[47] Of course there was no exact line between the plantation belt and the yeoman-dominated economy to its north. There were yeomen in the plantation belt and small planters in the upper piedmont. But the predominant economic and cultural characteristics of the two regions were more different than they were alike.

Moonshine whiskey, the province of the poorest yeomen, was indicative of the economic structure and isolation of many communities in the upper piedmont. As a United States attorney explained, the moonshine economy arose because "of the difficulty and expense of" transporting corn and grain to market "over roads almost impassable." It was a common saying in moonshine districts that "it is worth two loads of corn to haul one to market." Thus, the prosecutor described the economic pressure that led to making whiskey: "The price of a bushel of corn is

46. For the best work on the effect of transportation in local economics, see George Rogers Taylor, *The Transportation Revolution, 1815–1860* (New York, 1951).

47. This pattern is apparent in all the local histories of the area, the best of which is James C. Bonner, *Georgia's Lost Frontier: The Development of Carroll County* (Athens, 1971), but perhaps more illuminating is Frederick Law Olmsted, *A Journey in the Back Country* (1860; rpr. New York, 1970), Chap. 6, esp. 221–24.

GEORGIA RAILROADS, 1860

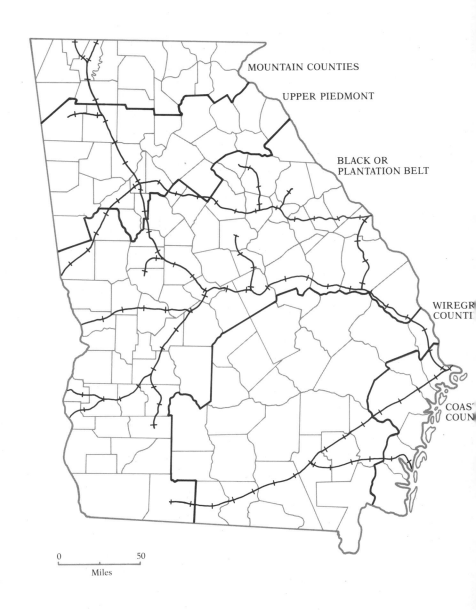

MOUNTAIN COUNTIES

UPPER PIEDMONT

BLACK OR
PLANTATION BELT

WIREGR
COUNTI

COAST
COUN

0   50
   Miles

GEORGIA RAILROADS, 1890

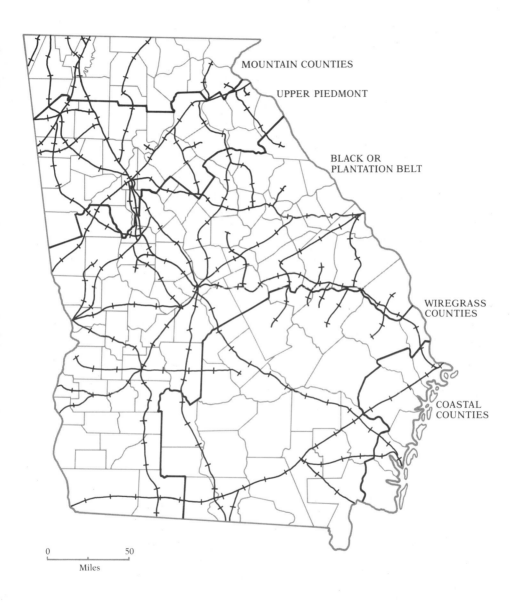

MOUNTAIN COUNTIES

UPPER PIEDMONT

BLACK OR
PLANTATION BELT

WIREGRASS
COUNTIES

COASTAL
COUNTIES

0   50
      Miles

sixty cents, of a gallon of whiskey two dollars, and three gallons of whiskey can . . . be distilled from one bushel of corn."[48] Two-dollar jugs of whiskey were easier and less expensive to transport to market than were bulky sixty-cent bushels of corn.

After the Civil War, moonshiners had a problem. Their stills were illegal under federal tax law. Thus a sporadic but very serious Ku Klux or White Cap war between hill folk and federal revenue officials spanned the late nineteenth century.[49] This violence, like Ku Kluxism in general, was a form of vigilantism through which communities, and yeomen communities in particular, fought hostile values and authority. Moonshiners were too poor to pay the tax on their whiskey and therefore fought the revenue agents of a government that threatened their livelihood. They believed that theirs was a moral cause. In that, even those whites who did not bootleg supported their often poor neighbors who did. The moonshiners and their sympathizers were so numerous that aspiring state politicians without exception pledged themselves to vote for the repeal of the internal revenue laws. Even William H. Felton, a sanctimonious, vituperative preacher-politician who was active in temperance and prohibition movements, courageously supported repeal of the tax on whiskey.[50]

48. Atlanta *Constitution*, September 23, 1883; Horace Kephart, *Our Southern Highlanders* (New York, 1916), 119–90; Nixon, *Forty Acres and Steel Mules*, 12.

49. R. J. Caldwell, testimony, October 23, 1871, James Atkins, testimony, October 24, 1871, Joseph E. Brown, testimony, October 31, 1871, all in *Joint Committee Report on the Ku Klux Klan*, VI, 440–41, 524–25, VII, 812–13; A. W. Shrofine and William P. Ramsey to William Y. Atkinson, June 15, 1896, in Governor's Incoming Correspondence, Georgia State Archives, Atlanta; Atlanta *Constitution*, November 2, 1882, September 1, 8, October 27, 1883, January 24, 1884; Justice Department, General Records, Sources Chronological File, Georgia, 1871–1894, RG 60, National Archives.

50. J. E. Alsbrook to Alfred Colquitt, March 13, 1877, in Governor's Incoming Correspondence; *Cherokee Advance*, July 15, 1882; Ben H. Hill and William H. Felton to President, March 4, 1876, in Rebecca Latimer Felton and William Harrell Felton Papers, University of Georgia Libraries, Rare Books and Manuscript Department, Athens. See also "Interview with Hon. W. H. Felton of Cartersville, Ga., as Published Recently in the Chicago Tribune" (Flier, n.d. [*ca.* 1881], in Felton Papers); *Cherokee Advance*, October 14, 1882; Joseph E. Brown, interview, Columbus *Enquirer-Sun*, January 22, 1884 (Clipping in Scrapbook I, 1884, Joseph E. Brown and Elizabeth G. Brown Papers, University of Georgia Libraries, Rare Books and Manuscript Department, Athens); Americus *Weekly Recorder*, February 28, 1889; Athens *Banner*, n.d., quoted in James C. Bonner, "The Guber-

As railroads gradually made markets accessible to more and more farmers in the upper piedmont, moonshine and, more generally, the subsistence economy it symbolized retreated farther and farther into the hills. In the twentieth century, only the most isolated of mountain counties harbored many bootlegging farmers.[51]

White lightning was not, however, the only casualty of economic change. Transportation brought cheap manufactured goods that undercut the monopoly and, thus, livelihood of local artisans and that gradually ended the domestic manufacturing of many necessities, including, for example, textiles and clothes. Despite a rapidly growing population, small local manufacturers became rarer. In Cobb County, northwest of Atlanta, there were ninety-three small manufacturing establishments in 1880. They included shops that made, among other things, paper, boots, furniture, and woolen, cotton, and leather goods. By 1890 only sixty were left. During the late nineteenth century, this decline was repeated in many upper piedmont counties. Between 1880 and 1890, the number of manufacturers in Cherokee went from fifty-five to twenty-four; in Hall, from fifty-five to twenty-three.[52] Gradually, riverside towns with industrial mills (usually making textiles) would more than replace artisanal employment in piedmont counties, but of course, the mills meant a very different way of life.

Perhaps the most numerous victims of economic change were in the class of its most numerous beneficiaries: the farmers. Improved transportation broke local monopolies, provided markets for crops, and released farm families from the endless toil of

natorial Career of J. W. Northen" (M.A. thesis, University of Georgia, 1936), 14; *Acts*, 1877 (Resolution No. 7), 366.

51. Reflected in the decreasing frequency of reports on bootlegging to the attorney general of the United States, in Justice Department, General Records, RG 60, NA.

52. U.S. Department of the Interior, Census Office, *Report of the Manufactures of the United States at the Tenth Census, 1880*, Table 5, pp. 207–11; U.S. Department of the Interior, Census Office, *Report of Manufacturing Industries of the United States at the Eleventh Census; 1890*, Pt. I, *Totals for States and Industries*, Table 6, pp. 382–85. See also Forrest McDonald and Grady McWhiney, "The Antebellum Southern Herdsman: A Reinterpretation," *Journal of Southern History*, XLI, 147–66.

POPULATION DENSITY OF GEORGIA
UPPER PIEDMONT, 1880–1890

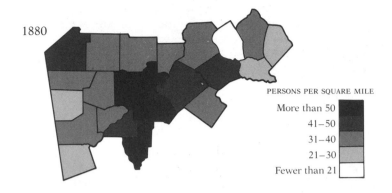

1880

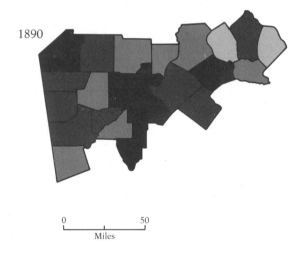

PERSONS PER SQUARE MILE

More than 50
41–50
31–40
21–30
Fewer than 21

1890

0   50
└─────┴─────┘
      Miles

IMPROVED FARMLANDS IN GEORGIA
UPPER PIEDMONT, 1880–1890

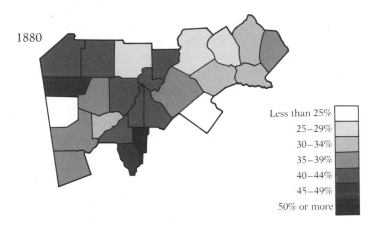

1880

Less than 25%
25–29%
30–34%
35–39%
40–44%
45–49%
50% or more

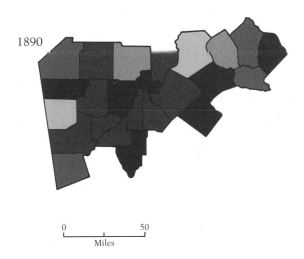

1890

0   50
Miles

home manufacturing. It encouraged farmers to increase the size of their fields and plant crops for sale. And it encouraged them to plant cotton, the most valuable of southern staple crops. But the opportunities that railroads brought to subsistence farmers also meant a new vulnerability. The weather had always been an unpredictable adversary, but the market, in which hard labor and bumper crops might be crushed by low prices, seemed even more capricious and, like federal revenue agents, more unjust than God's nature. Yeomen were cautious as they committed themselves to raising cotton. Many farm owners, renters, and share hands in the upper piedmont continued to devote a greater share of their fields to corn and other grains than did their counterparts in other sections of the state. But bad years and the famous crop-lien system still conspired to trap many formerly independent landowners in a cycle of endless debt and dependence upon merchants. Many yeomen sold their farms and moved elsewhere (often to wiregrass counties) to escape bankruptcy. Others held on until their debts exceeded their assets and merchants, unable or unwilling to extend credit further, foreclosed their mortgages.

Transportation was not, however, the only agent of economic change. The rapid population growth that affected the black belt was an even greater force in the upper piedmont. There by 1890 many counties had over forty persons per square mile. Landholdings too small to be divided among sons, debt-ridden yeomen who had lost their lands, and perhaps most numerous, migrants from the always poor mountain counties to the north meant that white renters, share hands, and wage laborers were increasingly common in the upper piedmont during the late nineteenth century. The yeomanry was giving birth to a large white laboring class.

Expanding population and quickly expanding cultivation meant that the woodlands that fed large numbers of swine and cattle were quickly disappearing. As in the black belt, this pattern brought laws (though fewer and less rigorous) redefining customary rights of property by limiting hunting, fishing, and gathering. And the fence-law fights, which in the early 1870s were limited to the black belt and a few counties bordering it, expanded to include most of the upper piedmont in the 1880s.

The arguments heard in the fence-law battles of the upper piedmont were the same as those in the black belt. Proponents of no-fence spoke endlessly of the expense and inefficiency of enclosing crops and of the injustice of allowing nonlandowners to share in the decision. Opponents complained bitterly that their rights as landless men would be denied. An increasingly large white laboring class added another dimension to the fight that could, in the black belt, be too simplistically described as a contest between white land and black labor.

In the upper piedmont, two overlapping patterns of division were important: one geographical and one class-related. The geographical pattern arose because the internal frontier retreated gradually. The especially broken terrain or infertility of one neighborhood, for example, could perpetuate traditional patterns longer than more accessible or fertile neighborhoods. In the latter, commercial farming, the size of individual landholdings, and consequently, tenancy and sharecropping expanded quickest. Thus neighborhoods of very small farmers, the poorer end of the landowning class, tended to oppose the stock law longer than districts of larger and more commercially oriented proprietors. This pattern of division was reflected incidentally in local debates over whether the no-fence law was yet necessary: "Mr. Pitts says we have a good range," wrote one proponent of no-fence. "I would like to know where it is. . . . Surely he has not been anywhere but on the Oak mountains."[53]

As in Baldwin County, there were reasons for the very smallest landowners to oppose the stock law even after the woods of their neighborhood were depleted. As many with little land pointed out, they were unlikely to have access to water for their stock, and they had insufficient land to devote to pasture. For them, poor open woodlands were better than no pastures at all. In Cherokee County, for example, a proponent of no-fence reported that "its strongest opponents" were small farmers. "Their complaint was that it would deprive them of pasturage, and that they would be forced to despair of their stock."[54]

Legislators could not ignore the opposition of yeomen as

53. *Carroll County Times*, September 1, 1882.
54. "Plow Boy," letter, in *Southwestern News* (Dawson), April 29, 1887; F. L. G., letter, in *Cherokee Advance*, June 9, 1881.

lightheartedly as they could that of black workers. Small farmers held considerable collective political influence. Rather than impose the stock law upon upper piedmont counties, the general assembly, dominated by large landowners, extended the principle of local option. In 1881 it empowered militia districts (the political subdivisions of county government) to hold referenda to adopt the no-fence system.[55] Although this change worked against the interests of small landowners by allowing the gradual extension of the no-fence area, it nevertheless possessed the legitimizing air of democracy.

The pattern of class divisions evident in the controversy is interesting. Unlike their counterparts in the black belt, proponents of no-fence in the upper piedmont could not generally ignore their landless white opponents as numerically insignificant. But no-fence men still called for the disfranchisement of all landless men, white and black, whom they classified together. "Poor white folks and niggers should have no voice in government," they said or, if more circumspect, implied. The bitterness of no-fence men was proportionate to the number and strength of their landless opponents. "Renters and negroes" prevent a change in the law, complained John Dent. These "men, white and negro, who own not a foot of land, nor a stick of timber in the world, are an agrarian party who oppose capital and capitalists on the grounds of envy and jealousy." (Dent used *agrarianism* in its antique sense as it referred to republican Levellers in England during the seventeenth century.) "The spirit of communism is fully displayed," he wrote on the same occasion. "There is a natural antagonism between labor and capital, . . . and the one that has the power . . . will oppose the other. Consequently capital will rule until Revolution upsets law and order."[56]

In the upper piedmont, even more than in the black belt, calls for the disfranchisement of landless whites were a serious violation of the white social cosmography. The caste line was supposed to be the primary division of southern society. Class was

55. *Acts*, 1880–81 (No. 401), 79–80.

56. "Zoilus," letter, in Sparta *Ishmaelite*, October 3, 1883; L., letter in *Carroll County Times*, May 3, 1878; Mathis, Mathis, and Purcell (eds.), *Dent Journals*, XIV, September 27, 1880, XVIII, November 17, 1886, and see XV, April [?], May 9, 1882.

not supposed to supersede race. Faced with a challenge to their caste faith and their economic interests, landless whites in the upper piedmont, like those in the black belt, spoke out in defense of both. "Because of my opposition to the stock law Mr. L. accused me of being in favor of negro equality," wrote a landless man. "I am about as far from that as the east is from the west." Why, then, the man asked, does Mr. L. say the landless white men should not be able to vote? "Not every man that is poor in purse is poor in mind," wrote another. "Many have more genuine love of country at heart than a thousand such puppets as would abuse a man for his poverty by classing him with a 'nigger.'" Like their yeoman forebears during Reconstruction, such men showed the depth of their commitment to white democracy not only in their rhetoric but by occasionally resorting to moral vigilantism against their opponents.[57]

If there is any irony in this debate, it is that the landowners had already adopted a program of gradual disfranchisement that would, among other things, expedite the victory of no-fence. Unable to exclude blacks from the polls because of the Fifteenth Amendment, the Redeemer constitution established a cumulative poll tax. After 1877 any man who had not paid his annual tax in any year, no matter how long past, lost his vote until he paid all past taxes due. The one-dollar poll tax kept many poor men from the polls each year, but the cumulative tax gradually disfranchised many, perhaps most poor whites and blacks. By the 1890s, a period of passionate political conflict, fewer than 50 percent of Georgia's electorate participated in elections. Participation of whites and blacks was substantially below that in southern states with no cumulative system.[58]

During the 1880s no-fence men won an increasing number of elections not only because the internal frontier continued to retreat from neighborhood after neighborhood but also because opponents of no-fence gradually became less and less powerful.

57. *Carroll County Times*, June 21, 1878; "Zoilus," letter, in Sparta *Ishmaelite*, October 3, 1883, and see June 19, 1885; Atlanta *Constitution*, September 8, November 6, 1883.

58. J. Morgan Kousser, *The Shaping of Southern Politics: Suffrage Restriction and the Establishment of the One-Party South, 1880–1910* (New Haven, 1974), 65, and see Tables 3.2, 3.3, 3.4, pp. 67, 68, 72.

Similarly, political discourse during the 1880s increasingly reflected divisions only above the indistinct line that separated landowners and the most prosperous of renters and share hands from the poorer ranks of Georgia society. Politics continued to reflect divisions between upper piedmont and black belt, planters and yeomen, town and country. But it reflected only one side of the division between landowners and laborers.

Perhaps the landowners' violation of the white social cosmography was a sign of calculated insincerity, a sign that landowners were only using racism as an instrument of class control. But there is such voluminous evidence of the extreme racism of landowners to discount that view as facile if not doctrinaire. Landowners did use racism as a political tool, but that is hardly the whole story. During Reconstruction, in black codes and in violence, powerful white landowners and their poorer white counterparts had both shown themselves committed to a racially bifurcated society. Because of federal law, the line between white and black could not be as rigorously maintained as most, perhaps nearly all, white southerners wished. Therefore, the other divisions among southerners—divisions based on property and long evident even under the slave regime—became potentially more tense than they had been before. This was first apparent in the Ku Klux violence, which showed whites without black employees more determined to maintain the "ideal" racial order rigorously than were employers economically vulnerable to the disruption of black labor. It was apparent as white landowners redesigned labor law. Unable to place blacks in a racially defined category of labor, landowners adopted self-serving statutes that would apply to white as well as black workers. It was apparent in the exclusion of poor whites as well as blacks from the polls. And it was apparent as white landowners redefined property rights to secure their own interests while displaying ostentatious indifference to the fate of their landless neighbors.

But certainly actions based upon division of property did not mean that divisions of race had been replaced. There was a great deal of class oppression in the New South, but as innumerable and redundant studies pointing out the obvious have shown, racial discrimination remained potent in every aspect of southern life. The sacrifice of landless whites to the interests of property meant that two overlapping systems of social division—one of class and one of caste, one tied to property and one to race— both of which had always existed in Georgia, were coming into conflict far more than the white social cosmography meant to allow. At times these two systems reinforced each other, as the white cosmography said they should. Surely this was the case with racial discrimination. But whiteness was not and had never been synonymous with property, capital, and membership in society. The potential for conflict had always existed in a widely shared social ideology that erroneously equated the class and caste systems. After Reconstruction, federal law promoted conflict, for the Fourteenth and Fifteenth Amendments limited the ability of white southerners to reconcile their two divergent systems of social order in the way their white social cosmography said they should. After 1890, legal and mandatory segregation would offer a partial practical and ideological solution, but it was geared primarily toward urban and industrial life. Southern agricultural society, without the hierarchy of labor created with mechanized production, remained caught midway between its class and caste systems.

Chapter VI

CASTE, CLASS, AND THE PERSISTENCE OF SOUTHERN POVERTY

This is no Country for a man who has to start from the bottom rung of the ladder, no room for enterprise. You make but little and must hold on to that little to keep your ground. . . . It naturally *makes men close* and *selfish*, as one can not afford to be liberal.

—John H. Dent, 1884

C ONTROVERSIES ABOUT fence law exemplified a more general pattern of socioeconomic conflict among rural whites. Unable to define the caste barrier as rigidly as they wished, white southerners struggled to reconcile their class interests and their caste faith. Different groups adopted different strategies. Planters tended to interpret any challenge to their selfishly conceived class interests as a challenge to the caste system upon which the plantation economy was based. But white resistance to class abuse was also predicated upon caste norms. White landless laborers and small-to-middling white proprietors fought abusive planters in terms of what Pierre van den Berghe and George Fredrickson have called *Herrenvolk* democracy.[1] Claims of equal membership in the supposedly superior race justified and defined the resistance of poor-to-middling whites and inextricably tied their notions of equality and justice to black subordination. The *Herrenvolk* mentality, in defining the terms of dissent, inevitably defined the caste limits of possible social and economic reform. Those limits were responsible for the persistent, unnecessarily dense poverty of the New South. All southerners, white and black, prominent and destitute, remained poorer than they need have been. Ultimately, the self-interested

1. Pierre van den Berghe, *Race and Racism: A Comparative Perspective* (New York, 1967), 17–18; Fredrickson, *The Black Image in the White Mind, passim.*

bigotry of the caste system oppressed not only black southerners but also their white oppressors.

The commitment of landless whites to the caste system seems, perhaps, least explicable. Many historians have described racial oppression as simply a subset of more general class oppression. They have stressed the similarities between the fates of white and black labor. Reiterating the greatest fears of prominent Democrats, including many planters, these historians have therefore been prone to interpret the resistance of white workers to abuse and, most dramatically, the Farmers' Alliance and the Populist Revolt as challenges to the caste foundation of the plantation economy: as incipient class coalitions traversing, if tentatively, the barrier of race.[2] On its face, this view seems plausible enough. Because agriculture, unlike industry, did not entail an elaborate hierarchy of skills, the fate of white and black workers was in many ways the same. Both could be wage hands, sharecroppers, share tenants, and renters. Patterns of violence, arson, and theft indicate that they felt similar grievances and took similar revenge.[3] They seem to have aspired to the same relative economic independence. And they both resisted, as best they could, exploitation by landlords.

Nonetheless, this view depends on a mistaken exaggeration of the similarities between the fates of landless whites and blacks. There were also crucial differences between them, differences very important in their own minds. To understand the interplay between the culturally defined caste barrier and the economically defined class divisions among whites, one must recognize that the South's elaborate system of racial etiquette and prejudice preserved an important degree of respectability for landless whites and placed them apart and above their black counterparts. For a white tenant to be called "Mister" while a black, if he were aged and white-haired, at best received the honorific title "Uncle" reflected different social status and a different lati-

2. Woodward, *Tom Watson*; Lawrence Goodwyn, *Democratic Promise: The Populist Movement in America* (New York, 1976).

3. Smith, "Violence in Georgia's Black Belt," 66–67; *John Hammock v. State*, Quitman County, January, 1874, *Charles Allen v. State*, Sumter County, April, 1892, Supreme Court File Nos. A-6744, A-17397; Atlanta *Constitution*, September 5, 1883.

tude in behavior that had real substance. Landless whites received a social and economic dividend from discrimination that reinforced their long-standing commitment to the caste system. Nor were they merely passive recipients of that dividend. Their caste faith led them to expect it and, when it was not forthcoming, often to try to insist upon it. As in the case of fence laws, their resistance to abuse by landowners invariably entailed demands that the caste system be strengthened.

The tension between abusive landowners and landless whites may be seen in the case of immigration schemes. Despite the racial distinctions that helped to elevate whites and subordinate blacks, countervailing class interests and prejudice worked simultaneously in the minds of large and middling landowners to push landless whites into the category of irresponsible, indolent, ignorant, and unreliable workers. Landowners defined the ideal worker as abjectly subordinate and unfailingly industrious—an extreme definition born in slavery. They used racist doctrine to explain the failure of blacks to match unrealistic expectations. But slavery had, as Republicans charged, debased not only the labor of blacks but also labor in general. Landowning employers understood all labor in terms of the standards established for the ideal black slave and, in a peculiar inversion, expected white labor, by virtue of supposedly racial superiority, to fulfill their expectations better than blacks ever could. They were, of course, horribly disappointed.

As white landowners complained about black labor and attributed the economic problems of the South to it, they periodically demanded a "superior" work force. "Negroes are by nature indolent and superstitious," they would say. The "utter worthlessness of labor such as ours . . . [is proven] each recurring year;" we "need to make ourselves independent of the *negro*."[4] One theoretical solution that was popular among planters was to seek white or, occasionally, Oriental "immigrant" workers. (*Immigrant* meant anyone from outside the South.) During Reconstruction, for example, Sidney Andrews reported widespread

4. S. H. Bassett, address to the Georgia State Agricultural Society, in *Southern Cultivator*, November 1884; "Sigma," letter in Dawson *Weekly Journal*, March 13, 1877; Edgefield (S.C.) *Advertiser*, June 17, 1868, quoted in Vernon Burton, "Race and Reconstruction," 36, emphasis in the original.

sentiment in favor of securing white workers from the North. Frances Butler joined with her neighbors to "order" seventy Chinese coolies as a substitute for "negro labour." And over and over, whites expressed the same opinion: "We can drive the niggers out and import coolies that will work better, and at less expense, and relieve us of this cursed nigger impudence." In 1886 a professor at the University of Georgia repeated the same proposal with the usual professional solemnity. "To be able to improve farming," he declared knowingly, "intelligent and scientific laborers must be brought to work in place of the unskilled laborer—the negro—who is incapable of receiving scientific instruction." After the beginning of the twentieth century, planters continued to attempt this sort of immigration scheme.[5]

As one historian has noted, the results on campaigns to replace blacks with immigrants were "pathetic." Some planters, as always, blamed the failure on blacks themselves. In 1893, for example, one wrote that immigrants would not come to the South until blacks were colonized abroad. Abhorrence of the "manners, color, etc." of blacks supposedly kept whites away. Actually, few white or Chinese immigrants would come to the South on the terms that planters offered. As one Georgia employer testified in 1899, "the Italian or Chinaman can not do [field labor] . . . for less than [we pay] the negro."[6] Planters were surprised and disappointed. White laborers, whether immigrant or southern, commonly demanded more than blacks received. They would not usually agree to live in the same quarters, work the long hours expected of them, or settle for rations of fatback and cornmeal. And not only did racial etiquette allow whites to resist the demands of employers with a vehemence denied their

5. Andrews, *The South Since the War*, 359–60; Leigh, *Ten Years on a Georgia Plantation*, 146; 168; Reid, *After the War*, 301, quoted in Oscar Zeichner, "The Transition from Slave to Free Labor in the Southern States," *Agricultural History*, XIII (January, 1939), 25; Americus *Weekly Recorder*, February 25, 1886, and see August 28, 1885; Hart, *The Southern South*, 267. On immigration schemes in other states, see Wharton, *The Negro in Mississippi*, 97–102, 212: Vernon Burton, "Race and Reconstruction," 36; Hoffman, *Race Traits and Tendencies of the American Negro*, 252.

6. Willard Range, *A Century of Georgia Agriculture, 1850–1950* (Athens, 1954), 79, and see 80; *Southern Cultivator*, January, 1893; James Barrett, testimony, in Industrial Commission, *Report on Agricultural Labor*, 100–101.

black counterparts, but whites were also too obviously ambitious, too obviously anxious to escape their status as laborers and become independent farmers.[7] White laborers shared the same goals as blacks and were freer to pursue them vigorously.

The reaction of large and middling employers to assertive white southern and immigrant workers was striking. "I thought that white labor was the most reliable," wrote one in 1872. "But I have fairly tested it this year and the Nigger is best. . . . [Blacks] are more tractable and most easily satisfied. . . . Not so with the white man. They are captious, fault-finding, suspicious and . . . contentious." Another employer wrote, "I prefer the Negro to any of them [Dutch, Canadian, Irish, Swedish, or Yankee]. The Negro is not so quick as many white laborers, but he demands so much less in the way of supplies, is more acclimated and generally easier to get along with." Contemporary scholars summarized the opinion of white employers. "The negro is preferred to the native or foreign white [wage] hand by a large number of Southern landowners," wrote one; "he gives less trouble than a white man because he is content with less comfortable lodgings, with coarser food, and with smaller wages." Another explained that "the white man . . . demands a good house, stoves [sic], and a diversified diet, while the negro seems content with a log cabin and a fire place, and with corn, bacon and molasses as articles of food."[8]

Of course blacks were no more content than the whites, but members of the growing white laboring class were freer to make demands, and they demanded that they be treated better than the black workers around them. Just as urban whites in Georgia refused to work beside blacks and insisted that whites hold the superior positions, just as white members of the Knights of Labor in Georgia kept their chapters lily-white over the objections of black workers, so too, landless whites insisted that they be in

7. Wharton, *The Negro in Mississippi*, 100–102; Hart, *The Southern South*, 267.

8. Mathis, Mathis, and Purcell (eds.), *Dent Journals*, X, July 8–9, 1872; Letter in the Louisville [Ky.?] *Journal*, n.d., quoted in Asa H. Gordon, *The Georgia Negro: A History* (Ann Arbor, 1937), 70–71; Bruce, *The Plantation Negro as a Freeman*, 27; Hammond, *The Cotton Industry*, 185. See also Hoffman, *Race Traits and Tendencies of the American Negro*, 252; Somers, *The Southern States Since the War*, 76.

positions on the agricultural ladder superior to blacks on the same plantation.[9] Just as racially defined subordinate labor was the foundation of planter power, so too, it was the basis of class awareness among poor-to-middling whites and the demands they made to employers.

White workers insisted on important privileges, such as gardens, that were denied to blacks on the same plantation. They insisted on superior houses.[10] And they vigorously resisted attempts to supervise their work on the same terms that blacks were supervised. An agent of the Census Bureau reported, "the principal cause of dissatisfaction with them is due to the higher standard of living. . . . They are unwilling to live in the two room houses furnished negroes and cannot get along on the allowance for food the black man finds sufficient. . . . [They are known] for complaining of their surroundings and being hard to please. . . . [And they are known for] resenting the imperious manner so natural to the planter accustomed to be obeyed by an inferior people."[11]

This conflict between landowners and landless whites helped to produce a rural equivalent to urban segregation: a class structure among landless men that inexactly followed racial lines. White renters, share hands, and perhaps even wage hands tended to be a bit more prosperous than their local black counterparts. Landowners, with rare exceptions, ran their farms with all white or all black labor.[12] And although in Georgia as a whole a great many whites and blacks fell into each category of labor, and while statistics for the state as a whole obscure local differences, within each region of the state, within each county, within each

9. Atlanta *Constitution*, March 28, 1883; Maurice S. Evans, *Black and White in the Southern States: A Study of Race Problems in the United States from a South African Point of View* (London, 1915), 63–65; Gordon, *The Georgia Negro*, 72–73; Hoffman, *Race Traits and Tendencies of the American Negro*, 278; Raper, *Preface to Peasantry*, 148–49; Savannah *Tribune*, February 5, 19, July 30, August 6, 13, September 17, 24, 1887.

10. Atwater and Woods, "Dietary Studies," 11; O. B. Stevens, testimony, in Industrial Commission, *Report on Agricultural Labor*, 911; Bruce, *The Plantation Negro as a Freeman*, 27; Hammond, *The Cotton Industry*, 185.

11. Robert Preston Brooks, "Economic Conditions" (MS dated 1911, in Brooks Papers), Vol. II, Sec. 8, p. 7.

12. Hart, *The Southern South*, 254–55.

Status of Whites and Blacks in Sample Census Districts, 1880

	Whites			Blacks		
	Owners	Renters	Share Hands	Owners	Renters	Share Hands
Black Belt						
Baldwin (District 5)	27	0	20	14	2	73
Greene (District 33)	36	7	6	9	21	35
Quitman (District 95)	25	5	5	5	6	8
Sumter (District 72)	102	2	36	14	1	96
Upson (District 137)	194	11	8	4	7	2
Upper Piedmont						
Floyd (Districts 71 and 62)	169	18	113	29	8	96
Gwinnett (District 115)	84	4	35	4	0	2
Haralson (District 141)	146	1	77	0	0	1
Coastal						
Glynn (District 55)	29	5	2	118	5	2
TOTALS	812	53	302	197	50	315

SOURCE: Eighth Census, 1880: Agricultural Schedules (microfilm).
NOTES: These statistics do not include wage hands, who were overwhelmingly black and who were on the bottom rung of the agricultural ladder. Share hands include both sharecroppers and share tenants.

neighborhood, landless whites clustered on the higher rungs of the agricultural ladder while a greater proportion of blacks occupied rungs farther down. Where there were many white renters, share tenants, and croppers, blacks were mostly croppers and wage hands. The hierarchy was even more noticeable in the upper piedmont, where landless whites were relatively more numerous, than it was in the black belt. This is why John Dent could inexactly but understandably refer to renters and Negroes as if they were two separate categories. The divisions were not as absolute as landless whites wished. The constraints of federal law did much to prevent that. But within each locality the results were clear enough to show why landless whites felt and in fact were divided from blacks by superior status and income. As a northerner farming in Georgia explained, white and black landless men did "not come in contact very much on the same lines of work."[13]

The *Herrenvolk* expectations of landless whites and the pressure they put upon landowners did not by themselves create the racial hierarchy of rural labor. Differences in the productivity of white and black workers helped. The productivity of whites, even when they were poor, tended to be superior to that of blacks, who suffered from greater imposed ignorance. Therefore, even those landowners who shunned white wage hands and sharecroppers as too intractable preferred whites, where they could get them, in the less closely supervised positions of share tenant and renter.[14] In the late nineteenth and early twentieth century, as population grew and mountain and up-country whites moved south in search of work, they were able to push blacks off some old plantations.[15] An agent of the Census Bureau reported in 1911 that, whether in the black belt or in the upper piedmont, differences in productivity contributed to the pattern by which blacks were hired as wage laborers and sharecroppers, while whites farmed as share tenants and renters.[16]

At first these differences in productivity were the legacy of slavery, but they persisted. Indeed, they increased over time, as whites continued to receive superior education and training. By the late 1920s and early 1930s, when there were several excellent studies of the plantation system in Georgia, the social and economic dividend that the caste system gave to landless whites was rather large. Whether comparing white and black wage hands, or sharecroppers, or share tenants, or renters, whites were substantially better off than blacks in the same county. There

13. J. H. Hale, testimony, in Industrial Commission, *Report on Agricultural Labor*, 401.

14. DeCanio, *Agriculture in the Postbellum South*, 12, 209–19, 224; Robert Higgs, *Competition and Coercion: Blacks in the American Economy, 1865–1914* (Cambridge, Mass., 1979), 71–72; Nixon, *Possum Trot*, 104; Brooks, "Economic Conditions," Vol. II, Sec. 1, pp. 1–2, Sec. 2, pp. 3–4, Sec. 4, pp. 2–4, Sec. 8, pp. 3–4.

15. Raper, *Preface to Peasantry*, 105, 187–90; Wharton, *The Negro in Mississippi*, 104.

16. Brooks, "Economic Conditions," II, *passim*; Raper, *Preface to Peasantry*, 197, Table 39; W. B. Hill, "Rural Survey of Clarke County, Georgia," 19, and Table 3; Woofter, *Negro Migration*, 65–67, Table 11.

were large differences in cash income, the quality of housing, the size of farms, and the value of homegrown food between whites and blacks in the same categories of labor.[17] This dividend from discrimination ratified the long-standing caste norms of land-less whites, but it is important to remember that white and black laborers endured different degrees of poverty, not wealth. Whether in 1880 or 1930, the dividend came to whites who were stuck in an unreformed plantation system—a system that kept white and black landless men and the South in general poor.

Although the plantation system remained unreformed, the continuing racial pattern of relative productivity and, therefore, relative prosperity among whites was a result of the small measure of reform that did come to the New South. As one planter wrote on the eve of World War I, "After '65 we had a few white[s] . . . [who] were mostly worthless and the negro man from slavery was the better man. [A] few things have changed. We have more whites and they have improved by education and farm instructions of various institutes and they are far superior to the negro."[18] Landless whites were, of course, not responsible for reforms like farmer institutes. Nor were reforms targeted to help landless men. Rather, a few benefits from reforms instituted by and designed to serve small-to-middling white proprietors trickled down within the caste system to poorer whites.

Small-to-middling white proprietors and their *Herrenvolk* faith played a crucial role in reform and in the southern economy. Agricultural reform depended upon these men, first, because they were not protected from the poverty that was one result of the plantation economy and, second, because they (unlike landless whites) were politically powerful enough to force action, however slow, upon the New South creed. This is not to suggest that the small-to-middling farmers sought agricultural reform over the objections of planters and planter-merchants. The fight among competing interests was not that clearly drawn. If the available choices had been clearly understood and self-consciously made, perhaps they would have been made differently. However, small-to-middling farmers did seek self-interested

17. Raper, *Preface to Peasantry*, 35, 64, 42, 51.
18. No name, Bulloch County (Questionnaire, "Inquiries I," 1912, in Brooks Papers).

forms of social investment, such as improved education, farmer institutes, and in the twentieth century, improved roads, the expense of which planters opposed. Through these reforms, small-to-middling farmers slowly created areas of New South agriculture within the stagnant plantation economy and improved the necessary rural base for regional economic development.

The most important pattern of relative prosperity within the South distinguished poorer areas dominated by planters from relatively more prosperous areas dominated by small-to-middling white proprietors. This pattern held true within the black belt. More important, it held true in comparing the planter-dominated black belt to the upper piedmont, dominated by small-to-middling white proprietors. According to the federal census, this pattern was obvious in the late nineteenth century, and it was increasingly marked in the twentieth.[19] It meant that small-to-middling white farmers, concentrated upon poor lands, "produced greater yields per capita and per acre" than white and black sharehands and renters, "concentrated upon the most fertile soil." Paradoxically, the best soil produced inferior yields (hence more poverty) "and was rapidly being exhausted."[20]

Of course, one should also not exaggerate the well-being of small-to-middling white farmers. In the late nineteenth century they were poor, and improvements came to them only at an excruciatingly slow pace. Some lost their farms before improved methods and credit facilities could save them. Decentralized plantations, feeding on the failure of small-to-middling farmers, followed cotton culture into the upper piedmont and had the same harmful effects on agriculture there that they had in the black belt.[21] In both regions the productivity of plantations generally lagged behind that of small-to-middling holdings of inferior soil farmed by proprietors.

In plantation districts, the effects of caste and class arrogance were concrete. Assumptions of caste and class superiority were so deeply and pervasively held that they skewed the socioeconomic behavior of most large landowners into patterns that,

19. Hilgard, *Report on Cotton Production in the United States*, II, 332; Nixon, *Forty Acres and Steel Mules*, 21.

20. Woodward, *Origins of the New South*, 208.

21. Nixon, *Lower Piedmont Country*, 54–55.

while rational, were less than optimal, that were culturally immune to substantial reform, and that seriously hampered southern economic development. Although large landowners paid a heavy price for specious selfishness, many of them, unlike laborers, renters, and small-to-middling proprietors, were sufficiently cushioned by profit from the most painful consequences of their own error to avoid contemplating even economically self-serving elementary change. Although reform was in the economic self-interest of large landowners, it would have threatened the social and economic hierarchy of their communities. For that reason, agricultural reform came to plantation districts later than to those areas dominated by small-to-middling white farmers. For that reason, the black belt, which was dominated by plantations, lagged behind the upper piedmont, which despite the incursion of plantations continued to be dominated by small-to-middling white proprietors. And for that reason, most of the South remained too poor to sustain the broad industrial development necessary for regional prosperity.

Responsibility for this tragedy is not attributable solely to planters. The caste conception of southern society afflicted every group of whites. Many white southerners had a reasonably sophisticated understanding of their region's economic problems, but there were debilitating gaps in that understanding. Even New South reformers who criticized the effects of plantation agriculture succumbed to the caste prejudices upon which it was predicated and therefore failed to prescribe an adequate remedy for the behavior of many planters and planter-merchants. The failure to understand assured the failure to act; so there was little or no reform in plantation districts in the late nineteenth century or, for that matter, much of the twentieth. Most important, the caste conception of reform limited the efforts of the one collectively powerful reform group: small-to-middling white proprietors. They instituted changes to benefit solely themselves, adamantly excluding blacks. In thus contorting the New South creed of middle-class whites, the caste faith limited the potential for regional economic growth to the detriment of all southerners.

Historians have tended too often to tie the New South creed to the personality of its most effective spokesman, Henry Grady, the insufferably ingratiating Pollyanna who edited the Atlanta *Constitution*.[22] In fact, the New South creed was a widely shared and espoused understanding of the South's problems and owed less to Grady's originality than has been conventionally assumed. Grady's self-promotion, tedious ebullience, and often groundless optimism have been, however, a worthy symbolic target for agrarian-minded writers who lament the very lamentable fate of many farmers and farm workers in the late nineteenth century and who, rather irrelevantly, celebrate the values of a pastoral ideal that never existed.

In pastoral allegories, the New South creed has been cast as an apostasy to southern values; its popularity among poor white groups has been described as a "delusion," and fault for the fate of poor farmers has been attributed to "oppressive" capitalism—the same force that Grady and others supposedly championed. In attributing responsibility for southern poverty to capitalism and capitalists, critics of the New South creed have written tales of inspiring combat between the forces of light and the forces of darkness, but they have offered little to explain the chronic problems of the South, and they have systematically ignored the validity, indeed, the practical imperative of much of the New South creed.[23] The primary reasons for southern poverty lay within the South.

Critics have stressed the industrial part of the reformers' program and its apparent failure to deliver the South from poverty. In the standard interpretation of New South industrialization, the "colonial" status of the South is described as a product of "foreign" northern investment. To serve their own regional interests at the expense of southern regional prosperity, northerners allegedly both concentrated investment in extractive industries and expropriated or exported southern profits rather than reinvesting them locally. "Cut off from the better-paying jobs and the higher opportunities" by northern investors, claims his-

22. On Grady, see the worshipful Raymond B. Nixon, *Henry Grady, Spokesman of the New South* (New York, 1943). On the New South creed, see Gaston, *The New South Creed*.

23. Both Woodward's *Tom Watson* and his *Origins of the New South* fall into this category. So do more recent works, including most notably Goodwyn, *Democratic Promise*.

torian C. Vann Woodward, "the great majority of Southerners were confined to the worn grooves of a tributary economy. Some emigrated to other sections, but the mass of them stuck to farming, mining, forestry, or some other low-wage industry, whether they liked it or not. The inevitable result was further intensification of the old problem of worn-out soil, cut-over timber lands, and worn-out mines."[24] Thus the well-intentioned southern appeal for northern capital supposedly deepened regional dependence and poverty.

Southern advocates of diversified manufacturing had a more cogent understanding of their region's tributary status. They frequently complained that southern stores were "filled with articles that are brought from a distance." Southern industries, "home manufactures" as they were called, promised regional "prosperity and growth" by relieving southerners from their dependence upon imports from the North and by creating an expanding cycle of local trade that would multiply the number of times profits from "exported" cotton changed hands within the South.[25] "It is desirable that we should keep our money at home," reformers said, for when southerners "purchase from abroad and from strangers . . . the earnings of the State go to build up other States" instead of the home economy.[26] Reformers said that local service industries, such as insurance companies, and factories, whether producing textiles, carriages, brooms, stoves, sewing machines, or something else, all helped to deliver the South from chronic poverty.[27] "Southern enterprise" promised to keep money "in Southern hands."[28]

As reformers recognized, profits were a secondary consideration. Wages and other corporate expenditures were the most important regional benefit from industry. The expenses of manufacturing were the most important part of the cycle of trade that reformers hoped to create. The Atlanta *Constitution* supported

24. Woodward, *Origins of the New South*, Chap. 6, esp. 310–11, 319–20.
25. Americus *Weekly Recorder*, October 23, 1885, September 12, 1884.
26. Mathis, Mathis, and Purcell (eds.), *Dent Journals*, X, May [?], 1872.
27. See Atlanta *Constitution*, May 9, 16, 1883, February 17, 1884; Americus *Weekly Recorder*, August 12, September 12, November 12, 1884, or a run of any weekly or daily newspaper.
28. Atlanta *Constitution*, May 16, 1883.

this argument while contending that the Gate City was the fore-most industrial center in the state. In 1883 Atlanta's industries accounted for $2,468,456 in capital, employed 3,655 workers, paid $889,282 in wages, paid $3,159,267 for raw materials (many or most of which were purchased from nearby suppliers), and sold their output for $4,867,727. For Atlanta's industries as a whole, the expenses of production, excluding depreciation, exceeded profits nearly fivefold. The statistics were similar for Richmond, Bibb, Muscogee, and Chatham counties, the homes of Augusta, Macon, Columbus, and Savannah.[29]

It may be emotionally or ideologically satisfying to blame capitalism for the persistence of southern poverty, to blame north-erners for patterns of investment allegedly meant to preserve the South's tributary status, or as at least one historian has done, to blame capitalist planters for limiting industrial devel-opment in order to prevent competition for black labor, but these claims are simply wrong. From all indications, southern-ers were the heaviest investors in southern industry, and they in-itiated most projects even if (as one historian has stressed) they occasionally raised some of their capital in the North. There is no evidence that either they or northerners hesitated to invest wherever it seemed profitable to do so.[30] But to say these things leaves two important questions unanswered. Why was invest-ment concentrated in low-wage industries, and why was the in-dustrial development of the piedmont much more marked than that of regions below the fall line? The textile industry, the most important and successful part of the late nineteenth-century drive for southern industrial development, provides answers to both questions—answers closely related to each other.

In the textile industry, southern production was limited chiefly "to yarn and coarse or unfinished cloth."[31] The South

29. *Ibid.*, March 18, 1883.

30. Dwight B. Billings, Jr., *Planters and the Making of a 'New South': Class Politics and Development in North Carolina, 1865–1900* (Chapel Hill, 1979). Even the historian who blames capitalist planters for inhibiting industrial develop-ment in order to prevent competition for black labor shows that they were re-sponsible for a substantial part of the development that did take place. Wiener, *Social Origins of the New South*, 142–46, 182.

31. Atlanta *Constitution*, June 19, 1884; Woodward, *Origins of the New South*, 308.

came to monopolize production of coarse materials and also manufactured unfinished goods, while finer grades continued to be produced in the North. Southerners claimed that the relative sophistication of northern labor accounted for this pattern, but their explanation seems implausible. Textiles, in general, are a low-skill industry, and the differences between skills required to produce coarse and fine grades are minimal. In any case, the production of unfinished materials showed the capacity to produce a finer grade of goods. Similarly, the pattern cannot be explained by differences in the amount of capital available to invest in the marginally superior equipment necessary to produce finer goods. The substantial investment made in southern textile factories and the transfer from the North to the South of the production of coarser goods reflect sufficient capital and sufficient flexibility to produce fine goods in the South had it been profitable to do so.

The pervasive poverty of the South explains the pattern, for the same regional economic weaknesses that limited industrial development before the war limited it after. Before the war, the planter class consumed goods of relatively high quality but in small quantities; slaves received rude and meager supplies; and small-to-middling whites, whether in the upper piedmont or the black belt, engaged in a nearly subsistence agriculture and thus added somewhat but not massively to consumption. The South overall consumed relatively few goods and services.[32] Antebellum southern industrial production (what little there was of it) concentrated logically enough on the few goods consumed in large quantities—things such as brogans, coarse textiles, and a few more sophisticated items, including cotton gins. After the war, widespread poverty preserved the old pattern.[33] Local markets were simply insufficient for broad industrial development. Therefore in the late nineteenth-century South, as in less-developed countries in the late twentieth century, investment concentrated on those few goods for which there was a substantial local market, on semifinished goods in which the region had

32. Douglas C. North, *The Economic Growth of the United States, 1790–1860* (Englewood Cliffs, N.J., 1961), 122–37, 110–14.
33. See, for example, Wiener, *Social Origins of the New South*, 138–40.

some competitive advantage (such as varn and unfinished cloth to be shipped to producers elsewhere), and on extractive industries (such as lumbering and mining).

Small or weak southern markets do not, however, explain why industrial development was more marked above the fall line than below. At least one historian contends that planters opposed potential competition for black labor and therefore hindered industrial development in the black belt.[34] This argument is simply incorrect. Much of the black belt was in the lower piedmont (above the fall line), where there was considerable industrial development. In Georgia three of the four largest textile centers—Augusta, Macon, and Columbus—were in the middle of the black belt (on the fall line) with smaller centers scattered more heavily to their north than to their south.[35] A major part of the explanation for this distribution of industrial development is the traditional one. Textile centers first developed at or above the fall line because water power was most readily accessible there. Even after other forms of energy became available, further development followed where development started. It often does. That is one reason why there are industrial cities.

Although industrial development was important, alone it would not bring regional prosperity. Throughout the South, industry remained the stepchild of the agricultural economy. Patterns of industrial growth alone are therefore insufficient to explain the at first marginal but increasingly substantial general prosperity of northerly sections of the piedmont in comparison to plantation districts. Black belt industrial centers, like Augusta, Macon, Columbus, and Athens, remained islands of New South industry in a stagnant plantation economy, while the major region dominated by small-to-middling proprietors gradually improved its agricultural as well as its industrial economy.[36] The relative poverty of plantation compared to nonplantation districts arose, not because of industry, but because small-to-middling white farmers gradually improved their methods

34. *Ibid.*, 142–46, 182.
35. Atlanta *Constitution*, January 31, 1883.
36. Werner, "Hegemony and Conflict"; Brooks, "Economic Conditions," Vol. II, Sec. 9, pp. 1–4; Hill, "Rural Survey of Clarke County, Georgia."

while planters—some of the same men who invested in New South industry—incongruously failed to introduce its rural counterpart: New South agricultural reform.

Contrary to conventional belief, preachers of the New South creed were not blinded by dreams of an industrial paradise, did not describe industrialization as a simple solution for rural poverty, and did not ignore the problems of agriculture.[37] Preachers of the creed had a program for rural prosperity that, like the program for home manufactures, had been propounded by southern nationalists before the Civil War.[38] The continuity between antebellum and postbellum times was reflected not only in the admonishments of reformers but also in the degree to which their program was both necessary and unheeded and in the degree to which it was limited in ultimately self-defeating ways by its caste orientation and its concern for white landowners alone.

The agricultural program of New South publicists included two catchphrases: "diversified crops" and "intensive farming." The first was an attack upon the burden that "time prices" for supplies bought under the crop-lien system placed upon farmers. Articles about successful truck farms, orchards, and dairies appeared in weekly and daily newspapers but were not the focus of this modest reform message. When most Georgians spoke of diversified crops, they meant that farmers should raise their own supplies of corn, meat, and vegetables in order to avoid the crushing interest rates and debt associated with "all cotton farming." "Until the people of Georgia learn to raise what we eat . . . we will be bondsmen of the crop mortgage," wrote one preacher of the creed. The claim was standard that farming was profitable but that under the credit system the increase in wealth all went to the merchants, to the towns, and to the North. "The cities and towns are building up and the farms running down," wrote one advocate of diversified crops, because farmers are "planting all cotton, raising so little provisions, and raising no meat. And

37. Paul Gaston's treatment of the relationship between industry and agriculture in the minds of New South reformers is typical and erroneous in *The New South Creed*, 67.

38. James C. Bonner, *A History of Georgia Agriculture*, is largely concerned with antebellum reform movements. See also Avery O. Craven, *The Growth of Southern Nationalism, 1848–1861* (Baton Rouge, 1953), 248–49, 264–69.

if the agricultural system is not changed . . . and the farmers do not raise their own food supplies and make their farms self-sustaining, their doom will ever be [to remain] 'the hewers of wood and the drawers of water' to the commercial classes. . . . As they are now doing, they are merely making cotton to exchange for bread and bacon."[39]

While raising "hog and hominy at home" promised to relieve the South in general of a colonial dependence on western corn and bacon, advocates of diversified crops stressed that raising supplies at home would also protect the individual farmer's profits.[40] Even cotton brokers spoke out in favor of this system. If a farmer raises his own provisions, wrote one, "his cotton crop then represents surplus; he need owe no burdensome debt." Farmers who raise their own supplies "make cotton for themselves," wrote the editor of the Savannah *News*; others make "cotton on which all sorts of middlemen . . . thrive." Raising feed and food at home meant no debt, and thus even depressed prices for cotton would not threaten bankruptcy. According to an editor in Jackson County, "the successful farmer" followed a simple rule: "make what you eat at home and a little to spare and then make all the cotton you can."[41]

"Intensive farming" concerned agricultural methods rather than the selection of crops. It was a call to increase productivity through scientific cultivation. Inevitably, discussion most commonly concerned cotton. During the 1880s, for example, the average yield of cotton in Georgia was "hardly better than one

39. R. J. Redding, testimony, in Industrial Commission, *Report on Agricultural Labor*, 446; Americus *Weekly Recorder*, March 14, 1884; Mathis, Mathis, and Purcell (eds.), *Dent Journals*, XVIII, January 20, 1886; Sparta *Times and Planter*, May 13, 1881.

40. *Jackson Argus*, n.d., quoted in Atlanta *Constitution*, April 18, 1884; Americus *Weekly Recorder*, March 14, 1884; Mathis, Mathis, and Purcell (eds.), *Dent Journals*, XIV, February [?], 1882, XIII, March 16, 1880.

41. William F. Alexander to the Committee on Agriculture and Forestry, in "Letters from Merchants of the South," *Report of the Committee on Agriculture and Forestry*, Pt. I, p. 410; Thomas D. Clark, "The Furnishing and Supply System in Southern Agriculture Since 1865," *Journal of Southern History*, XII, 37–39; Savannah *News*, n.d., *Jackson Argus*, n.d., both quoted in Atlanta *Constitution*, September 29, 1883, April 18, 1884. See also *Report of the Commissioner of Agriculture for the State of Georgia* ([Atlanta], 1877), Appendix, p. lxx.

bale to three acres." Advocates of reform agreed that with relatively simple changes of method average yields could "be easily increased to a bale an acre." Experimental farmers had raised five bales to an acre, and so many Georgia publicists thought that three need not be uncommon. Federal officials agreed. One reported that the average yield of one-third bale "could be greatly increased . . . as is shown in the many experiments made under the direction of the Georgia department of agriculture and by individual persons."[42]

The poor methods of farming that brought pathetically low yields were reflected in the elementary advice that advocates of reform repeated endlessly and, during the nineteenth century, mostly without effect. Deep plowing, seed selection, ditching, the use of barnyard manures, composting, ensilage, terracing, contour plowing, and crop rotation were among the most frequently discussed needs. Advice was striking in its simplicity and in retrospect seems remarkably like training offered to peasants in developing nations in the late twentieth century. Farmers were told to do things one would have assumed they already knew, such as feeding garbage to hogs, collecting, saving, and spreading manure, or even tying up tomato plants and pinching back the vines to encourage fruitfulness.[43]

Deep plowing and seed selection adequately illustrate the general resistance to improved methods. Even during the 1890s, after decades of discussion, the *average* depth to which land was plowed in a majority of plantation-dominated counties was three inches or less. Hoeing would have done as well.[44] As a result, soil could seem far worse than it was. Some reform-minded farmers testified that the apparently exhausted soil in their counties was in fact not exhausted at all. "Only the surface is scratched off," said one. "So many people" just turn over "two or three inches of the surface" that "it has never been tilled very thoroughly and there is a great deal of fertility in much of the

42. Henry W. Grady, "Cotton and Its Kingdom," *Harper's Monthly Magazine*, LXIII, 720; Hilgard, *Report on Cotton Production in the United States*, II, 322.

43. Sandersville *Mercury*, June 22, 1880; Americus *Weekly Recorder*, January 11, 1884; *Carroll County Times*, June 14, 1878. Similar examples can be found in a run of any weekly or daily newspaper.

44. Hilgard, *Report on Cotton Production in the United States*, II, 429.

subsoil."[45] Seed selection was similarly promoted and ignored. Although it would have cost little but effort, few farmers chose to save seed from their best cotton to plant for the coming year. "Cotton seed is cotton seed" they were prone to say well into the twentieth century.[46]

Advocates of diversified crops and intensive farming argued that farmers had to be more systematic—that business methods were as necessary in farming as in other enterprises. "It is one of the unfortunate facts about farming that it is not regarded as a business, either by the farmers or by others," wrote the editor of a plantation belt newspaper. "Very few farmers keep any books, and therefore cannot tell at the end of the year whether they have made anything or not, except as they may or may not have any money on hand." Too many farmers do not count "improvements as profits capitalized," and under the crop-lien system "in too many cases [the farmer] cares not so much about the price as the time, and as a consequence pays for his credit at a rate of fifty to one hundred per cent. per annum." Farmers ignore "improvements made by others" in trying to make money for themselves. "When we think of how farms are managed, as compared to other branches of business, the wonder is not that farming pays so little, but that it pays at all."[47]

To business-minded men the resistance of their tradition-bound fellows was bewildering. "We have labored hard with our pens," wrote one to a friend, but "old habits stick to our people. . . . Our letters will be more appreciated twenty-five years hence than they are now—for we are ahead of our" times. "We are not advocating theoretical farming," wrote another reformer with intense frustration. We only want farmers "to keep up with the time." Yankees "call us indolent and lazy," wrote a third, "but there is not a more thrifty people than the Southerners." The problem is, he continued, "our people don't know anything about

45. J. H. Hale, testimony, in Industrial Commission, *Report on Agricultural Labor*, 380.

46. Hart, *The Southern South*, 257–58; Hilgard, *Report on Cotton Production in the United States*, II, 324.

47. Americus *Weekly Recorder*, October 30, 1885. See also Milledgeville *Union and Recorder*, December 23, 1884; *Southern Cultivator*, March, 1874.

farming, and are growing poorer every year. Their land is being taken from them and their children will have nothing left."[48]

Indeed, an almost resolute ignorance was one obstacle to both diversified crops and improved methods. Like freshmen in English composition classes, many farmers were innocent enough to believe that good intentions and hard work, whether properly directed or not, would bring immediate rewards. They believed the marketplace would reflect their assumptions about what was just. These men found the plentiful advice of others galling. Their complaints reflected their own frustrations and formidable, unyielding ignorance. "Those who know all about the business [of farming] are engaged in other pursuits, especially the newspaper business," grumbled one such farmer. "The intensive system is a smart nice thing," wrote another, "but I will show you how it will hurt us. It reduces the acreage one-half or more. Now, land is no object with us. We all know, too, that double the rain falls on two acres compared with one. So it throws away half the rain we get, and with all of it we can't make both ends meet. . . . That system also plows deep.—We don't believe in deep plowing—[it] just kills the land—it is so." One can still hear the exhaustion of the editor of the *Southern Cultivator* as he replied "briefly to some of the points made by our correspondent." Other reformers had to convince fundamentalists that books and deep plowing were not un-Christian.[49]

Reformers were correct that ignorance contributed much to the poor methods of farming used on both large and small holdings. But curiously, as Paul Gaston has shown, prominent reformers had much to say about ignorance but little to say about education until the rise of the Farmers' Alliance at the end of the nineteenth century.[50] This obvious gap in the seemingly practical program of diversified crops and intensive farming reflected the most important limiting assumptions of the New South

48. John H. Dent to C. Wallace Howard, copied in Mathis, Mathis, and Purcell (eds.), *Dent Journals*, IX, December 31, 1871; Americus *Weekly Recorder*, October 30, 1885; L. B. Old, letter, in Milledgeville *Union and Recorder*, May 12, 1889.

49. Dawson *Weekly Journal*, January 16, 1878; O. F. C., letter, in *Southern Cultivator*, May, 1875; John R. Hopkins, "Dear Brethren," 1874, "Address to Gentlemen, Norcross, Ga.," n.d. (MSS in John R. Hopkins Papers, Georgia Department of Archives and History, Atlanta).

50. Gaston, *New South Creed*, 107.

creed. Whereas historians have tended to concentrate their concern upon poor, landless black and white share hands and renters, public discourse in the late nineteenth century included few statements of concern and many complaints about landless men. The program of agricultural reform addressed only the problems of proprietors—those considered legitimate members of society, legitimate objects of concern. When reformers addressed labor at all, their program was an attack (like the proposals and efforts to get immigrant labor) designed to liberate landowners from the "tyranny" of allegedly expensive, indolent, and unreliable black workers. Native white labor they left largely undiscussed.

Diversified crops and intensive farming realistically addressed the problems of small-to-middling proprietors, who cultivated their own fields and who gradually adopted scientific methods of farming as they learned more about them. But when reformers drew a connection among diversified crops, intensive farming, and the problems of plantation agriculture, their program served more as an attribution of blame to black labor for the financial problems of white landowners than as a plan for reform. Let farmers "concentrate their energies and manure upon half the acres" they now cultivate, "and they will dispense with one-third the amount of labor" they now use, advised one typical editor. "With the demand for labor lessened, labor will become better as there will be a surplus of labor and only the best" will secure employment. "Diversified as up-country crops are," wrote a Floyd County farmer, "they must become more diversified in order to do with less labor. More land must be sown down in small grains" (*i.e.*, crops that require no cultivation, hence less labor than cotton or corn) "until labor becomes more seasonable." Future governor William J. Northen repeated the standard wisdom before a farmers' convention: "A reduction in area [under cultivation] will not only bring us better income by reducing expenses and increasing yields. . . . It will very much lessen the hardships of life" by easing our "labor problem." Diversify the crops, he advised.[51] When innumerable reformers, including these, conceived of diversified crops and intensive farm-

51. Americus *Weekly Recorder*, March 5, 1886; Mathis, Mathis, and Purcell (eds.), *Dent Journals*, X, December 25, 1873; "Patrons of Husbandry: Coopera-

ing as a means of dispensing with undesirable black labor, they simply ignored the cultural and practical mechanics of plantation poverty.

During recent years there has been a debate among scholars about the economics of the plantation and the causes of persistent southern poverty.[52] Economic historians Roger Ransom and Richard Sutch best represent one side of the argument; Stephen DeCanio, the other. Ransom and Sutch explain the persistent poverty of blacks—and thus of the black belt as a whole—in terms of racist exploitation. DeCanio, while not denying the persistence of southern poverty, argues that the market was free and performed well and that, when exploitation is defined narrowly in terms of a just apportioning of marginal increases in product, blacks were not exploited. Rather, he says, blacks were treated similarly to whites in the same positions.[53] There is a danger in seeking truth in the no-man's-land between irreconcilable positions: the danger of conceptual mushiness. Yet in the work of these scholars, it is possible to see their positions as less irreconcilable than they first appear.

Ransom and Sutch contend that monopolistic merchants used the club of the crop-lien system to impose a less-than-optimal crop mix on "farmers." Merchants then charged usurious interest rates on supplies purchased "on time"—supplies "farmers" would best have raised for themselves. In their text, Ransom and Sutch treat "farmers" as a lump sum, but their accompanying statistics show that proprietor-cultivators (usually small-to-middling whites) had a substantially more advantageous crop mix than share hands and renters.[54]

To explain this pattern it is important to remember that share-

---

tion—We Propose Meeting Together, Talking Together, and in General Acting Together" (Unascribed clipping, n.d., Scrapbook III, 68, in Northen Papers).

52. For critical essays on this literature, see Harold D. Woodman, "Sequel to Slavery: The New History Views the Postbellum South," *Journal of Southern History*, XLIII, 523–54; Jonathan M. Wiener, "Class Structure and Economic Development in the American South, 1865–1955," *American Historical Review*, LXXXIV, 970–92.

53. Ransom and Sutch, *One Kind of Freedom*; DeCanio, *Agriculture in the Postbellum South*.

54. Ransom and Sutch, *One Kind of Freedom*, 98–99, 156–58, 160–62.

croppers and most share tenants were not farmers in a conventional sense. In Georgia and several other southern states, they were legally defined as laborers and could receive credit only through their employers.[55] In other southern states, such as Alabama, croppers might retain their legal status as tenants but, as was true of renters in Georgia, were legally eligible for crop liens only through their landlords.[56] It was not share hands, black or white, who reduced the self-sufficiency of their farms by choice. Nor was it merchants, unless they doubled as employers. The pattern arose because many employers had their laborers raise cotton (the most commercially valuable staple crop), while workers, whether black or white, had to support themselves with supplies purchased on credit.

The common practice of having workers pay for their own supplies explains a major part of the decline in the production of foodstuffs across the South after the war.[57] Proprietor-cultivators, sometimes after luckily surviving an experiment in all-cotton farming, generally tried to raise supplies at home, as preachers of the New South creed advised. But where antebellum masters had benefitted from raising food for their slaves instead of buying it on credit, the postbellum labor system took the advantage of raising foodstuffs away from the landowner, shifted the cost of credit to the worker who supplied his own family and thus shifted the production of supplies for workers outside the South.

Not only did an employer save the cost of credit and gain from raising cotton in place of grain, but also, whether doubling as a merchant or not, he often gained a share of the profit from supplies sold to his employees at credit prices. The employer who was not a merchant could receive a kickback from the merchant to whom he assigned his workers' and renters' trade. The planter-merchant, of course, profited directly. Employers and merchants designed this system as a way of obtaining a greater share of the wealth that workers produced. Captain J. N. Montgomery of Madison County explained as much to a state agricultural society convention in the 1870s: "There are two ways by

55. Hill, "Rural Survey of Clarke County, Georgia," 27.
56. Wiener, *Social Origins of the New South*, 104–105.
57. Ransom and Sutch, *One Kind of Freedom*, 152–62.

which the farmer can make up the difference" between paying
hands one-third of the crop ("which . . . is the proper share") and
paying one-half (which is what hands were getting). The first
way, said Montgomery, is to "sow down one-third of each farm"
in small grains, so "you will not require so much labor." The second method was the one more commonly adopted across the
South: if you "turn to be your own commission merchant . . .
and furnish your hands at moderate rates of interest, [it] will
fully make up the difference." [58]

As any Georgia Allianceman could explain, the "moderate interest" that the planter-merchant or both landlord-employer
and merchant were eager to charge became truly usurious partly
because credit facilities throughout the South were inadequate.
Ransom and Sutch attribute the high interest rates across the
region to monopolistic merchants, but merchants also suffered
from inadequate credit facilities. It has been repeatedly shown
that, like their debtors, they paid very high rates of interest to
their creditors and suffered from a good many bad debts on their
books.[59] On the ladder of creditors, no one made a lot, but the
cropper, renter, or proprietor-cultivator with a crop lien found
himself at the nether end of the ladder and thus bore the greatest burden. He paid the costs of everyone above him.

While consistent with the general conclusions of Ransom and
Sutch, nothing in this argument contradicts the findings of Stephen DeCanio. As DeCanio himself states, his study is "insufficient to settle the question of exploitation of farmers by merchants." DeCanio studies the "agricultural sector" rather than
the competing interests of groups within it. With that major lim-
itation, his conclusion that cotton was not "overproduced" is
perfectly valid. It was not overproduced as far as employers or
merchants were concerned. The advantage to workers of raising
their own supplies instead of buying them at high interest rates
is beyond DeCanio's analysis, which proves only that cotton was

58. *Transactions of the Georgia State Agricultural Society from August, 1876, to
February, 1878* (Atlanta, 1878), 406–407. See also Tindall, *South Carolina Negroes*,
59.

59. Clark, "The Furnishing and Supply System," 24–44; Jacqueline P. Bell,
"The General Supply Merchant in the Economic History of the New South,"
Journal of Southern History, XVIII, 37–59; Williamson, *After Slavery*, 174.

the most profitable staple crop to raise for sale.[60] By dealing solely with "the aggregate," DeCanio slips over the real point at issue.

DeCanio also argues that merchants did not create an inflexible system of crop mix. "Southern cotton farmers were as flexible and price responsive as wheat farmers in the rest of the United States," he says.[61] This is a valuable contribution consistent with the evidence that landlord-employers, not merchants, determined the crop mix. Unless a merchant doubled as an employer or landlord or both, his interests would not vary. Cotton remained the most valuable security for debts, and if the merchant were worried about low cotton prices, he could simply shorten the line of credit. But the interests of employer-landlords could vary considerably. During the 1890s, for example, when the price of cotton fell catastrophically low, it was advantageous to employers to raise supplies for hands. With cotton selling at five cents a pound, share hands and renters were unlikely to pay large debts in full at the end of the year. Employers who did not have croppers raise their supplies and landlords who did not allow their renters to do so would be left at the harvest owing debts for which they had stood as security. The production of foodstuffs in plantation districts therefore increased markedly when the price of cotton fell. According to the Georgia Department of Agriculture, for example, the acreage devoted to cotton in the middle of the black belt increased 4 percent after the good prices of 1889. After the very bad year of 1891, however, the acreage devoted to cotton in the same region shrank a startling 17 percent. In 1890 landowners also sought to protect themselves from debt by increasing the area devoted to corn by 17 percent and the area devoted to wheat by 12 percent.[62]

This pattern of plantation agriculture was rational only to the degree that landowning employers maximized their yearly income given static resources of land and labor. The pattern was less than optimal to the degree that it denied the possibility of economic growth. Landowning employers sought to increase

60. DeCanio, *Agriculture in the Postbellum South*, 13, 180.
61. *Ibid.*, 257.
62. *Publications of the Georgia Department of Agriculture* V–XXI, esp. XVIII, 37.

their income by increasing their share of a poorly cultivated crop rather than by increasing productivity (which would have benefitted landowners, laborers, and the regional economy). Many landowners even supervised only so far as to assure a minimum profit.[63]

As agricultural reformers described their program of diversified crops and intensive farming, they showed that the caste values upon which the plantation was based pervaded the South and limited the possibilities for regional economic growth. Reformers shared the urge for increased exploitation. It was, indeed, an old pattern, for in hard times before the war, slaveholders had attempted to achieve their own financial salvation by increasing already severe demands on their slaves rather than by reforming poor methods.[64] During Reconstruction and in complaints voiced well into the twentieth century, landowners, small to large, rhetorically displayed the same unchanging urge. "The negro is a kind of animal," wrote one white, complaining that the days of slavery were past. He "will not work without force. When force leaves him, then he is no longer a good worker. He fears nothing but the lash. He cares nothing for law or God."[65]

It was this habit of mind that small-to-middling white proprietors brought to their reform of southern society. They shared the caste values of the plantation even as they opposed the selfishly exercised power of planters. In fierce political battles dating from before the Revolution, large planters had frequently opposed the ambitions of yeomen. Improved transportation, public education, inequitable systems of taxation, and greater democracy among whites had all been issues. They still were issues in the late nineteenth and early twentieth century. In every instance, as in fence-law fights, planters interpreted each challenge to their interests as an affront to the system of subordinate black labor upon which they depended. At the same time, small-to-middling white farmers, like landless whites, showed their

63. Barrow, "A Georgia Plantation," 833.
64. Stampp, *The Peculiar Institution*, 84–85.
65. No name, Putnam County (Questionnaire, "Inquiries I," 1912, in Brooks Papers).

commitment to *Herrenvolk* democracy, demanded justice by virtue of their race, and sought to harden the caste line further.

The collective political awareness and strength of small-to-middling white landowners developed gradually during the late nineteenth century and the Progressive Era, but as historians have long recognized, it grew most dramatically with the rise of the Farmers' Alliance. The hysterical reaction of the traditionally powerful to the farmer insurgency in Georgia is well known.[66] It should be remembered, however, that Georgia's famous political battles of the 1890s were primarily battles among landowners. The cumulative poll tax had already taken a heavy toll. The ballot was overwhelmingly the province of landowners and the most prosperous share tenants and renters. So, too, was the Alliance. Its foremost historian, Robert McMath, describes its membership as drawn from the "middle range" of white landowners.[67] Membership lists from rare, surviving minute books confirm McMath's conclusion with hard evidence. In Taliaferro County, for example, a majority of Alliancemen owned farms of from 51 to 950 acres. All but three members seem to have lived on family-owned land. Only two applicants were excluded from membership. Both were landless. And while officers of the Taliaferro Alliance tended to own a bit more land than the other members, none had a plantation. The officers "ran" between one and fifteen hands. In other counties the pattern was similar.[68]

It is a tradition among historians to describe the Farmers' Alliance and the Agrarian Revolt as, if anything, a repudiation of the New South creed and a threat to the caste system. In fact, like all major movements in the rise of "poor" whites, the Alliance was thoroughly imbued with the New South creed and *Herrenvolk* assumptions. The state Alliance in Georgia and sub-alliances throughout the state not only repeated but also stressed

66. See Woodward, *Tom Watson.*
67. Robert C. McMath, *Populist Vanguard: A History of the Southern Farmers' Alliance* (New York, 1977), 66.
68. Crawfordsville (Taliaferro County) Farmers' Alliance No. 1437, Minute Book, 1888–1893, Georgia Department of Archives and History, Atlanta; Taliaferro County Tax Digests, 1888–1891, Georgia County Property Tax Digests; Werner, "Hegemony and Conflict," 243.

the program of diversified crops and intensive farming. According to some historians, Alliancemen used the New South "shibboleths" only as a tactic, as an effort to placate the traditionally powerful.[69] There is substantially more evidence, however, to support the insight of one lonely historian who observed that landowners "responded enthusiastically to the Alliance" because it "seemed to provide a vehicle for attaining prosperity through the very reforms" long urged by proponents of the New South creed. "If the Alliance was hostile to the crop-lien system, railroad discriminations, and middle men in the cotton economy, so too were New South intellectuals, and these men had been hostile far longer."[70]

Intellectuals is certainly a misnomer, and it is doubtful anyone had been hostile to middlemen longer than farmers, but the insight is still quite valid. Many national, state, and local leaders of the Alliance were long-standing, sincere advocates of diversified crops and intensive farming. Leonidas L. Polk, editor of the *Progressive Farmer*, was the most notable national figure. In Georgia, both William J. Northen (the Alliance governor) and Leonidas F. Livingston (the father, some claim, of the subtreasury plan) were presidents of the state agricultural society and propogandists for New South reform well before they became leaders of the Alliance. Neither these three prominent men nor other Alliance leaders abandoned the New South program after 1888. And these men were in harmony with the rank and file. The Alliance was, after all, a rather democratic organization. In the lectures that suballiances regularly gathered to hear, instruction on improved agricultural methods, the advantages of home-grown supplies, and the importance of avoiding debt played as prominent a part as calls for "cooperation" and explanations of the evils of the national banking system.

In 1888 the state Alliance printed a twenty-three-point canon of its faith. Dedication to "improved methods of farming," "scientific agriculture," "education for our class generally," and "labor saving machinery" came right after "the Supreme Being," the Bible, and the "dignity of agriculture."[71] In both 1888 and

69. McMath, *Populist Vanguard*, 43.
70. Werner, "Hegemony and Conflict," 243.
71. *Henry County Weekly*, June 15, 1888, quoted in Lewis Nicholas Wynne,

1889 the president of the state Alliance cited instruction about agricultural reform as the organization's principal achievement. "In order to survive," he said, the farmer "must diversify his crops as well as rotate. . . . he must give his farm the same close, everyday, personal attention that a merchant gives to his business."[72] Local Alliancemen made innumerable similar pronouncements to each other. "If we try we can" raise all we "need at home," declared George Smith of the Milton County Alliance. In counties nearby, Alliancemen boasted that the movement had led farmers finally to raise enough "corn, meat and provisions to weather the winter" and to last until the wheat and oats ripened in spring. "Plant supply crops and make cotton our surplus," was still the familiar refrain.[73] Others could cite the use of cotton bagging during the jute boycott as an impetus to southern textile development or talk of building other "home manufactures," such as oil mills, banks, or even cigarette factories.[74]

Alliancemen also frequently repeated to each other the conventional New South wisdom that blamed black labor for many of the South's troubles. The old hostility of small-scale employers toward planters and planter-merchants was common in Alliance rhetoric and was, as always, tied to the belief that unsupervised farms provided an escape hatch that kept all black labor less tractable than it should be. While Tom Watson gave speeches about the problems posed by "working Free niggers," the Alliance program of "cooperation" took on a significant meaning in labor relations.[75] Leonidas F. Livingston and William J. Northen were rivals within the Alliance, but both were

---

"The Alliance Legislature of 1890" (M.A. thesis, University of Georgia, 1970), 30–32.

72. Atlanta *Journal*, n.d., quoted in *Southwestern News* (Dawson), June 6, 1888; Augusta *Chronicle*, August 29, 1888, June 6, 1889, quoted in Werner, "Hegemony and Conflict," 245.

73. *Cherokee Advance*, December 14, 1888; *Carroll Free Press*, December 27, 1889. See also Mathis, Mathis, and Purcell (eds.), *Dent Journals*, XIX, October [?], 1890; unascribed clipping, September 21 [1890], in Joseph E. Brown and Elizabeth G. Brown Papers; *Cherokee Advance*, March 21, April 4, 1890.

74. *Cherokee Advance*, June 7, 1889, March 7, 1890; Americus *Weekly Recorder*, November 22, 1889.

75. Tom Watson, speech, November 7, 1889, quoted in Werner, "Hegemony and Conflict," 321–22.

long-standing advocates of "laws by which labor could be made reliable." They and less prominent Alliancemen promoted efforts to increase control and exploitation of workers as a means to increase the prosperity of landowners. "The management of labor is the most important element in farm economy," declared one. Farmers must stop competing with each other and become "uniform and cooperative." A "laborer who leaves the farm and abandons his contract [at] . . . a very hurtful time for the farmer, ought not to [receive a] . . . paying position on another farm . . . until his wages are adjusted." That rule "should be enforced by the uniform management of the neighborhood." Indeed, calls to control black labor through what New South publicists termed cooperation had been heard for decades.[76]

The Alliance commitment to the New South creed, its caste limits, and *Herrenvolk* democracy was more than rhetorical. Alliance proposals for national reform met only frustration and defeat, but on state and local issues, the Georgia General Assembly took action. The "Farmer Legislature," elected in 1888, and the "Alliance Legislature," elected in 1890, both reflected the increasing political strength of small-to-middling white farmers, and their concern with both New South reform and the caste barrier.[77] Sometimes the issues were well-worn. In 1889 the general assembly imposed fence laws on no fewer than twenty-two districts and adopted no fewer than fifteen laws restricting hunting and fishing.[78] In 1887 W. L. Peek, who would run for governor as a Populist in 1892, had unsuccessfully fought for a bill of questionable constitutionality to make workers criminally liable for unpaid debts. In 1890 the legislature adopted a similar statute— a law that would help to create the peonage cases of the twentieth century. And in 1891 the Alliance Legislature also adopted the state's first Jim Crow law, a fairly concrete symbol of the *Herrenvolk* faith. Like wealthier whites, those unable to afford first-class railroad tickets were guaranteed segregated cars.[79]

76. Atlanta *Constitution*, August 16, 1883; *Southern Cultivator*, February 1889; Mathis, Mathis, and Purcell (eds.), *Dent Journals*, XI, August–September, 1874, XIII, August 19, 1878.

77. Americus *Weekly Recorder*, January 10, 1889; Wynne, "Alliance Legislature of 1890," *passim*.

78. *Acts, passim.*

79. "Peek's Slavery Bill" (Broadside, *ca.* August 19, 1892, in Northen Papers);

The general assembly also paid unusual attention to education. In 1889 it created farmer institutes to give training in scientific cultivation. As a prominent black politician later reported, blacks were not supposed to attend. Similarly, when both sessions of the legislature increased expenditures for public schools, blacks were not expected to benefit. There were a few lonely southern voices that called for the education of blacks. Atticus G. Haygood of Emory College, and, most notably, Booker T. Washington were among them.[80] Other opinions were more common. Some, like the professor from the University of Georgia who called for immigrant labor, denied even the possibility of educating blacks. The president of the Georgia State Agricultural Society forcefully espoused that position in 1899. Those blacks who could be educated were mere "exceptions to the rule," he said.[81] But the strongest testimony to the pervasiveness of this view is the well-known discrimination against blacks in the public schools that lasted long after the United States Supreme Court ordered it ended in the 1950s. It was this discrimination, of course, that perpetuated and enlarged the disparity in productivity between landless whites and blacks. The caste barrier did not provide for excluding landless whites; so a few benefits from reform trickled down to them.

The Georgia Alliance, and the legislative action its constituency influenced, reflected the mentality of reform in the New South. A complete history of the transition from the redeemed South to the progressive South, including all the ambiguities of caste and class divisions, has yet to be written. But by 1890, a long-lasting pattern had been established. Reform for small-to-middling white landowners was coupled with their caste faith. Rather indirectly, in small ways, reform benefitted landless whites and ratified the caste system, but reformers were not con-

---

Americus *Weekly Times-Recorder*, July 24, 1891; Woodward, *Origins of the New South*, 212.

80. *Acts*, 1889 (No. 606), 166; George Henry White, testimony, in Industrial Commission, *Report on Agricultural Labor*, 423–26; On Haygood, see Harold W. Mann, *Atticus Greene Haygood: Methodist Bishop, Editor, Educator* (Athens, 1965). Timothy Thomas Fortune, *Black and White: Land, Labor and Politics in the South* (1884; rpr. Chicago, 1970), 28–54.

81. J. Pope Brown, testimony, in Industrial Commission, *Report on Agricultural Labor*, 65.

cerned with landless whites. They were concerned solely with themselves. In this Progressive coupling of class interests and the caste system lay the opportunity to be simultaneously an insurgent, a reformer, and a demagogue, to be a Ben Tillman, a Tom Watson, a Eugene Talmadge, or a Ross Barnett. In the calculus of New South reform, demands of "justice" for whites were a function of the exclusion, indeed the hatred of blacks. Planters were not, therefore, solely at fault for southern injustices or for persistent southern poverty. Small-to-middling white landowners, increasing their political strength, embraced the caste-based assumptions of the plantation and joined in selfishly dooming themselves and their region. Because of the *Herrenvolk* justification and limits of reform, the great mass of landless men, white and black, remained trapped in the plantation system and poorer than they need have been. They remained too poor to be consumers, too poor to provide adequate markets for diverse manufacture, and thus, too poor to allow a regional economic development that would have benefitted every echelon of southern society.

The results of the caste system were, of course, not foreseen or understood. When the Civil War ended and Reconstruction began, white southerners knew that slavery was dead but did not question its caste premises. They believed that "southern prosperity" (by which they meant white prosperity) depended upon the "proper" subordination of black labor. Indeed, white southerners had every expectation that a rigid caste system would be maintained. But they were disappointed because Republican "interference" during Reconstruction changed much. Despite the violent resistance of a broad cross section of southern whites, Republicans made it impossible to maintain the caste line by absolute law as well as by custom. They thus created or greatly enhanced numerous opportunities for friction between economically defined class interests and culturally defined caste norms. That friction increased during the late nineteenth century as some blacks achieved a measure of independence and as the number of landless whites increased rapidly. In a hierarchy of class selfishness whites uncertainly struggled to unbind the friction, which they supposed should not exist. Planters never questioned the sacredness of caste, never stopped wanting the greater subordination of "idle and unreliable" black labor, never questioned the superiority of whites over blacks (something not to be confused with a belief in white equality). And poor-to-middling whites demanded equality with those above them while ignoring the needs of those below. Their resistance to class abuse was inseparable from their caste values. Whether planter or poor, whites continued to believe that a "proper" caste system would assure their own prosperity. They were all exactly wrong. Their resolute commitment to their caste values limited their region's economic growth and their own fortunes.

Selected Bibliography

PUBLISHED WORKS

Newspapers

Americus *Times-Recorder*, 1891–1896
Americus *Weekly Recorder*, 1883–1891
Atlanta *Constitution*, 1880–1896
Carroll County Times, 1872–1873, 1876–1884
Carroll Free Press, 1883–1896
Cherokee Advance, 1880–1896
Covington *Georgia Enterprise*, 1873–1874, 1883–1885, 1887–1890
Dawson *Journal*, 1878–1887
Dawson *News*, 1889–1896
Dawson *Weekly Journal*, 1872–1878
Milledgeville *Union and Recorder*, 1872–1896
Sandersville *Herald*, 1882–1887
Sandersville *Mercury*, 1880–1887
Savannah *Tribune*, 1886–1888
Southern Cultivator (title varies), 1874–1896
Southern Farm: A Journal of Practical Agriculture, 1887–1890
Sparta *Ishmaelite*, 1883–1884, 1887–1896
Waynesboro *True Citizen*, 1883–1884

Books and Articles

Andrews, Sidney. *The South Since the War, as shown by Fourteen Weeks of Travel and Observation in Georgia and the Carolinas.* Boston, 1865.
Arnett, Alex M. *The Populist Movement in Georgia: A View of the "Agrarian Crusade" in the Light of Solid-South Politics.* New York, 1922.
Banks, Enoch M. *The Economics of Land Tenure in Georgia.* New York, 1905.
Barrow, David. "A Georgia Plantation." *Scribner's Monthly*, XXI, 830–36.
Bonner, James C. *A History of Georgia Agriculture, 1732–1860.* Athens, 1964.
Brooks, Robert Preston. *The Agrarian Revolution in Georgia, 1865–1912.* University of Wisconsin, *Bulletin*, No. 639, History Series, Vol. III, No. 3. Madison, 1914.
Bruce, Philip A. *The Plantation Negro as a Freeman: Observations on His Character, Condition, and Prospects in Virginia.* New York, 1889.

Burton, Vernon. "Race and Reconstruction: Edgefield County, South Carolina." *Journal of Social History*, XII (Fall, 1978), 31–56.

Cohen, William. "Negro Involuntary Servitude in the South, 1865–1940: A Preliminary Analysis." *Journal of Southern History*, XLII, 31–60.

Cutler, James Elbert. *Lynch-Law: An Investigation into the History of Lynchings in the United States*. London, 1905.

Daniel, Pete. "The Metamorphosis of Slavery." *Journal of American History*. LXVI (June, 1979), 88–99.

Davis, Natalie Zemon. *Society and Culture in Early Modern France: Eight Essays by Natalie Zemon Davis*. Stanford, 1975.

DeCanio, Stephen. *Agriculture in the Postbellum South: The Economics of Production and Supply*. Cambridge, Mass., 1974.

Escott, Paul D. *Slavery Remembered: A Record of Twentieth-Century Slave Narratives*. Chapel Hill, 1979.

Evans, Maurice S. *Black and White in the Southern States: A Study of Race Problems in the United States from a South African Point of View*. London, 1915.

Fredrickson, George M. *The Black Image in the White Mind: The Debate on Afro-American Character and Destiny, 1817–1914*. New York, 1972.

Friedman, Lawrence M. *A History of American Law*. New York, 1973.

Gaston, Paul M. *The New South Creed: A Study in Southern Mythmaking*. Baton Rouge, 1970.

Gottlieb, Manuel. "The Land Question in Georgia During Reconstruction." *Science and Society*, III, 356–88.

Graham, Hugh D., and Ted R. Gurr, eds. *Violence in America: Historical and Comparative Perspectives. A Report to the National Commission on the Causes of Violence and Its Prevention*. Washington, D.C., 1969.

Haden, C. J. "The Spectre of the Negro." *Southern States: An Illustrated Monthly Magazine Devoted to the South*, I, 458–60.

Hammond, Matthew Brown. *The Cotton Industry: An Essay in American Economic History*. Ithaca, 1897.

Hart, Albert Bushnell. *The Southern South*. New York, 1910.

Higgs, Robert. *Competition and Coercion: Blacks in the American Economy, 1865–1914*. Cambridge, Mass., 1979.

Hill, W. B. "Rural Survey of Clarke County, Georgia, with Special Reference to the Negroes." *Bulletin of the University of Georgia*, XV, No. 3, (March, 1915).

Hoffman, Frederick L. *Race Traits and Tendencies of the American Negro*. New York, 1896.

Holmes, William F. "Whitecapping: Agrarian Violence in Mississippi, 1902–1906." *Journal of Southern History*. XXXV, 165–85.

Johnson, Charles S. *Shadow of the Plantation.* Chicago, 1934.

Kephart, Horace. *Our Southern Highlanders.* New York, 1916.

Kessler, Sidney. "The Organization of Negroes in the Knights of Labor." *Journal of Negro History,* XXXVII, 248–76.

Kolchin, Peter. *First Freedom: The Responses of Alabama Blacks to Emancipation and Reconstruction.* Westport, 1972.

Kousser, J. Morgan. *The Shaping of Southern Politics: Suffrage Restriction and the Establishment of the One-Party South, 1880–1910.* New Haven, 1974.

Kremm, Thomas W. and Diane Neal. "Clandestine Black Labor Societies and White Fear: Hiram F. Hoover and the 'Cooperative Workers of America' in the South." *Labor History,* XIX, 226–37.

Leigh, Frances Butler. *Ten Years on a Georgia Plantation Since the War.* London, 1883.

Litwack, Leon F. *Been in the Storm So Long: The Aftermath of Slavery.* New York, 1979.

Mandle, Jay R. *The Roots of Black Poverty: The Southern Plantation Economy after the Civil War.* Durham, 1978.

McMath, Robert C. *Populist Vanguard: A History of the Southern Farmers' Alliance.* New York, 1977.

McWhitney, H. Grady, and Francis B. Simkins. "The Ghostly Legend of the Ku-Klux Klan." *Negro History Bulletin,* XIV (February, 1951), 109–12.

Mathis, Ray, Mary Mathis, and Douglas Clare Purcell, eds. *John Hory Dent Farm Journals and Account Books, 1840–1892,* Microfilm (University, Ala., 1977).

Merriman, John. "The Demoiselles of the Ariège, 1829–1831." In John Merriman, ed. *1830 in France.* New York, 1975.

Meyers, Frederic. "The Knights of Labor in the South." *Southern Economic Journal,* VI, 479–87.

Nixon, Herman Clarence. *Forty Acres and Steel Mules.* Chapel Hill, 1938.

———. *Lower Piedmont Country.* New York, 1946.

———. *Possum Trot: Rural Community, South.* Norman, Okla., 1941.

Novak, Daniel A. *The Wheel of Servitude: Black Forced Labor after Slavery.* Lexington, 1978.

Otken, Charles H. *The Ills of the South.* New York, 1894.

Range, Willard. *A Century of Georgia Agriculture, 1850–1950.* Athens, 1954.

Ransom, Roger, and Richard Sutch. *One Kind of Freedom: The Economic Consequences of Emancipation.* Cambridge, 1977.

Raper, Arther F. *Preface to Peasantry: A Tale of Two Black Belt Counties.* Chapel Hill, 1936.

Reid, Whitelaw. *After the War: A Tour of the Southern States, 1865–1866.* Ed. C. Vann Woodward. New York, 1965.

Roark, James L. *Masters Without Slaves: Southern Planters in the Civil War and Reconstruction.* New York, 1977.

Rosengarten, Theodore. *All God's Dangers: The Life of Nate Shaw.* New York, 1975.

Somers, Robert. *The Southern States Since the War, 1870–1.* London, 1871.

Stagg, J. C. A. "The Problem of Klan Violence: The South Carolina Upcountry, 1868–1871." *Journal of American Studies,* VIII, 303–18.

Stampp, Kenneth M. *The Peculiar Institution: Slavery in the Antebellum South* (New York, 1956).

Taylor, George Rogers. *The Transportation Revolution, 1815–1860.* New York, 1951.

Tebeau, C. W. "Some Aspects of Planter-Freedmen Relations, 1865–1880." *Journal of Negro History,* XXI, 130–50.

Thompson, C. Mildred. *Reconstruction in Georgia: Economic, Social, Political, 1865–1872.* New York, 1915.

Thompson, Edward P. "'Rough Music': Le Charivari Anglais." *Annales: Economies; Societés; Civilization,* XXVII (March–April, 1972), 285–312.

Tindall, George Brown. *South Carolina Negroes, 1877–1900.* Columbia, 1952.

Trelease, Allen W. *White Terror: The Ku Klux Klan Conspiracy and Southern Reconstruction.* New York, 1971.

Unwritten History of Slavery: Autobiographical Accounts of Negro Ex-Slaves. Social Science Source Documents, No. 1. Nashville, 1945.

Wharton, Vernon L. *The Negro in Mississippi, 1865–1890.* New York, 1965.

Wiener, Jonathan M. "Class Structure and Economic Development in the American South, 1865–1955." *American Historical Review,* LXXXIV, 970–92.

———. *Social Origins of the New South: Alabama, 1860–1885.* Baton Rouge, 1978.

Williamson, Joel. *After Slavery: The Negro in South Carolina During Reconstruction, 1861–1877.* New York, rpr. 1975.

Winston, George T. *The Relation of the Whites to the Negroes.* Publications of the American Academy of Political and Social Science, No. 310. Philadelphia, n.d.

Woodward, C. Vann. *Origins of the New South, 1877–1913.* Baton Rouge, 1951.

———. *Tom Watson: Agrarian Rebel.* New York, rpr. 1970.

Woofter, Thomas Jackson, Jr. *Negro Migration: Changes in Rural Organization and Population in the Cotton Belt.* New York, 1920.
Zeichner, Oscar. "The Transition from Slave to Free Agricultural Labor in the Southern States." *Agricultural History,* XIII (January, 1939), 22–32.

Public Documents

Acts of the General Assembly of the State of Georgia. Milledgeville and Atlanta, 1866–1896.
Atwater, W. O., and Charles D. Woods. "Dietary Studies with Reference to the Food of the Negro in Alabama in 1895 and 1896." U.S. Department of Agriculture *Bulletin* No. 38. Washington, D.C., 1897.
The Code of the State of Georgia. Atlanta and Macon, 1867, 1873.
"Conditions in Georgia." *House Miscellaneous Documents,* 40th Cong., 3rd Sess., No. 52.
Du Bois, William Edward Burghardt. "The Negro in the Cotton Belt: Some Social Sketches." U.S. Department of Labor *Bulletin,* No. 22 (May, 1899), 401–17.
———. "The Negro Landholder of Georgia." U.S. Department of Labor *Bulletin,* No. 35 (July, 1901), 647–777.
Eleventh Census, 1890.
Hilgard, Eugene W. *Report on Cotton Production in the United States; Also Embracing Agricultural and Physio-Geographical Descriptions of Several Cotton States and California.* 2 vols. Washington, D.C., 1884.
Industrial Commission. *Report of the Industrial Commission on Agriculture and Agricultural Labor. House Reports,* 57th Cong., 1st Sess., No. 179.
Industrial Commission. *Report of the Industrial Commission on Agriculture and on Taxation in Various States. House Reports,* 57th Cong., 1st Sess., No. 180.
Publications of the Georgia Department of Agriculture, V–XXI, 1879–1895.
Report of the Committee on Agriculture and Forestry on the Condition of Cotton Growers and the Remedy; and on Cotton Consumption and Production, February 23, 1895. Senate Reports, 53rd Cong., 3rd Sess., No. 986.
Schurz, Carl. "Report of Carl Schurz on the States of South Carolina, Georgia, Alabama, Mississippi and Louisiana," in "Message of the President of the United States . . . in Relation to the States of the Union Lately in Rebellion, December 19, 1865." *Senate Executive Documents,* 39th Cong., 1st Sess., No. 2.

Stanton, Edwin M. "Letter of the Secretary of War Communicating . . . Reports of the Assistant Commissioners of Freedmen and a Synopsis of Laws Respecting Persons of Color in the Late Slave States, January 3, 1867." *Senate Executive Documents*, 39th Cong., 2nd Sess., No. 6.

Tenth Census, 1880.

Testimony taken by the Joint Committee to Inquire into the Condition of Affairs in the Late Insurrectionary States: The Ku Klux Klan Conspiracy. House Reports, 42nd Cong., 2nd Sess., No. 22, Vols. VI, VII.

UNPUBLISHED WORKS

Manuscripts

Duke University Library, Durham, North Carolina
    Tenth Census, 1880: Agricultural Schedules.
National Archives, Washington, D.C.
    Justice Department, General Records, Sources Chronological File, Georgia, 1871–1894, RG 60.
Georgia Department of Archives and History, Atlanta
    Campbell, Tunis G. Papers, File II.
    Crawfordsville (Taliaferro County) Farmers' Alliance No. 1437. Minute Book, 1888–1893.
    Executive Rewards, 1883–1889.
    Georgia County Property Tax Digests.
    Hopkins, John R. Papers.
    Negro File.
    Northen, William J. Personal Papers.
    Petitions and Memorials, Records of the House and Senate.
    Supreme Court of the State of Georgia Files.
University of Georgia Libraries, Rare Books and Manuscripts Department, Athens
    Brooks, Robert Preston. Papers.
    Brown, Joseph E. Papers.
    Brown, Joseph E., and Elizabeth G. Brown. Papers.
    Felton, Rebecca Latimer, and William Harrell Felton. Papers.
    [Mohr?], "Labor History of Georgia."
University of North Carolina at Chapel Hill
    Tenth Census, 1880 (microfilm).

Dissertations and Theses

Smith, Albert Colby. "Violence in Georgia's Black Belt: A Study of Crime in Baldwin and Terrell Counties, 1866–1899." M.A. thesis, University of Georgia, 1974.

Ward, Judson C. "Georgia Under the Bourbon Democrats, 1872–1890." Ph.D. Dissertation, University of North Carolina, 1947.

Werner, Randolph Dennis. "Hegemony and Conflict: The Political Economy of a Southern Region, Augusta, Georgia, 1865–1895." Ph.D. dissertation, University of Virginia, 1977.

Wynne, Lewis Nicholas. "The Alliance Legislature of 1890." M.A. thesis, University of Georgia, 1970.

Index

Agricultural reform: attitudes toward, 73–74, 171–72; New South program for, 160, 165–68; effectiveness of, 171, 176–77

Agriculture: condition of, 3, 8, 22–28; increased productivity versus exploitation of labor in, 3, 22–28, 73–74, 159–60, 172–76; productivity of whites and blacks in, 21–24, 80–81; methods used in, 73, 167–69

Agriculture, U.S. Department of, 81, 119

Alliance Legislature, 96, 180–81

Andrews, Sidney, 34, 59

Arp, Bill, 13–14

Arson: motivations for, 62–63, 98–101; labor conflict and, 93–94; laws on, 94; buildings burned, 99–100

Assault. *See* Murder and Assault

Atlanta *Constitution*: on colonization of blacks overseas, 26; on black parents, 62; on murder of black union sympathizer, 106; on industrial development, 162–63

Black codes, 3, 12, 35–37, 56, 60; compared to subsequent laws, 110–114

Blacks: attitudes of toward work, 6, 9, 10–12; and white paternalism, 6, 16–21; white characterization of labor of, 7–9, 14, 21–28, 68–69; agricultural techniques of, 21–24, 80–81; as vigilantes, 43; wage labor and, 63–64, 67–69, 72; landownership by, 64–66, 103–104. *See also* Agriculture; Caste system; Labor; Unions

Brooks, Robert Preston, 7

Brown, Joseph E., 36

Butler, Frances, 6, 19, 25, 32–33, 64–65; and arson, 101; and hunting, fishing, and gathering by employees of, 118–19

Caste system: caste defined, 1; social doctrine of, 1–2, 7, 13–28; and class relations among whites, 2–4, 28, 115, 154–60, 179–83; and agricultural reform, 3, 22–28, 73–74, 159–60, 172–76; and labor relations, 3–5, 53, 77, 152–58; and labor law, 85, 87, 109, 113–14; and property law, 135–36. *See also* Class relations among whites; Federal law; *Herrenvolk* democracy; Ku Klux Klan; Labor

Census of 1880 and 1890, 67–68

Charivari, 44–45; connection of to the South, 45–46; and sex roles, 45–47; and economic grievances, 47; localism of, 49

Charles Jones v. *State*, 99

Christy, John, 50

Civil Rights Act of 1866, 37–38

Clarke, John F., 104–107

Clarkson, E. M., 111

Class relations among whites, 1–2, 4, 28; and labor law, 113–14; and property law, 131–32; and vigilantism, 54–56; and agricultural prosperity, 159–60. *See also* Caste system; *Herrenvolk* democracy; Ku Klux Klan; Labor

Cobb, Howell, 133

Collins, J. D., 57–58

Colonization of blacks overseas, 26

Conservation, 122, 124–25

Couper, Robert, 85–86

Davis, Natalie Zemon, 45

Dawson *Journal*: on supervision of black labor, 76

Deaver v. *Rice*, 90

DeCanio, Stephen, 172, 174–76

Dent, John H.: on paternalism, 18–19, 21; on black labor, 70, 75, 78, 119–20; on black tenancy, 75–76; on labor law, 84; on arson, 100; on